Jersey Women Mean Business!

Big Bold Business™ Advice from New Jersey Women Business Owners:

Practical Pointers, Solutions, and Strategies for Business Success

D1082328

Edited by Joyce Restaino

Woodpecker Press, LLC
Bayville, NJ

Jersey Women Mean Business!
Big Bold Business^{TM} Advice from New Jersey Women Business Owners:
Practical Pointers, Solutions, and Strategies for Business Success

Copyright © 2012 Woodpecker Press, LLC
and Grow Your Business Write, LLC
All rights reserved.

Published by
Woodpecker Press, LLC
P.O. Box 316, Bayville, New Jersey 08721-0316
www.WoodpeckerPress.com
info@woodpeckerpress.com

To order additional copies of the book, visit www.WoodpeckerPress.com.

ISBN: 978-1-937397-07-4 (sc)
ISBN: 978-1-937397-08-1 (ebk)
ISBN: 978-1-937397-09-8 (ebk)
ISBN: 978-1-937397-10-4 (ebk)
ISBN: 978-1-937397-11-1 (ebk)

Printed in the United States of America

Cover design: Hit Designs, www.HitDesigns.com

Dedication

To my husband, Pat, and children, Nicole and Scott

–Joyce Restaino
Editor

To my husband, Peter, son, Ben,
and in memory of my parents, Julia and Hugo

–Donna R. Thompson
Publisher

Acknowledgments

Publishing is my passion, as is the case with so many others involved in this wonderful field. Thus, producing this book—the first in a series of Big Bold Business Books—is exhilarating and provides me with a deep sense of satisfaction and pride that comes with any great accomplishment. The smell of that new book right out of the box from the printer never gets old.

When Joyce Restaino, the owner of Grow Your Business Write, LLC, brought the idea for this book to Woodpecker Press, we together embraced the concept. She and I have worked closely on the book, gotten to know our authors through their words, expanded on our vision for Big Bold Business, and are excited about where this concept will take us. In all our endeavors, we intend to showcase the ingenuity and insight of our authors—each of whom is a business owner—with the ultimate goal of helping the reader or audience learn new ideas or better understand how to succeed in his or her own business.

A book compilation, such as this one, can only be achieved with the cooperation, input, dedication, creativity, talent, and skill from those directly involved. Thus, the following are acknowledged for their participation in and contributions to this book:

Editor: Joyce Restaino, Grow Your Business Write, LLC

Proofreaders: Peter Thompson, Cheryl Iannarella, Hedi Molnar

Graphic Artist: Raquel Bonassisa, Hit Designs

Writers: Caryn Starr-Gates, Maria-Elena Grant, Hedi Molnar, Lisa Romeo

Printers: Jim Harris and Gerry Burstein, G & H Soho, Inc.; Holly Kaplansky, Minuteman Press of Newark

Social Media Marketing and Website Specialists: Gene Sower, SamsonMedia.net; Pattie Simone, WomenCentric.net; Rosanna Imbriano, RI Consulting; Donna Price, Compass Rose Consulting

Videographer: Erik Galuppo, Galuppo Productions

I sincerely thank every one of these professionals and look forward to the possibility of working with them again on future volumes of the Big Bold Business Book Series. And, last but certainly not least, thank you to each of the seventy-two New Jersey business owners who took the time to write a chapter for this book. Congratulations as you enjoy the benefits of being a published author!

Donna R. Thompson
Publishing Director
Woodpecker Press, LLC

Table of Contents

Introduction

Everything starts with an idea...a concept...a vision...a dream. Create the next hot fashion trend. Pursue a career as a professional athlete. Put an end to worldwide hunger. Find a cure for the deadliest diseases. Change the way people work and communicate with the next great advance in technology. Own your own business.

Ideas are everywhere—there certainly is no shortage. Triggered by a conversation, a movie, a picture, a story—they come easily. The difficulty with ideas is turning them into reality, especially when you have to deal with the naysayers—the doubters—the skeptics—and the laughers. Those who move forward have confidence, courage, conviction—and support. The support typically comes from one or two people who believe in the idea.

That's how this book came to be. It started with an idea to compile the collective wisdom of New Jersey women business owners eager to share their expertise, knowledge, and know-how with entrepreneurs, small business owners, start-ups, and would-be business owners around the world. When I brought this idea to Donna Thompson, of Woodpecker Press (the publisher of this book), and her then-partner, Brenda Hendrickson, they jumped on board. Although I had the experience and know-how on the writing and editing end, I did not have the ability to—nor did I want to—publish a book of this nature by myself. The result of our collaboration—this book—is very 21st century business.

The Power of Many and How One Person Can Make a Difference

To publish this book, we needed many New Jersey women business owners willing to fill its pages with lessons, advice, tips, and inspiration that would both encourage and elevate business owners: women and men. This book is a reality because of the 72 New Jersey women business owners who contributed chapters. They range from start-ups to well-established companies. Yes, all of them, combined, made this book possible. However, each business owner you meet on these pages makes a difference in the lives of the people her business serves.

Big and Bold—A Jersey Thing

Big and bold is a Jersey thing. Reality TV has certainly played up the "Jersey" attitude. After all, we have *The Real Housewives of New Jersey*, the *Jersey Shore*, *Jerseylicious*, and of course, the fictitious Sopranos—to name a few. So the spotlight shines on New Jersey's big, bold "characters." But here's reality: Owing your own business is a 24/7 commitment filled with risks, responsibilities, and rewards. Owning your own business is a big, bold accomplishment.

This also speaks to the character of the women behind each business. Their reasons for starting a business vary. Whether it was driven by passion, a desire to control their own destiny, the result of downsizing, or frustration with a corporate position (many of these women business owners have rich corporate backgrounds), each business owner took the big, bold step that others only dream about. In doing so, their companies support their families and the families of their employees.

On these pages, you'll find lessons, inspiration, encouragement, proven tips, and action steps that you can use in your business. Each time you implement or adapt what you have learned from these women business owners, you take a big, bold step and move closer to your goals. This book is a team effort, yet each business owner is an expert in her own right. Use the members of this team to guide you as you make your next big, bold push to move your business forward.

How to Get the Most Out of this Book

- Start anywhere—with any chapter. There is no particular sequence to follow.
- Rich in "show-how" and inspiration, with hundreds of tips, techniques, and ideas—try or tweak those that will make your business more efficient, create a community, attract more customers, ramp up demand for your product/service, reach new markets, and more.
- Contact the contributors for more resources and information, and connect with them on social media platforms. You'll find contact information in each author's bio box.
- Let the contributors know how their advice and expertise helped you.
- Spread the word about this book to other business owners and entrepreneurs.
- Write a review of this book on Amazon.
- Connect with the "Big Bold Business Community" http://www.facebook.com/bigboldbusiness

Now, on behalf of the 72 women business owners who appear on these pages, here's to your BIG BOLD business success!

Joyce Restaino
Editor

Financial and Legal

Take Charge of Your Future with a Supercharged Retirement Strategy

by Jaime Raskulinecz

As an entrepreneur, you organize, manage, and assume the risks that come with running your own business. You make decisions, build teams, and form strategic partnerships to grow your company. Put simply, you're in control of your professional future—and that's the way you like it.

But what about your financial future and your retirement plans? Are you in control? You can be with a self-directed IRA, which is a retirement account with a slew of unique investment options with tax advantages that you control. Harnessing these tax-advantaged accounts is a smart way to supercharge your retirement with investments you are familiar with and/or interested in.

What is a Self-Directed IRA?

These nontraditional retirement accounts, which include the Roth IRA or SEP IRA (simplified employee pension), let you implement a more aggressive strategy and build a more diverse portfolio by investing in vehicles you have experience with and understand.

Although self-directed IRA accounts are not for everyone, savvy investors with knowledge or expertise in a particular area enjoy the broader variety of investments (with certain restrictions) that a self-directed IRA has to offer. These include real property, loans, partnerships, commercial paper, and certain commodities not typically allowed in common IRAs.

How Does It Work?

Are you a real estate investor? You can purchase residential or commercial property, vacant or developed land, or invest in a renovation or new construction with funds from your self-directed IRA—and take advantage of sheltered income from the rental or sale of that property.

Example 1: Sheila used funds in her self-directed IRA to purchase a vacation home, which she rents out most of the year. The account earns tax-free rental income, and when she sells the property, the sheltered proceeds will go back into the IRA. Sheila cannot use the property personally, so she is using the investment to help grow her retirement account with a strategy she knows and understands.

Do you play the gold market? You can buy and sell precious metals within your self-directed IRA and let the appreciation grow tax deferred in your retirement nest egg.

Would you like to make loans to others with terms you set? Or be an angel investor in a start-up company? Instead of laying out your hard-earned cash, you can invest within a self-directed IRA and earn tax-deferred interest or sheltered income in an account you direct. You can even roll over an old 401(k) or existing IRA to get started on this lucrative, less restricted kind of retirement account.

Example 2: Didi loaned her brother $10,000 from her self-directed IRA to set up a new business. He is repaying the loan at 10% interest over four years. This rate is less than what his credit card offered, and Didi's account is earning much more interest than many regular IRAs earn.

Is a Self-Directed IRA Right for You?

How do you know if this type of tax-advantaged account is right for you? For starters, if you're interested in getting off the roller-coaster ride of the stock and bond markets and breaking free of the restrictions at typical brokerage firms, then you would benefit from learning more about self-directed IRAs.

The more you know and understand, the better you can respond to economic downturns and take advantage of investments more quickly than you would by going through a traditional IRA custodian.

Three Little-Known, Surprising Facts about a Self-Directed IRA

1. **Net worth is not a factor.** It used to be that self-directed IRAs were the domain of high–net worth individuals, but not anymore. You can get started with an initial investment of a few thousand dollars.

2. **Age doesn't matter.** You could be a young investor in your 20s, just starting your retirement plan and looking to do something more aggressive with investments you are comfortable with. Or, you could be taking distributions from your Roth or traditional IRA. (To take distributions from all IRAs without a penalty, you must be 59½.) Regardless of age, you can open a self-directed account.

3. **You can roll over funds**. Maybe you want to open this type of retirement account for your SEP IRA or to roll over the funds from a traditional IRA or an old 401(k) plan. You can even choose to keep your existing IRA account for stock and bond transactions, and open a self-directed account for your supercharged investment strategy.

The bottom line: You want to be actively involved in your investment decisions—or have a trusted advisor (accountant/CPA, independent fee-based financial planner, or real estate agent) who is knowledgeable about the options available for these nontraditional accounts.

How Do I Open a Self-Directed IRA?

The first step is to work with firms that specialize in administering self-directed retirement plans and serve as custodians of these accounts' assets. Although they are not investment advisors—your investment strategies and choices are entirely up to you—make sure the firm you work with offers support to help you make informed, safe decisions about your investment.

Because there are special processes, documentation, and regulations for these accounts, as account administrators, these firms see that your transactions are handled properly. And to make sure your investments are completed and maintained according to IRS regulations, they take care of the necessary paperwork.

If you understand certain markets and investments, or are already investing in ones outside of your retirement plan, think about applying what you know to this investment strategy with a self-directed IRA. Besides supercharging your retirement, this strategy puts you in control of your future.

Jaime Raskulinecz is the CEO and founder of Next Generation Trust Services in Roseland, New Jersey. The company specializes in comprehensive account administration and transaction support services for self-directed retirement accounts. Jaime entered the business in 2004 because she wanted to make real estate investments within her retirement accounts. A long-time real estate investor, she is a certified property manager and licensed real estate broker in New Jersey. For information on self-directed IRAs or to open an account, contact Jaime at 973-533-1880 or JaimeR@NextGenerationTrust.com.

How to Stop the Financial Bleeding and Push through the Chaos of a Financial Crash

by Debra A. Courtright

You are speeding along the highway of small business entrepreneurship: you have clients—money is coming in, money is going out. But this balance is precarious, so you move cautiously through the yellow light—and then *bam*! You are hit from behind. Your cash flow is sideswiped and your business is bleeding everywhere. Enter chaos: telephone calls, collection agency letters, and threatening letters to shut you down.

How do you stop the bleeding? What strategies can you use to get through this financial crash? First and foremost, *do not pay anything based on harassment* until you can look at the whole picture to better understand your situation—then follow these step-by-step instructions. It could save the life of your business.

- *Do not* pay bills as they arrive. You need to strategize how you will make payments based on available cash flow, or you could run short for necessities.
- Prioritize your expenses (vendors) by listing the absolute necessities first (rent, utilities, staff, etc.). Do not forget any automatic charges deducted from your checking account.
- Create a cash flow projection by the week, for each month, including anticipated income and expenses. Create the following columns:
  1. Anticipated income
  2. Bills expected to arrive
  3. Actual funds received
  4. Percentage of revenue to be put in savings
  5. Actual bills received
  6. Difference
  7. Wish list column (meetings, advertising, special projects) in case there is a surplus
- To help keep track of pending debt, enter all invoices into an accounting program to track accounts payable.
- Figure out your breakeven point. Simply put: how much money you need each week, and ultimately, at the end of the month, to pay all of your expenses. Don't forget to include any miscellaneous expenses, such as networking, travel, meetings, etc.

- Run your accounts receivable report and work diligently in collecting all outstanding invoices. If you have anything due over ninety days, consider using a collection service (fees range from twenty-five percent to thirty-three percent).

- A short-term option to increase cash flow is to use factoring—selling your accounts receivable or invoices to a third party at a discount.

- Run reports that can help you analyze your cash flow. Do the majority of your funds arrive around the tenth to fifteenth, or at the end of the month?

- Based on your cash flow analysis, pay your monthly expenses twice a month: for example, the tenth and twenty-fifth normally work; however, your business obligations may indicate that you need to change these dates. Changing dates allows you to deposit income, so you know what funds are available to pay the expenses, instead of projecting the receipt of income.

- If payments are due that do not fit into your semimonthly payment strategy, call the vendor and request a change of the due date. Most of the time, the vendor can work with you.

- Before you pay any bills, balance or reconcile your bank account.

- Before you pay anything, calculate the amount of income received during the previous half month and put aside a minimum of 2.5 percent into a no-touch savings account for severe emergencies. (Ideally, you want to put away more, but be realistic).

- If you fall behind with vendor payments, call them and work out a strategy for partial payments. If you reach out to them before they call you, you have a better chance of working things out. Make sure you can meet your payment promises.

- As you review each vendor invoice, check for irregularities and mistakes. Telephone, Internet, and credit card processing statements are notorious for hidden fees or increasing fees without your knowledge. Scrutinize each invoice, and research alternatives.

- Get rid of any service you do not need. Be careful with any service that might have a termination clause: telephone and cell phone companies are famous for charging early termination fees that can be quite costly.

- Check credit card charges regularly. It is easy to forget to discontinue an automatic charge.

- Try and obtain a no-interest credit card to transfer any current interest-bearing credit card debt.

- Take a look at your payroll periods. Depending on your cash flow, you may find it easier to cover payroll on the fifteenth and last day of the month instead of biweekly. Be advised that semimonthly payroll amounts will be higher because there are only twenty-four pay periods instead of twenty-six pay periods.
- Review your insurance policies and try to spread payments over time.
- Workers Compensation can be paid at the time your payroll is run instead of paying one or two large lump payments.
- If cash flow permits, pay more than the minimum balance on any long-term debt or credit card payments. For example, if you pay $50 a month additional on your five-year car loan, you can save interest and finish paying the debt approximately six to nine months early.
- If rent becomes difficult to pay in one lump sum, talk to your landlord and negotiate paying half at the first of the month and the balance midmonth.
- If your utilities peak during the summer and are lower in the winter months (or a variation of this), have your utilities averaged over the year. Warning: watch for unexpected heat waves or cold weather since your end-of-the year invoice could include a large catch-up balance.
- Treat your revenue like gold!

What if your crash is life threatening to your business, and you are unable to answer the phone or open another envelope or sit anywhere near your desk for fear of coming face-to-face with past due invoices? The smartest move you can make is to find someone to take over these tasks for you. It does not have to be a paid consultant. It could be a friend, a colleague, a spouse—but I highly recommend someone who can be objective in helping you stop the bleeding.

Debra A. Courtright is president of D.A.C Management, Inc., which came into existence a long time before it was officially a named business. Her early beginning was running the finances of her father's small pizzeria and then taking on the challenge of running two fast-food venues while in high school. From there, her accounting and bookkeeping skills have taken her on many roads and journeys, serving profit and nonprofit organizations and small- and medium-sized businesses and their special cash flow needs. To reach Debra, contact her by phone at 973-618-9288 or e-mail at debra@dacmanagement.biz, or visit www.dacmanagement.biz.

Divide and Conquer: Use Segmentation to Control Your Business and Boost Your Profits

by Brenda Hendrickson

Do you know if your business is profitable? Do you know which product or service brings in the most revenue? Do you know the net profit for each of your products or services?

If you answered "No" to any of these questions, you're not alone. In fact, during my twenty-plus years of bookkeeping and accounting work for small business owners, I have found that although they have an intuitive sense of how their business is doing, many *do not* know how each of their products or services is performing. Unfortunately, without this information, businesses waste time, resources, and money on poor or losing performers. This is true, even when total sales (the numbers) show a profit.

Of course, the bottom line in any business is in the numbers. But numbers can tell different stories. It depends on how you look at them. If you want to know where to spend your hard-earned dollars to get the maximum return on investment and generate more profits, segmentation will help you see clearly.

Segmentation: What It Is and Why You Should Use It

Segmentation shows you how each of your products or services is performing. The beauty of segmentation is that it gives you the ability to closely monitor the effectiveness of a marketing or sales campaign so you can make timely management decisions to alter a plan or discontinue a product or service. Any savings from losing performers can be used for your more profitable products or services. Most important, you don't have to wait until tax time to catch mistakes and missed opportunities. (Oops!)

Almost every business can benefit from segmentation. But since it takes some thought about the products and/or services you offer, the first step is to determine how to segment them to reflect the profitability of your company. For example, you can segment by product, service, customer, region, or any other attribute. Second is to work with a QuickBooks (accounting software) expert to revise or set up your chart of accounts. The chart of accounts is a list of accounts that is used to classify each transaction.

To see how segmentation can benefit your business and boost your profits, let's look at two scenarios for a client of mine who uses QuickBooks.

Scenario 1

Although my client reconciles her bank statement to account for all cash that comes in and goes out, and she generates a profit and loss statement so she knows if there is a profit or loss, the report tells her nothing about the three services (consulting, training, seminars) she sells. Why? Because her three services are lumped together and classified as *sales*, as seen in the following report:

	Sales	Expenses	Profit and Loss
Totals	$59,300	$42,900	$16,400

This report shows that the company made money—approximately twenty-eight percent ($16,400/$59,300). Is my client happy? Yes. But putting all revenues in sales limits her ability to analyze her business. Because the expenses are not classified for each of her three services, scenario 1 tells her nothing about the individual services she offers and whether she is making or losing money on any of them. What my client does not know is that a segment of her business is losing money, so her assumptions about her business could be misleading.

How can she remedy this? By revising her chart of accounts to include an income account for each of her three services—which you can see in scenario 2.

Scenario 2

Remember, the three services she provides are consulting, training, and seminars. But unlike scenario 1, this report uses segmentation to show revenues, expenses, and profits and losses for each service.

Services	Revenues	Expenses	Profit and Loss
Consulting	$25,500	$10,800	$14,700
Training	$15,100	$12,100	$3,000
Seminars	$18,700	$20,000	−$1,300
Totals	$59,300	$42,900	$16,400

Another benefit of using segmentation is that my client can match the revenue for each of her profit centers (services) with the related expenses. This is called the matching principle. Using the matching principle to show the profit and loss (before taxes) for each of the services she provides, you can see that one of her services—seminars—shows a loss.

With this information, my client can make important and timely management decisions as she moves forward. For instance, is the loss significant? No. Can a reduction in seminar expenses make seminar services profitable? Yes. Or, my client can eliminate the seminar services and put the seminar expenses into increasing the profitability of the two remaining services. My client has many options. It will be up to management to analyze and make those decisions. As you can see from this example, segmentation gives my client the information (numbers) she needs to position her business for growth.

A Single Product or Service
Can Benefit from Segmentation

Does segmentation work if you sell just one product or service? Yes. Let's say you want to identify your best customers to reward them with a special discount. Segmentation allows you to identify them. (Maybe you want to reward those who spent $1,000 in the last six months or those who spent $100 in the last thirty days.) And once you identify your best customers, you can allocate more funds and devote more time to keeping them coming back and referring you to others. That's how it works.

Segmentation does take a little brainstorming, but it is well worth the effort. Best of all, it can be adapted to all types of businesses to increase profitability. Of course, it's worthwhile to work with an experienced professional who can structure your chart of accounts to segment your business to give you the best possible control over your profitability. Wouldn't you like to put your money and effort into the products and services that will produce the most profit? Now you know how.

Brenda Hendrickson is an award-winning businesswoman. Changing times and environment have helped her to be more educated, resolved, and successful. Her various careers encompass the sciences, where she received a patent, to entrepreneurship, where she founded several businesses and sold a very successful tax practice. Her experiences as a certified senior advisor, accountant, and tax preparer have earned her major acclaims and awards, such as NJAWBO 2008 Business Woman of the Year, NJBIZ 2009 50 Best Women in Business, and the NJAWBO Teal Heart Award for going above and beyond. Brenda has held elected positions as treasurer and president of the Essex County Chapter of NJAWBO, treasurer of the Cedar Grove Education Foundation, and vice president of the Cedar Grove Lions; and she volunteers with a food kitchen and pantry for local churches. She also wrote a book, *How To Be A Frugal Millionaire*, which was published in 2008. For more information or to contact Brenda, visit www.brendahendricksoncsa.com.

Eight Steps to Retirement Planning and Financial Security

by Elise Feldman

Business owners face many challenges. Whether you are just starting out or planning to expand your business, you have to deal with financing, managing human capital, marketing, and exploring ways to become more profitable. Along the way, you may have sacrificed "you" by spending what little free time you have focusing on others.

Well, it's time to spend some of your energy thinking about yourself and your future. And my goal is to help you create financial security for your future—however you envision your lifestyle. Of course, in order to live the lifestyle you envision, you must be able to afford it. The big question is how do you get there? Let me guide the way.

Time Keeps on Slipping into the Future

To plan for your financial future, you will need information. So plan to use common sense, do some research, and consult with knowledgeable advisors. Your advisors can tell you if your expectations are reasonable and then steer you in the right direction so you reach your retirement goals. Here are eight steps to put you in control of your financial future:

1. **Determine your ideal future lifestyle.** Create a mental image of how you want to live when you are no longer working full time, and answer the following:

- Do you plan to fully retire or work part time?
- Will part-time work be in your current field or an area you are interested in but haven't had time to pursue?
- What will that future lifestyle cost? Create a budget and factor in inflation—an increase in costs and expenses based on the rate of growth in the economy. (While inflation is minimal now, you might want to increase amounts by one to five percent to be sure you have enough to meet your expectations.)
- Will you be sharing your lifestyle with anyone? If so, will they contribute financially?
- Where do you want to live, and in what type of housing (town house, own your home, apartment, senior community)?
- What activities do you want to participate in? What will they cost?
- Who else (people or charities) must you provide for, and when?

2. Assess your current financial situation and create a budget by doing the following:

- Tally your current assets (those that are available for spending) such as cash, checking accounts, securities, and salable assets. You may be planning to sell items collected or acquired such as art, jewelry, and real estate.
- Determine when your assets will be liquid or "spendable."
- Do a statistical projection at a moderate rate of interest to see what those assets will actually be worth at the time you plan to use them. Get a statistical calculator to calculate these figures on your own. HP and TI are popular calculators. My calculator of choice is the HP 12c.
- Compare these figures to your future financial needs from step 1 to see if there is a difference.

3. Evaluate if the "difference" you need is reasonable and attainable. Creating an unrealistic goal is a surefire way to not reach your goal. If your goal is unrealistic, rethink it.

4. Research your options. You can go this alone. After all, the Internet is a wonderful tool with tons of information at your fingertips. I have found, however, that uninformed research yields incorrect conclusions. The first source I suggest you turn to is your accountant. Query her on her knowledge of retirement planning. If she is not an expert in this area, ask her if she can recommend consultants or advisors who specialize in retirement planning.

5. Determine if you want to do personal savings with after-tax dollars or qualified retirement plans and other such programs with before-tax dollars. Knowledgeable advisors can provide quantifiable analyses on what each version can accomplish. An educated decision is often based on the following factors:

- Your available budget.
- The employees on your payroll, including their age, compensation, and length of service.
- The number of years you will contribute to a plan.
- Your tolerance for paying fees to consultants, working with various advisors, and dealing with the required paperwork.

6. Analyze qualified and nonqualified plan options. Saving in a tax-deferred environment usually allows the contributions to compound and grow larger than when saved outside of these plans. A credentialed consultant can show you the options that are best suited to your needs.

- Ask for feasibility studies. The plan design is crucial.
- Compare the plan features, contribution and benefit limits, and implementation and annual administration processes.

Such plans include 401(k) programs, Profit Sharing, Defined Benefit, Section 125 Cafeteria Plans, Non-Qualified Deferred Compensation Plans, and Individual Retirement Accounts. In some instances, it makes sense to use more than one.

Qualified Retirement Plans offer you a tax deduction for contributions made each year. This privilege comes by following the U.S. Federal rules for Qualified Plans including plan limits, plan entry, vesting, and distributions. In addition, they have set procedures for adoption and annual maintenance.

- Defined Contribution plans such as 401(k) and Profit Sharing have contribution limits. In 2012, the salary deferral limit is $17,000 plus $5,500, if over age 50. The total contribution limit is $50,000 (plus the $5,500 deferral) and covers employer contributions of match and profit sharing.
- Defined Benefit plans have benefit limits. For 2012, you can fund to a benefit at retirement (earliest age 62) of $200,000.
- A variety of these plans are simpler. They include SIMPLE IRA or SIMPLE 401(k) plans, and Simplified Employee Pension Plans (SEPs). Rules on limits and entry vary.

7. Create the plan and stick to it. Retirement savings must be methodical and ongoing. You will need to continually evaluate the program you select—monitoring the laws of a plan and the investments chosen in coordination with your investment tolerance—and adjust for changes in your employee demographics, budget, and business structure.

8. Project the accumulation of new assets and add to your existing ones. Finally, plan for how and when you will take those monies. Research the rules again. It makes sense to evaluate the tax-deferred distribution options along with tax-preferential distribution options.

These eight steps are indeed a project, but one worth doing. They will yield an education and an orderly way to develop your retirement plan, and the financial wherewithal to live your dream.

Elise Feldman, a Certified Pension Consultant (CPC), created Feldman Benefit Services, Inc., to solve employee benefit and tax issues by designing, implementing, and administering retirement, deferred compensation, and other employee benefit programs. She lectures to financial professionals and business owners on retirement planning, employee benefit programs, entrepreneurship, and leadership. A certified sponsor of the State Board of Accountancy, she offers CPE credits to accountants and insurance agents. Elise is a member of the American Society of Pension Professionals and Actuaries, FPA, Vistage, and VP of the Small Business Council of America. You can reach Elise at efeldman@feldmanbenefit.com or 973-376-6777 or by visiting www.feldmanbenefit.com.

Reduce Your Risks:
Legal Advice for Your Business Life

by Sandra L. Cohen

Even though you might not think of yourself as a risk taker, the fact that you own a business proves otherwise. In fact, running your own business may be your dream come true. Although there are many things you can do to keep your dream alive and reduce your risks, consider the following four, and take the necessary steps to protect your business.

Who Owns Your Website?

One of the first things many businesses do is create a website. While this is usually an easy decision—call a Web master and have the website developed, designed, and loaded—there are issues to address with your Web developer and/or designer.

First, be sure that you own all code or software, or have a license to use it. Just because you pay for the design and development does not mean you own the product. Make sure you have a written agreement transferring the ownership of the website and every facet (code, graphics, text, designs, etc.) of it to you. If the developer cannot transfer ownership of the software, be sure you have a license to use it. If you need passwords to access the code, then get them from the developer and/or designer, and test them to make sure they work. Otherwise, if you want to change something on your website, you will have to call the developer or the designer. What will you do if you can't find him or her?

Second, have your Web developer and/or designer transfer and assign all copyright ownership to you, and state that he or she is not using someone else's materials (photographs, copy, music, etc.). It is very easy for developers/designers to obtain information, design, graphics, or text, then copy it and post it to your site. Without assurance that the material is original work, you run the risk of copyright infringement on another's work. To keep your business up and running, make sure you own your website and all of its parts.

Third, post the specific terms and conditions that apply to your website. For example, specify the permitted uses of the site and your ownership of the website; state that the user is responsible for all activities under his or her password, whether authorized or not. Since each business is a little different, terms of use may need to be customized and may need to comply with certain laws or guidelines in order to protect you and your business. Have users agree to your terms and conditions by requiring them to click an "I accept" button or a box that contains the terms and conditions.

Office Space

A major step for business owners is signing a lease for office space. Clearly, it will include the term of your lease, the rental amount, and payment terms. Make sure you understand whether you are responsible for your utilities or if they are included in the rent. Review the lease to see if you are paying the landlord's real estate taxes and insurance. It is not uncommon for tenants to pay the real estate taxes, but be sure you are only paying your proportionate share (the percentage of the building that your space represents to the entire building). Usually, a landlord shifts all expenses it has to pay for the care and maintenance of the building to the tenant, including the common areas (areas shared by all tenants). The lease should also specify who is responsible for repairs to the premises. Keep in mind that a commercial lease is often drafted in favor of the landlord. These are just some of the key provisions to consider.

Protect Your Products and Services

If you use a word, phrase, symbol, or design that identifies your product or service, consider trademark registration. A trademark is a word or design that indicates you as the source of the product. Similarly, a service mark identifies the source of the service. (Note: trademark is used here to refer to both service marks and trademarks.) For example, we all know that a product bearing a "swoosh" is made by Nike. A trademark that is similar to another mark may be refused registration because it is likely to cause confusion for the consumer if both marks are used in similar channels of trade.

You can legally protect your mark on a state or federal level. If you only do business in one state, a state registration may be enough. However, if you do business nationwide, federal trademark registration is a good idea. Doing so protects your mark and prevents others from using the mark in connection with similar goods or services. Once the mark is used in commerce, you can add the trademark symbol ™. You can use this designation without any registration. However, the symbol ® can only be used after you obtain federal registration of the trademark. Consider applying for trademark registration to protect your rights and enhance your business brand and its assets.

Keep it Confidential

A confidentiality agreement or nondisclosure agreement (NDA) can be critical to a business. These agreements protect confidential and proprietary information. The type of information covered is set forth in the agreement and can range from specific product information to marketing strategy.

An NDA can be between you and an employee or consultant. Or it can be between you and another party with whom you seek to do business. For example, you might evaluate if you want to perform services for one another, or if the information is being disclosed so the other party can manufacture a product for you. Before disclosing information or ideas, ask the other party to sign a confidentiality agreement or NDA. By entering into such an agreement, the other party cannot disclose or use information you provide if it is considered confidential under the agreement. The agreement should state that your information remains confidential, even if your relationship with the other party ends.

Running a successful business includes taking risks. But failing to legally protect your business assets is risky business. That is why safeguarding your business is a major key to success in today's competitive world.

NOTE: The points raised are general in nature and should not be taken as legal advice or as a substitute for careful review of your business concerns with an attorney and the preparation of appropriate documentation. Every business and its situations are unique, and different approaches may be necessary in different circumstances. This information is intended as a guide. To make sure you are in compliance, consult individual state laws as well as federal laws.

Sandra L. Cohen, Esq., is an attorney and partner at Epstein Cohen & Gilberti, LLC, in Red Bank, New Jersey. She practices in the areas of corporate, transactional, real estate, trademark, and franchise law. Sandra has been an instructor of Corporate Law at Farleigh Dickinson University, Paralegal Studies program. She received her J.D. from Seton Hall Law School, cum laude, and her B.A. from Douglass College, Rutgers University, cum laude, and studied at Notre Dame University, London, England. She is a member of the New Jersey State Bar Association. For more information, contact Sandra by phone at 732-212-0400 and at cohen@ecg-law.com.

Prenups—Not Just for Marriages

by Geralyn Gahran Humphrey

I'm sure you've heard why it's a good idea to have a prenuptial agreement (fondly referred to as a prenup) before getting married, particularly if one or both spouses have significant assets or children from a prior relationship. Well, owning and running a business with a partner(s) can be as emotional and complicated as any marriage. Having an agreement—a prenup—with your business partner is even more crucial than having a marital prenup, especially if your business partner is your spouse or another family member.

What is a business prenup? A business prenup is an agreement between the business owners that establishes how they will set up and run the business. The exact name of a business prenup will vary with the form of the business. It may be called a partnership agreement, an operating agreement, an LLC agreement, a shareholders' or stockholders' agreement, or a buy-sell agreement.

Recipe for a Business Prenup

A business prenup typically deals with the following:

Money in—what each owner will contribute to the business at start-up.

Dividing the pie—each owner's percentage interest in the business, and whether there are multiple classes of ownership interests with different owners and/or voting rights. For example, there may be class A ownership interests, which have voting rights, and class B ownership interests, which have no voting rights.

Who does what—each owner's title and area of responsibility in the business, as well as the types of decisions where some or all of the owners have veto rights.

Future funding—what happens if the business needs more money. This could include additional contributions from some or all of the owners, as well as loans or other outside funding.

Money out—how the profits (or losses) of the business will be divided, and how the distributions to the owners will be handled.

Disaster planning—what happens if an owner dies or becomes disabled. This is the part of the prenup that is frequently referred to as a "buy-sell" because it typically involves the mandatory or optional sale of the interest of the deceased or disabled owner in the business.

New owners—how new owners are added to the business.

Exit strategy—what happens if an owner wants to leave the business or transfer all or part of her interest in the business.

Lights out—what happens if the business is sold or liquidated.

Advantages of a Business Prenup

"But we get along so well, I'm sure we'll figure it out." "Why do we need to define our relationship?" "I'm sure we're going to be successful. Why do we need to think about negative things?" "We don't need no stinkin' paper!" These are all things engaged couples say. But prospective business partners say the same things. The same optimism and euphoria that an engaged couple feel at the start of their marriage are present when people start a business together. So why interrupt all of these good feelings to prepare an agreement? Here are three key reasons:

1. Planning for success. Like premarital counseling, preparing a business prenup requires the business owners to think about how to deal with the various steps of starting and running a business, including some of the day-to-day aspects that may have been glossed over during the "courtship" phase of the relationship.

For example, will all of the owners be involved in all phases of the business, or will each be in charge of a certain area? Will all of the owners have to agree on every decision, or are there certain decisions that an owner can make without needing approval from the other owners? If the business needs more money, will all of the owners have to contribute? What if one or more of the owners do not contribute?

These issues may not be as interesting as deciding how to divide all the money that the business is sure to make, but working them out is essential to the smooth operation of the business. It is better to work them out before a crisis arises—when stress and emotions may keep the owners from thinking clearly. I'm sure you've heard this before: If you fail to plan, you are planning to fail.

2. Protecting your investment. The business owners will be investing significant time and money to start the business. It only makes sense to decide how to protect that investment if the unexpected happens. For example, what if one of the owners dies? Will the deceased owner's family take over that part of the business? Will the other owner(s) be required or have the option to buy out the deceased owner's share of the business? How will any buyout be funded? Again, it is better to think about these issues before the crisis hits. Some possible protections, such as insurance, need to be in place before the event occurs.

3. Getting a different perspective on your business partner.
Observing how each owner acts in the course of preparing a business prenup often provides valuable clues about how that owner will act when running the business. This may reinforce the decision to start the business, or lead the owners to rethink their decision. If so, it's better to have this occur before the owners invest more time and money.

A business prenup should be part of the standard documentation for any multiowner business, regardless of size. Does it guarantee that the business will be successful? Of course not. But it makes it more likely that the relationship of the owners during the life of the business will run more smoothly and in line with each owner's expectations.

Disclaimer: The information in this chapter is not, nor is it intended to be, legal advice. The law changes frequently and varies from jurisdiction to jurisdiction. You should consult an attorney for advice regarding your particular situation.

Geralyn (Lynn) Gahran Humphrey, Esq., is the founder and principal attorney at The Humphrey Law Firm, LLC. Lynn represents smaller, growing businesses in all phases of business life, including business formations, business loans, sales and purchases of businesses, and the preparation and review of business contracts. She also represents businesses and individuals in connection with the purchase, sale, and financing of commercial and residential real estate. Lynn is licensed to practice in both New Jersey and Pennsylvania. Want more information? Check out Lynn's website at www.humphreylawnj.com. She can also be reached at 973-287-6616 or ghumphrey@humphreylawnj.com.

Marketing: Strategic

Cooperative Marketing: A Smart Strategy That Ends Costly Marketing Mistakes

by Robbi Hershon

Does the following sound familiar?

You're an intelligent person—a professional—a doctor, lawyer, chiropractor, accountant, etc. You open or relocate your office, fitted with the latest equipment, to best serve your patients or clients. You even put a sign out front, so people know where you are and what you do. So, why doesn't the phone ring? Why aren't people lining up outside your door?

I'll tell you why: your prospects don't know about you or your business. *You* have to tell them where you are, what you do, and why they should stop by to meet you. And the way to do that is better known as marketing. Marketing, of course, is the lifeblood of any practice or business, but with so many marketing techniques and promotional materials to try, it is not always as effective as you would like it to be.

From my experience, marketing at its best can be good, bad, or downright ugly. What worked in the past doesn't necessarily work the next time. Yet, in order to reach new and existing customers, clients, or patients, you must market your services and products. If you don't reach out, then certainly your competitors will.

Of course, there are costs to market your products or services, which add up quickly. And remember, the medium you use to get your message across has a big impact on the overall cost of your marketing campaign. But one resourceful and cost-effective way my partner and I use to promote our practice, The Hearing Group, and to reduce the cost of marketing, is to partner with a manufacturer or vendor with whom we routinely do business.

The Perks of Partnering with Manufacturers

We partner with the manufacturers of the products we recommend for our patients. Not only does the manufacturer provide us with a wide selection of marketing materials to choose from, but they also customize their ads to our practice and coordinate the delivery of the marketing piece, whether it is direct mail or print advertising. One of the biggest benefits we receive by partnering with our manufacturers is that most of them will reimburse our practice up to fifty percent of the cost of the advertisement, up to a certain dollar amount.

For example, if we decide to execute a direct mail piece that will cost our practice $5,000, a manufacturer could reimburse us up to the maximum amount of $2,500. Some manufacturers will actually give us a check for that amount; others will issue coupons totaling fifty percent of the advertising costs. We, in turn, use the coupons to purchase products at a reduced price, which results in a greater profit on the sale of those particular products.

Opportunities to Increase Income

Some vendors or manufacturers offer us a business-enhancement service. This type of program allows a practice or business to "bank" some of the money spent on the cost of the products. This money can be used to defray the cost of marketing. It can also be used to purchase equipment for the office. By combining cooperative dollars with the money in the "bank," the cost of marketing becomes much more affordable.

For one open house, we partnered with a hearing aid manufacturer. We placed a four-page insert, which was customized to our practice, into a statewide newspaper. We selected the zip codes we wanted to target. The total cost was $4,400, which included the printing and insertion.

The manufacturer reimbursed our practice $2,200. We then recouped the remaining fifty percent from our previously earned business-enhancement funds, bringing the cost of the insert to zero. The manufacturer also sent a technology specialist to our office to assist us during the open house. Most of the people who responded to the ad were new to our practice. Not only did we grow our practice by gaining new patients, but we also generated income by selling hearing aids to the patients who needed them.

Another effective marketing method is to hold an information session conducted by the manufacturer's representative. In one instance, we part-nered with another one of our vendors. We sent a direct mail piece to several thousand homes, once again using demographics to specifically target our potential patients. This manufacturer customized the marketing piece—an oversized postcard—to our practice.

At the information session, with the help of the manufacturer's repre-sentative, we presented a slide show to the twenty attendees who responded to the direct mail piece. We also provided a light meal. As a result, we scheduled appointments and sold about $36,000 worth of hearing aids. Again, because this direct mail piece was co-oped at fifty percent in coupons to be used toward the purchase of their products, we were able to purchase the hearing aids for less than what it would normally have cost us, which significantly increased our profits.

Cooperative marketing can be a win-win situation—especially in a slow economy—because both the manufacturer and the business benefit. The business reduces the amount of money spent on the marketing campaign and has the chance to sell more products. In addition, the business drives more sales to the manufacturer.

After nearly eight years in private practice, although I am certainly no marketing expert, I have learned these methods allow us to market our business at a reasonable cost, attract more patients, provide a range of quality hearing aids so our patients have a better quality of life, and grow our business and that of our vendors.

 **Robbi Hershon, Au.D., CCC-A**, is a doctor of audiology and a partner in The Hearing Group, located in West Orange, New Jersey. Her practice provides hearing solutions to people of all ages. She is there to help you every step of the way, in identifying hearing loss to dispensing the hearing aids to help you hear better. With over twenty-five years of experience, she is a member of the American Speech Language and Hearing Association, the New Jersey Academy of Audiology, and the Rotary Club of West Orange, and is a board member of the nonprofit Help the Children Hear. To find out how Dr. Hershon and The Hearing Group can help you, visit www.thehearinggroupusa.com, phone them at 973-243-8860, or send an e-mail to hearinggroup@comcast.net.

Developing Strategic Alliances to Build Your Business

by Rosanna Imbriano

Unless you just won the lottery, chances are you are careful about the way you spend your marketing dollars to earn the greatest return on investment. Of course, the whole purpose of marketing is to gain exposure for your business and ultimately grow it, which can be challenging under any economic circumstance. But did you know that one of the most effective ways for a company to handle its marketing and public relations—especially one on a shoestring budget—is to form strategic alliances?

A strategic alliance is formed between companies or organizations that share the same target audiences/markets and provide complementary products or services. They work together to help each other build their businesses through referrals and by outsourcing work to each other.

Forming a strategic alliance that builds business for all parties involved can be done in several ways. The easiest one is to identify other businesses that are compatible with yours, so you can partner for mutual benefit.

Increase Revenue—Not Marketing Dollars

Creating the right strategic alliance can help your business grow and increase its profits without spending additional marketing dollars. By building the right business relationships and partnering with them, you can develop a more cost-efficient way to increase revenue.

The first step is to identify your company's revenue streams and target markets by identifying where your revenue comes from and what kind of growth you want. Once you establish that, identify the strategic partners who can help you build your business and vice versa. Together, you can boost profitability because you are generating business for each other without spending media dollars.

For instance, in order to offer more services and grow, a printer could partner with a graphic designer, and a graphic designer could partner with a writer to work on client projects. If you run an auto body shop, you can benefit from a relationship with insurance agents or companies who are seeking a reputable shop where they can send their policy holders without hesitation. These are examples of how partnering with the right product or service provider can help companies accomplish their business-building goals effectively without spending unnecessary marketing dollars.

Once you have identified your strategic partners, you need to do the following:

- **Identify and clarify your marketing goals.** Do you want to increase business, develop alliances for the future, grow the business physically, boost its visibility in a certain area, or increase sales by a certain percentage? Whatever your goals, you'll want to network with those complementary businesses or organizations that can help you reach them more efficiently.

- **Figure out how to attain those goals within your marketing budget**. Forming strategic alliances means you will have other businesses or individuals marketing for you, making it much easier to stay within your budget. Together, you can work inexpensively and effectively, leaving more money to flow to the bottom line.

- **Consider hiring a consultant who specializes in strategic marketing.** Some business owners prefer the buffer of another professional who makes the connections as part of an overall marketing plan. Often that outside consultant can see potentially profitable connections between businesses that the owners do not see, suggest different ways for business owners to position themselves and their ability to work with others to boost their market share, seek out charitable organizations that align with a company's mission or goals for community outreach—or simply represent the business owner (who is busy running the day-to-day operations) in a polished, professional manner.

Note: If you do hire a strategic-marketing consultant, make sure that person does not merely offer you a cookie-cutter approach to this business development strategy. The consultant should take the time to truly understand your business, your target market(s), your goals, and your budget—and offer a customized approach to meet your needs.

Mutual Benefit is Key

Successful strategic alliances are two-way streets; therefore, before approaching businesses that can bring you new clients and additional revenue, make sure you can provide a product or service to help them meet their marketing goals as well. Your strategic partners should have a vested interest in helping your business grow, and you should demonstrate an equally strong commitment to their business development. That mutual cross-promotion and support through smart outsourcing is the hallmark of a successful alliance that creates a win-win relationship for all parties involved.

Perhaps your company provides website design and Internet marketing. A great way to expand your internal capabilities and attract more business is to offer copywriting services for your website clients. Instead of hiring a staff copywriter, you can strike a strategic partnership with writers you know and trust. Your company would expand its in-house services by providing website design and content creation. With additional services, you can take on more clients and increase billing. Of course, the writers you work with will see their revenue increase, too—thanks to the projects you refer to them.

Another example is in the real estate and mortgage fields, where real estate agents and mortgage brokers support each other by referring clients to home inspectors, home stagers, moving companies, financial planners, and other related professionals. These strategic alliances make sense because they are an appropriate match and serve as a way to expand each partner's market reach and referral base and improve customer relations.

Whether you develop these business-building relationships on your own or hire a marketing consultant to ally your company with complementary businesses, you will find that the power of two (or three or more!) is far greater than going it alone. After all, successful collaboration brings new knowledge, new markets, and new sources of revenue.

**Rosanna Imbriano**, owner of R.I. Consulting, LLC (www.riconsultingllc.com), in Cedar Grove, New Jersey, is a marketing strategist and consultant who helps clients grow their businesses through nontraditional marketing methods. She speaks to nonprofits and companies about strategic marketing campaigns and presents seminars on various marketing topics. Rosanna has worked in strategic marketing and public relations ever since she opened her own health spa at the start of her career in her twenties. She was named one of New Jersey's Best 50 Women in Business (2009) by NJBIZ. Along with running her own business, Rosanna is presently the marketing director for The Center for Italian and Italian American Culture (www.ciiac.org). She can be reached at 973-444-2317 or info@riconsultingllc.com.

On Target with Vertical Marketing

by Dawn Johnson

When it comes to marketing, business owners usually target the audience that can benefit most from using their products or services. Let's say, for instance, that your company offers fitness training programs. Since fitness training is not confined to a specific industry, your marketing plan will most likely focus on the audience, such as runners or college basketball players.

On the other hand, when you focus on a specific industry or niche market, your marketing strategy will target the industry before the audience. When you do this, you are engaged in "vertical marketing." To see how vertical marketing works, and how you can adapt it to extend your market reach, follow the eight action steps provided below.

Eight Action Steps to a Bigger and Better Market

Step 1: Review your client list and divide the list into different verticals (industries). The top vertical industries include business services, education, healthcare, hospitality, financial, government, manufacturing, not-for-profit, real estate, and technology. These industries can be segmented into subcategories. For example, healthcare can be broken down into medical, dental, senior or assisted living, biotechnology, pharmaceuticals, and hospitals.

Step 2: Develop a marketing plan to deliver your products or services to the top vertical markets and subcategories.

Step 3: Be creative in your plan. Use your marketing data and leverage campaigns around your target industries. For example, let's use VidaAire (www.VidaAire.com), an organic, all-natural, pure, lemongrass sanitizer spray, to see vertical marketing in action. Since the focus is on a specific industry, the goal is to understand *who* in this market uses the product and *why* they use it.

Let's start with the healthcare/medical industry. The "who" includes massage therapists, neuromuscular therapists, chiropractors, doctors, dentists, veterinarians, as well as health spa and fitness center owners. Why would they use this sanitizer spray? Because it's an organic, all-natural sanitizer that disinfects examination rooms and chairs, as well as fitness equipment. It can be applied directly to leather without causing damage.

VidaAire battles colds and flu, too. It can be applied directly to the skin as a hand sanitizer or sprayed into the air to eliminate germs. It is also an aromatherapy product that relaxes and calms. It can be sprayed to eliminate odors, as well as calm pets. VidaAire Sport was created to market the product to health spas, fitness centers, facilities with locker rooms, and athletes.

Hospitality is another top vertical market for VidaAire, so VidaAire Clean was created to sanitize and disinfect surfaces, while VidaAire Fresh was created to sanitize, disinfect, and freshen linens and upholstery. Because VidaAire repels bedbugs, VidaAire Travel is perfect for hotels, airplanes, cruise cabins, luggage, camps, outdoor activities, movie theaters, and more.

Other applications for VidaAire include use as a bug repellent that is safe to spray on plants to prevent deer and rabbits from eating precious plants and garden goodies. It keeps the bugs away at night, so spray it on your loved ones. Landscapers and gardeners are also good target markets for the product. And real estate agents can use it to freshen and clean homes for sale before showing them. (You get the idea.)

Step 4: Review each of your vertical markets and create an application (how your product or service can be used) for as many subcategories as possible.

Step 5: Dedicate resources to these applications and create marketing tools, including brochures, data sheets, campaigns, and taglines to increase sales.

Step 6: Understand how to farm the top contacts in an industry. Top contacts include C-level executives as well as key people in facilities management, financial, information technology, marketing, operations, safety, sales, training, and the warehouse. Assess these departments for at least three points of contact per department. For example, in the financial department, contact the CFO, controller, and accounts payable manager.

Of course, consider who your contacts know that you can connect with. At the very least, you should know five contacts from your clients and prospects. The more contacts you know in a company, the stronger your relationships with them will be. So, how do you find these contacts? Use social networking. For example, here are my links to social networking and referral sites that I am using to expand my market:

- LinkedIn (http://www.linkedin.com/in/dawnjohnsoncompass)
- Naymz (http://www.naymz.com/dawnjohnson2762163?preview=true)
- Jigsaw (http://www.jigsaw.com/join/DawnJohnson55145.xhtml)

Step 7: Explore how to cross market to your target markets. Once you have focused on an industry, examine your top twenty customers to understand why they bought your product or service. To expand your market, analyze who your customers' clients are and investigate if you have any verticals in common. Can you cross promote your services with your customers? Dig deeper by exploring the other services your customers buy. Can you create a strategic alliance with these companies?

Step 8: Think outside of the box by focusing on the industries that are not on your radar but can benefit from your products or services. VidaAire's hand sanitizer, for example, can be used as a promotional item, so it can partner with promotional companies. VidaAire can partner with florists or home garden stores because they could help customers prevent bugs, deer, or rabbits from eating or destroying their plants. It can also partner with airlines, cruise lines, camping grounds, and movie theaters to optimize healthy conditions for their passengers and guests. (VidaAire is currently used by hotels.)

Now it's time to identify VidaAire's consumers. They are holistic in nature. They may have allergies. They want organic, all-natural, pure, health-conscious products. They enjoy aromatherapy and are looking for nontoxic products. Therefore, VidaAire should look to partner with allergists or consumers who have conditions or diseases that require all-natural products. Foundations, not-for-profits, associations, and support groups for people with these allergies or diseases are additional markets for the product.

To expand the VidaAire market, let's see how it fits into the education vertical. VidaAire can be used in university health centers, to freshen dormitory mattresses and eliminate bed bugs, and in colleges and high schools that use sanitizer dispensers. To be more specific, VidaAire Sport is great for eliminating odors in high school locker rooms and on sports clothing and equipment—just a quick few sprays on those wrestling mats does wonders!

Now that you know how vertical marketing works, explore "new" industries that can benefit from using your products and services, and get ready for your business to grow.

 Dawn Johnson hosts Corporate Queens TV and radio shows to promote and assist women-owned businesses, entrepreneurs, and professionals. The shows offer resources and education to help women build strategic alliances and make connections that will increase their revenue. Dawn's Royal Court provides expert advice on topics such as beauty, marketing, sales, telephone techniques, technology, training, and much more. Visit www.CorporateQueens.com to get more information about tickets and show times, or contact Dawn at dawnjohnson@corporatequeens.com or 973-826-0760.

Numbers: The Secret Sauce to Consumer Marketing

by Monica C. Smith

When I started my business more than a decade ago, I was driven by the following three factors:
1. Entrepreneurial drive is in my DNA.
2. I thought the way most companies approached marketing was wrong.
3. Factors 1 and 2 made me unemployable.

It is fair to say that I view marketing through an unorthodox lens.

It has been my good fortune to have helped shape market approaches as well as analyze consumer and business-to-business data for a variety of brands—that is, companies or divisions with a set of products and/or services identified under a brand name. But after all of my years of focusing on delivering the best insight, I can tell you that marketing by the numbers (the data) is the basis for strong and vibrant results in the marketplace.

Let's travel back for a moment to the late 1990s when the "dot-com boom" was the marketing reality of the moment. Fundamentally, I knew marketers had it wrong. The Internet was not a place where new buyers magically appeared. It was, and still is, an alternative place to shop. The data showed that consumers simply shifted how they purchased. At that time, however, most marketing vice presidents were not interested in that obvious truth. They wanted an easy path, and believed the Internet was it.

The truth is, marketing to consumers is complex. It requires blending talent, passion, and extraordinary discipline, and in bad times—a steady, unemotional hand. The process is not elusive or impossible, but it is a never-ending cycle of change.

The Numbers

Marketing by the numbers is the key to a successful marketing campaign. Numbers will tell you almost anything you want to know about your consumers, for example, what they buy, how much they consume, and where and how often they buy. On the brand side, the numbers tell you how much it costs to communicate with your consumers and the most effective way.

When brands market with discipline—that is, when they identify the key data such as the true cost of all their marketing efforts for a campaign, their returns and cancels, and the costs associated with product, shipping, and credit card processing—they have a stabilized and consistent analytical view and baseline of real costs to start a tracking process.

With this consistently comparable view of the numbers, brand marketers achieve a better understanding of their consumers' reactions to almost any purchase channel. Purchase channels include at the point of sale in retail and online Web transactions, as well as purchases through a call center, a mobile phone, or TV set-top box. This understanding is critical, especially today, since the number of consumer purchase channels is outpacing the marketing technology that reads how consumers interact with and through new forms of media.

At the most basic level, there are the following two requirements for all marketing campaigns:

1. A complete understanding of all costs to acquire a customer, touch an existing customer, and sell each unit at point of sale through your website, direct mail, or direct response television. The numbers change constantly because costs (returns, cancels, communication channels, etc.) shift. Those costs are critical; thus, they must be accurate and up to date.

2. A marketing database that stores customer transactions, interaction, and other data in a standardized format—with easy access to the information. This data repository should store and record changes in customer information—specifically, all the transactions by a customer at the household or business level—and is the best starting point for informed marketing.

The Team

With the two foundation stones in place, you need a team that can work with the data. Ideally, the team should be made up of individuals with both right (creative) and left (logical) brain capabilities. Team members should be strong in math, masters of the Excel application, and have the ability to interpret the data and articulate how to turn the findings into an action plan. They need to be well informed and have an insatiable appetite to learn. I find that individuals who like to read typically bring broader expertise to the team.

Looking back on my track record of helping brands, I like to surround myself with smart teammates—those who have a point of view and are capable of sharing their findings on the brand or customer's stage. Not only do my team members share their voice directly with the brands and companies that are our clients, but they also defend their positions using trends, data points, outside research, and a collection of findings that are not just based on their own perspectives—but on facts.

No Guessing with Data

When pitching a business, I assess the scope of the work as I listen to the potential client discuss the company's objectives and challenges. To achieve a winning marketing campaign, massive amounts of data, along with consumer sentiment and product consumption, must be massaged, read, analyzed, and translated into actionable strategies. Although this is not rocket science, it is not simple.

However, when you have data, there is no need to guess. There is no need to sit behind a desk and pontificate, especially about what worked in the past. What matters? The information at hand and the ability to apply the proper analytical approaches to understand, for example, whether a price point, a new product extension, a brand pillar, or brand engagement strikes a chord and works. The assessment will pinpoint what is successful and should be replicated, and what should be isolated and eliminated.

After analyzing the results, marketers can come up with ideas, products, and brand engagements that move brands, products, or marketing campaigns from behind the corporate walls to the eyeballs they are seeking.

The truth is that consumer (and business) marketing does not stand still for any brand at any time, especially during a rocky economy. Some of the strategies that work today won't necessarily work tomorrow. Simply put, we are alone with our consumers, not only fighting for their attention and their dollars, but for a deeper understanding of what motivates them to buy.

Because marketing is in the numbers, everyone can participate, irrespective of budget size. But without the discipline and the proper tools to understand the impact of marketing dollars in every campaign, a brand is gambling with its marketing budget.

My grandfather, who was an entrepreneur, said, "If winning at the horse races was easy, no one would work." I say, "If all it takes to win customers today is to throw money into communicating with them, we would never have a recession." Consumers are in perpetual motion. To market to them effectively, brands must have the resources and analytical tools to serve up consumer data consistently and accurately. By understanding the numbers, brands can see the patterns of behavior that lead to strategic and actionable consumer marketing.

 **Monica C. Smith**, direct marketer, entrepreneur, and community servant extraordinaire (www.monicacsmith.net) brings strong convictions and a personal passion to all she does. Founding Marketsmith (www.marketsmithinc.com) in 1999, Monica has built it into an industry leader in multichannel marketing strategy, customer insight, analysis, and channel optimization serving DRTV, manufacturers, retailers, and catalogers. It was one of only two female-owned businesses selected as one of *New Jersey's Fifty Finest* in 2007. An independent thinker and industry guru, Monica blogs frequently, sharing insights and analysis of marketing's role in this difficult economy. She believes in giving back to her community through growing her N.J. business, championing the needs of foster children, setting up an intern program for young women, and cofounding "One More Smith" a nonprofit animal sanctuary.

Leadership

From Good to Great: Five Secrets That Separate the Best from the Rest

by Susan P. Ascher

You are doctors, lawyers, CEOs. Accountants, real estate agents, financial consultants. Publicists, business coaches, and salespeople of every kind. I know. I know. You think you are the "best of the best" in your field. And you may well be. But in today's competitive "new normal," being the best is no longer good enough. And to my point, good enough is only good enough. So, if you want to be the best, I'm going to let you in on the five secrets that separate the great from the good.

Secret Number One: IMAGE

If you want to make a million, you have to look like a million.

I don't care if you are fat, ugly, or on a budget. You have—as the conventional wisdom goes—thirty seconds to make a first impression. So do yourself a favor, unless your hair is a stunning shade of gray, color it and make sure you look coiffed. Generally speaking, if your hair looks like it did back in high school or college, you probably need a new style. Keep the makeup light (as Halston once said, "less is more"), but recognize that most successful businesswomen get a little help from their friends at the cosmetic counter.

A good-looking, well-fitting suit or dress (circa the twenty-first century—not from twenty years ago) speaks volumes about your professional image. If you can't afford the couture route (by the way, most of us can't), shop stores such as Annie Sez and Loehmann's—they carry designer brands at discount prices. Of course, you can always cash in on the constant barrage of sales and coupons offered by retailers.

If you are really clueless, I'm sure you have at least one friend who gets the whole image thing. Make her your go-to girl. If that doesn't work, hire an image consultant. She will be worth her weight in future business.

Secret Number Two: DEMEANOR = Poise + Confidence

Knowing how to enter a room (calmly), shaking a hand (it's a gender-neutral thing: firm, not bone crushing or wimpy), and making an introduction, speaks volumes in terms of differentiating you from your competition. Looking someone in the eye, acknowledging the presence of those around you, and engaging others in sincere conversation are the hallmarks of someone who stands out from the herd. After all, people want to associate with those who know how to engage others with authenticity, confidence, and respect.

Secret Number Three: MANNERS and CHARACTER, aka Charm and Disarm

Manners are the way you do things. Some people have good manners; some people have bad manners. You just cannot hide manners. Character, on the other hand, is what you do when no one is watching. It is comprised of the moral and ethical code by which you behave. Without getting too "preachy," the thing that is clear is that people don't live in silos. So you can't scream and yell at your suppliers and employees, but butter up potential clients because they have the power to pay future bills.

Everyone you come into contact with is a potential client or PR agent for you and your business. Never underestimate that you and your company are fully exposed at work and at play. The more often you practice good manners and define yourself with a high degree of ethics and morality, the more it becomes a way of life. If more people chose this standard of excellence, the fewer Tiger Woods and Anthony Weiner types of behavior we would have to excuse.

You get the idea. You cannot just do well or be nice in public—it has to become a way of life for you and your business. And trust me—you *will* stand out from your peers.

Secret Number Four: EXCELLENT COMMUNICATION, aka Building Trust

One of my favorite lines is, "Say what you mean and mean what you say." If I tell you I will call you at 5 p.m., that's when I will call you. Why? Because I want to build your trust in me. And every time I demonstrate honesty, I begin to build your trust. When I communicate clearly, concisely, and in a compelling way—be it in a one-on-one conversation, an e-mail, or a voice mail—I capture your attention, and you want to do business with me. Why? Because in today's world, it takes honesty, consideration, and thoughtfulness to be a good communicator, which is *rare* indeed.

Secret Number Five: FOLLOW UP

Someone calls. You *know* this person. Call back within twenty-four hours.
Someone calls. You *don't know* this person. Call back
within twenty-four hours.

The end.

Well, almost. The biggest mistake you can make is to not follow up on a lead, a phone call, or a meeting. A true professional differentiates herself by going the extra mile and following up on every possible opportunity. Remember, you never know where the next call leads. And if it's something you are not interested in or don't need, a polite "No Thanks" (see Secret Number Three: MANNERS) will suffice.

How do I know these secrets work? Because they are my daily code of conduct, and they have worked for me for three decades and countless others whom I have coached.

 **Susan P. Ascher** is the president and CEO of The Ascher Group, an award-winning company. She is also the founder of The Sphere of Excellence in Communications, a consulting firm that helps individuals and major corporations raise the bar in protocol and communications. Her first book, *Dude, Seriously, It's NOT All About You!* is a humorous rant on how communications and protocol have forever changed how we connect and interact with coworkers, friends, and family in the New Millennium. A sought-after national media resource, Susan has been interviewed on Bloomberg, ABC, NBC, CNBC, News 12, and My9TV, and is a frequent commentator on TV 8 in Vail, Colorado. She has presented workshops at universities throughout the country and has been published in *Forbes* magazine, *Crain's New York Business*, *The Star-Ledger*, *NJBIZ*, and *New Jersey & Company* magazine. For more information, contact sascher@aschergroup.com or go to www.aschergroup.com.

The Perfect Partner

by Laurel Bernstein

If you ride down any Main Street or through any office park, you see logo after logo and sign after sign announcing a business. You might not give it much thought, but for every logo and sign you see, someone with an idea started a business.

When the idea turned into a business, the business owner probably consulted with a lawyer to help with the legal issues. To be sure the business had every advantage in balancing the expenses against the revenues to reap the profits, the business owner hired an accountant. The business owner most likely also hired a designer to prepare a logo to put on a business card, a website, and the bricks-and-mortar building or office. In fact, successful business owners hire others to help with almost everything—from getting their nails done to borrowing money.

But as you ride down Main Street or through that office park, you might see a "For Lease" sign, which signals someone didn't make it. Every "Going Out of Business" sign represents a business owner who couldn't keep a great idea growing.

Smart Business Owners Rely on a "Success Partner"

The really successful business leaders realize they need a success partner to help bring out their full potential. A success partner makes sure business owners apply their ability, skills, and knowledge so they flourish and grow. Some business owners have a partner they trust to handle the things they know little about. Some turn to friends and other business owners for advice and ideas. But the most successful business owners are the ones who work with an executive coach—the success partner who brings out their best—so the business and the business owner shine.

If you leave it to chance and shoot from the hip, your idea may grow, you might be lucky, and your business might thrive. When it does, you may drift into areas you are uncertain about. In fact, you might be surprised by the places you wind up. As you grow, the need for your services or products typically changes. Without a success partner, you may not see the need to change until it's too late.

But if you have a plan, and use your full potential with the support of a success partner, you can go from good to great. You can rise above adequate. You could do more than just be "making it." You could be thrilling, magnificent, and above all, marvelous. With a success buddy who helps you identify your best voice, your widest reach, and your possible triumphs, you could be wildly successful.

A client recently told me, "Oh, I can do it myself!" After we spoke, she admitted there were times she was overwhelmed. It seemed people who had loved her work suddenly didn't appreciate her. Even though her confidence was shaken and her energy dwindling, she had to show up BIG.

I reminded her that people see her as optimistic. I reminded her of a memorable situation she had been in a few weeks earlier. I reminded her that she was upbeat and unstoppable. I reminded her that everyone in the room was energized by her ideas and her attitude.

Using me as a mirror, albeit one that reflected the past, she was able to muster her enthusiasm and energy. She remembered that when she's at the top of her game, she's a winner. With me as her success partner, she was ready to roll up her sleeves and get to work. And although she was capable of doing everything herself, she also knew the results would not be the best they could be.

> *To make a business dream come true,*
> *write it down, make a plan,*
> *and rely on a success partner.*

> –Laurel Bernstein

Are You Leading a Successful Business?

Everyone is talking about leadership and how it pertains to business owners. Do you have what it takes? Have you lost what it takes? Did you ever have what it takes? Are you the leader of your business, or are you the manager? What do you manage? Do you manage people? Do you manage change? Are you the money manager? Who is managing the process? If you're *managing*, you're not LEADING.

Leading is not about your title. You may be the president, CEO, owner— or all of those—and still not be the leader. Leadership is an attitude. A leader is the one who has the ability to stand up, stand out, and stand for what she believes in. She motivates those around her to jump on the bandwagon of enthusiasm. She inspires her clients, customers, and others in her life to be bold, to engage themselves fully, and to find and use their ultimate potential.

Imagine More Success

Do you want to be more than a satisfactory leader and business owner? Can you imagine more success? Are you sure you're performing at your highest potential?

Instead of doing "all right," with a success partner—an executive coach to guide you—you can follow a path that makes your business dreams come true. With an executive coach, you can create strategies that suit you and your business, and bring out your full potential as the leader.

Have you ever defined what success looks like? Is it a number? Is it a goal? Is it an objective? With an executive coach, your success partner is in your corner. Instead of worrying about the future, you will define your future. With a success partner, you'll follow a step-by-step plan that keeps you focused, gets you to use your best traits, and solidifies your confidence as you grow with your business.

So I ask you, why would you ever want to do it yourself?

 **Laurel Bernstein** is a credentialed executive coach. She works with small business owners and senior leaders in larger corporations who want to grow their businesses and reach their maximum potential as leaders. To find out how Laurel can help your business or career, call 201-927-5927 or e-mail her at bernstein.laurel@gmail.com. Mention the code BOGO, and she will provide a complimentary 15-minute consultation for potential new clients.

Eight Attitudes That Can
Change Your Business

by Carole DeLaOsa

When it comes to running a business, many things are out of your control—your attitude isn't one of them. After all, your attitude shows up in your words and actions, and it affects business success. As you grow your business, it is easy to become so involved in it that you never take the time to explore how your attitude influences your employees and customers—which ultimately impacts your bottom line.

> *Your life is a direct reflection of your attitude.*
> *If you don't like your life, change your attitude.*
>
> –David R. Meyer

So, what is attitude? Attitude is how you feel about yourself, others, situations, events, objects, and places. Essentially, attitude is a statement in words or actions—positive or negative—that makes a big difference in how much you gain or lose in a situation. Sometimes attitude is retiring or shy, other times it is bold.

Your attitude is formed over the years in various ways. At times it is based on experience and knowledge. Other times you pick up, then mimic, the attitude of those around you. For the most part, attitude is based on what is true for you or on your perception of truth. What you think, what you do, and how you feel forms your attitude.

Given all this, how much control do you think you have over how you feel? Can you change? That depends on your awareness and your willingness to make choices. I believe attitude is learned—and that it's possible to change or unlearn an attitude. Yes, doing so can be challenging, but you are in control. You *can* choose your attitude. In fact, I like to think that attitude is an action verb because you can change it.

It is easier to change your attitude when you think in terms of specific attitudes, instead of the broader lousy versus great attitude, or can-do versus no-way-can-do attitude. Below are eight common attitudes. Each includes an attitude issue and a suggested action that brings about change—a positive change in attitude *and* a positive change in the growth of your business.

1. Confidence Attitude Issue: You say you have a great deal of confidence about your business, yet the statement doesn't ring true. In fact, you feel doubt.

Action: Take time to expand your presence in your industry. Take on a new project. Reach out to new colleagues. Attend more meetings so people can get to know you, like you, and trust you. As you share your expertise, it will build confidence.

2. Optimism Attitude Issue: You are optimistic that your business will be making six figures within the next five years.

Action: Each day, take consistent action steps in the direction of a six-figure business. Consistency is the key to maintaining optimism and realizing your goals. Connect daily with clients and prospects through phone calls, e-mail, and social networking sites such as LinkedIn and Facebook. Positive feedback and new business boosts your optimism.

3. Interest Attitude Issue: You don't always feel like doing the task or work to grow your business.

Action: Be mindfully present. Take the time to put meaningful thoughts into each task. Realize that every moment you are doing something for your business you are taking it to the next level.

4. Gratitude Attitude Issue: There are some things about running a business that are distasteful and create obstacles to your success.

Action: Hate grunt work? Use it as an opportunity to clear your head while you shred the junk mail. Hate writing the newsletter? Be grateful for the power of words. Focus on the message rather than on the task. Remember, this is an opportunity to express yourself. Be grateful for the outlet that reaches other people.

5. Authority Attitude Issue: You are the authority on your business, but not necessarily the authority on every area necessary to run your business.

Action: You have the stage. Do research and delve into literature related to your business. Become familiar with everything that touches your business. However, understand that running a business is an ongoing learning process. You may not always know the answer to every question, but new ideas are born from questions, which lead to new products or services. Whether you know the answer or not is not the issue. Listening and learning enhance your ability to add to your business, and they show clients that you appreciate their questions and insight.

6. Persistence Attitude Issue: You don't want to make a pest of yourself.

Action: Use different methods to obtain the information you need. Rephrase a question until you get the desired information. Sprinkle your questions with humor. Also, being friendly helps.

7. Responsibility Attitude Issue: Being responsible isn't easy, and some days I'd rather not.

Action: Going to work every day, attending meetings, and making your company fiscally sound is the lifeblood of any successful business. A business reflects the strength of the owner. The more responsibly you work, the better the results—and the profits will follow.

8. Honesty Attitude Issue: Challenging times make you want to cut corners in areas that will adversely affect your business in the future.

Action: Charging a fair price for a quality product will ensure a steady customer base. Being honest establishes a trustworthy name so your customers will recommend you to others.

These eight attitudes also reflect the high standards you set for your business. Focus on changing one of them, or all of them. Yes, attitude is everything—and when you control your attitude, you control the success of your business.

*The subtle difference in our attitude can make a major difference
in our future. It can be as simple as the language we use.*

–Jim Rohn

Carole DeLaOsa, a business coach, has more than twenty years of experience in business and leadership positions. At her company, Transition4You, she consults with and mentors business owners, working with them on meeting key challenges in growing their businesses. She is adept at identifying client issues/inefficiencies, and offers tips, techniques, and time-tested applications as solutions. Carole enjoys having created a balanced life that includes spending time at the beach and indulging in black-and-white ice cream sodas on occasion. To learn more about Carole and how she can help you and your business, visit www.transition4you.com or contact her at 973-214-2127.

Leadership:
Navigating Your Business to Success

by Donna Price

Being the business owner or leader of an organization is like being the navigator on an adventure. You are the captain, steering your company's ship toward greater success. It starts with a solid vehicle, a specific destination, and top-notch navigation tools that include a reliable compass and a detailed map. To make sure your business is headed in the right direction, and you reach your destination successfully, prepare yourself for the journey.

The Vision: Before you can start the journey, you must be clear about your destination—your vision for the company's future. As you draw up the navigation plan, make sure you answer the following questions: Where is the company going? What will it look like in one year, two years, five years, and beyond? Often, a company vision is short. To really make it magnetic, it should be detailed, inspiring, and compelling. When a vision paints a clear picture of the future, you are drawn to it, and when it is shared, the entire organization is pulled by its magnetism. The vision becomes your *magnetic north*—the direction a compass points to naturally.

Leaders who want to achieve the vision must also share the vision. Remember, you are not on this journey alone; staff need to be inspired and committed to the vision as well. When staff members are unclear about where the company is going, they might work in different directions. As the leader, you want your entire team to move in the same direction, follow the same map, and head for the same destination.

The Vehicle: Think of your company as the vehicle—driven by its mission and purpose. To move your organization toward a specific destination, the mission and purpose must be solid, and everyone needs to be on board. If you lose your connection with your mission and purpose, you will drift, and your company will flounder.

Let's say your vehicle is a sailboat, and its core purpose is to travel through the water using the power of the wind. You decide to add an engine because it helps you navigate when the wind is weak. Wanting to reach your destination faster, you replace the engine with a *bigger* one, but the boat tips under the heavy load. Trying to turn your sailboat into a powerboat makes it unsteady—positioning it to sink. This is what happens when you lose sight of your company's mission and core purpose. You get pulled in a new direction, and suddenly, your solid business begins to falter. It is vital to keep your core purpose in mind as you evaluate new opportunities and strategies. Are they the right fit for your business? Do they blend with your core purpose? Be clear about your mission; review it regularly and check new strategies or destinations against it.

The Compass: A key tool for leadership navigation is a reliable compass. The compass represents the guiding values of your company—in essence, its moral compass. Using a compass along the journey to your vision keeps your organization on track and in alignment with your values and principles. When you are making decisions, referring to your compass helps you steer the company in the right direction. With a reliable compass, it is nearly impossible to veer far off course.

The Map: Every journey benefits from a detailed map. For leaders, the map is your strategic plan, which should be clear, focused on the destination, and simple to follow—for everyone. A complicated map causes confusion and is often discarded because it is deemed useless. Strategies that are simple, action focused, and assigned to specific staff members can be implemented more easily, which benefits your organization. Of course, building your strategic plan with your team is a highly effective approach because every member of the team is invested in the plan, which gives you buy-in, smoother sailing, and a better chance to reach your destination with fewer challenges.

The Action: No journey is accomplished with just a vision and strategies. You need implementation and accountability. Without these two components, the vision flounders. Leaders are the visionaries in organizations, but "secret" visions are hard for staff and teams to achieve. When leaders share their vision, collaborate on strategies, and achieve staff buy-in, implementation and accountability are more easily accomplished. Implementation takes daily action, which requires staff members to complete specific tasks. Remember, action drives the vehicle. When the actions are just busywork and not focused on the destination, they burn energy without purpose, and fail to move the company forward.

The Conversation: Being accountable and holding others accountable are often challenging because it can mean difficult or uncomfortable conversations, which make people uneasy. However, in order to produce results and accomplish what the team has outlined, individual members must follow through. When people fail to follow through, schedule "accountability" conversations. One effective approach is to hold accountability meetings at least monthly. At each meeting, based on the strategic goals they are working on, staff members establish their action goals for the month.

The Group: When people sit in a group and share what they plan to accomplish in the month, they are more likely to do it. The challenge comes when someone does not complete a task or an assignment. When this happens, individual team members or the team as a group must ask why. Often, when team members learn they will be held accountable and be asked what they did, what they accomplished, and at what level—they typically get on board and complete their tasks. Now you have a results-focused environment.

The Assessment: Finally, leaders navigating to success regularly assess where they are, how the strategies are working, what is going well, and what isn't. This is an essential part of reaching your destination. Is the map accurate? Do you need to change course? Is the vehicle holding up? Are there obstacles along the way that you didn't expect?

Navigating with the right tools makes it possible to achieve the vision to move your company where you want to take it. Leadership navigation— when everything is in place—is highly rewarding—and a rewarding journey is usually packed with adventure and fun.

 **Donna Price**, business success coach, speaker, and facilitator, is the president of Compass Rose Consulting. She is the author of *Launching Your Dreams*, *Coaching Staff for Success*, and a contributing author to several books and publications including the *Drake Business Review*. Donna developed and authored Bizology.Biz, a comprehensive, business-development system that guides owners step by step through her proven success process. Donna provides coaching, training, strategic planning, and speaking services. She is the host of two radio shows, *BizologyBuzz* and *Leadership Navigator*. Donna gets business owners and leaders moving their companies in the direction they want, producing transformational shifts in their business thinking and performance results. You can reach Donna at 973-948-7673 or dprice@compassroseconsulting.com, and learn more about her services by visiting www.compassrosecosulting.com.

Five Big E-Mail Business Busters— Are Your Messages DOA (Deleted on Arrival)?

by Joyce Restaino

E-mail—"It's a time suck," admits Joan Stewart, a publicity expert who receives hundreds of e-mail messages every day. Stewart, who speaks, blogs, tweets, and writes and sends her weekly "The Publicity Hound's Tips of the Week" e-newsletter to 7,000 subscribers looking to attract media attention for their organization or business, succinctly summed up how most businesspeople feel about e-mail. If you need more proof about the amount of time e-mail gobbles, *The New New Inbox: How Email and Social Media Changed Our Lives*, a 2010 survey by People-OnTheGo, found that business professionals spend an average of 3.27 hours a day on e-mail.

Yet, in spite of its time-consuming, interrupting nature—and the growing popularity of social media and other e-communication tools—e-mail remains a top way business owners conduct business and connect with their audience. But if you haven't given much thought to your e-mail lately, take note: Your e-mail represents you and creates an overall impression of your business. People often decide if they want to do business with you based on your e-mail image.

So, what does it take to stand out in a crowded in-box and avoid banishment to the trash bin? To find out, I conducted an unscientific survey of fifty business owners and professionals. From the office manager of an up-and-coming New York City photographer, to the chief of staff of a representative in the U.S. Congress, to some highly sought-after industry influencers, I asked these questions: (1) How many e-mail messages do you receive in a day? (2) Which do you look at first, "From" or "Subject"? (3) If you delete e-mail, why?

When it comes to opening e-mail, their answers revealed that the sender is more important than the subject; although for some, the subject helps determine the urgency of a message. The number of e-mail messages received every day ranged from thirty to hundreds. And although spam (marketing/selling) and not recognizing the sender were on just about everyone's list as reasons for deleting e-mail without reading it, the following five (in no order of importance) emerged as business busters:

1. Fuzzy thinking: "Your e-mail reflects your personality and thinking," says communication and productivity expert Dianna Booher, author of *Communicate with Confidence!* and founder of Booher Consultants. Long-winded e-mail without a purpose or a call to action leaves the receiver confused and frustrated. A poorly organized, rambling e-mail sends this message about you: sloppy thinking. Even when you don't get deleted, you will not be taken seriously.

Save yourself: For every e-mail, know your purpose, know your audience, and keep your message simple. Booher suggests sending fewer e-mail messages. "The more you write, the less people pay attention to you," she says. When crafting e-mail, a single-focused message with a clear call to action showcases your ability to summarize complex issues and move forward. (And it eliminates back-and-forth e-mail, which drives people crazy.)

2. Little regard for the relationship: It's not unusual to ignore e-mail from a stranger. But ignoring someone you are doing business with is shocking. Unfortunately, this is what happens when people can't meet a deadline or deliver what they promised. The irony is that by not responding, you still send a message. This is how it reads: I am not reliable; I do not value your time; you are not important.

Save yourself: If you cannot meet a deadline or deliver the goods—own up to it. To keep the relationship solid, a phone call explaining why, instead of e-mail, is in order. The worst thing is to ignore the person you are doing business with. Ignoring will not make a problem go away, but it will sink your reputation.

3. Always selling: There is no shame in selling, but when every e-mail message is a sales call, you can count on being deleted or blocked from in-boxes forever.

Save yourself: "E-mail is business for me," says Jeffrey Gitomer, bestselling author, whose expertise in sales, customer loyalty, and personal development is world renowned (500,000 subscribers to his "Sales Caffeine" e-newsletter). Always big on providing value, Gitomer says the best way to get e-mail opened and acted upon is to offer value. Sally Hogshead, author of *Fascinate: Your 7 Triggers to Persuasion and Captivation*, agrees. Her biggest pet peeve is "e-mailing without adding any value. It's better not to e-mail than to simply take up space in someone's in-box," she says. The problem is that many business owners don't think "value," although providing it is simple. In your next e-mail message, instead of selling, share: Offer resources and answer frequently asked questions. This builds trust and enhances your reputation.

4. Poor quality: Like shoddy products and unreliable service, poor grammar and spelling and a cold, uninviting tone create a negative impression. "I don't forgive basic grammar or spelling errors," says Ed Abel, a serial entrepreneur and founder of the ABEL Business Institute and the Skillpreneur Alliance. "It shows me the person is lazy and incompetent."

Save yourself: "As the leader of your company, clear, concise, error-free e-mail sends a message that you are a professional," says Booher. So, how do you boost your e-mail image? Keep your messages short, cordial, and to the point. Of course, it never hurts to brush up on your writing skills. Online and on-site writing courses are offered through community colleges and adult/community schools.

5. No connection: Asking someone you don't have a relationship with to "take a look at my next great thing and let me know what you think," really struck a nerve.

Save yourself: It's not that people don't want to help. In fact, most business owners say the amount of e-mail they receive reflects how robust their business is. Here's the thing: Reading and responding to e-mail takes time—which is often lost on the sender. So, how do you connect? Joan Stewart says to show her that you know her. With 11,000 subscribers on his mailing list, Mike Michalowicz, author of *The Pumpkin Plan* and *The Toilet Paper Entrepreneur*, agrees. "In the first sentence I look for something that identifies this person knows me personally," he says. To make a connection, let recipients know you subscribe to their newsletter, read their blog, follow them on Twitter, loved their book, heard them speak, etc. When you show a connection, you are more likely to get a response.

More and more, businesses are built up or brought down by words. As a business owner, your words—especially in e-mail—create an impression (that lasts forever) of you and your company. To avoid being deleted on arrival, keep your e-mail messages brief and friendly, and offer something of value by following Jeffrey Gitomer's advice: "Value in it for me, the recipient—not you, the sender."

Joyce Restaino, an award-winning writer and editor, leads Grow Your Business Write, is the editor of this book, and is one of the cofounders of the Big Bold Business™ book series. She works with business owners and professionals who want to increase their credibility and visibility through the power of the written word. To find out how Joyce can transform your knowledge and know-how into articles, blogs, books, and more; contact her at 973-697-1721 or joycerestaino@gmail.com, or visit www.growyourbusinesswrite.com.

To Expand Your Business
Far Beyond an Idea—Fill a Need

by Sonia Y. Scott

I'll never forget that morning in 2005. I woke up and declared, "I'm going to open a school." While most people debated what outfit to wear, poured themselves coffee, or searched for their car keys, I spent that morning sifting through the ideas crowding my mind as I attempted to answer the who, what, when, where, and how I was going to open a school.

Despite moving into unknown territory, the question, "Is it possible?" never entered my mind because seventeen years into my career in health care and three companies later, I refused to recognize the word *impossible*. As a result of this mind-set, I've managed to expand a small nanny placement agency into a home health-care company, a nonprofit organization, and, most recently, a vocational training school.

Dorson Baby Care is Born

In 1988, I was a Wall Street accountant, pregnant with my third child and looking forward to a career change. From a small makeshift office in my suburban home's basement, I developed a nanny placement agency, Dorson Baby Care, which recruited and placed housekeepers, nannies, and baby nurses with families. I upheld the budding company to high principles and made it the company's mission to provide quality services with a personal touch.

The goal was, and continues to be, to make each client feel like he or she is our one and only client. In the child care field, parents are often wary about letting just anyone around their children. So in doing placements, my recruits underwent rigorous background checks. In addition, I valued bi- and multilingual caregivers to cater to a multicultural client base, and I personally conducted face-to-face consultations with each and every family.

The Petersons were first-time parents for whom I provided a baby nurse. In recognizing the intense interviewing process I undertook to match the Petersons with their nurse (one who stayed with the family well beyond their first child), Mrs. Peterson inquired about finding help for her aging father. Soon after the Petersons sought my help, more and more of my clients, and others, expressed interest in finding elder care.

Dorson Home Care Fills a Need

In realizing the unmet demand for quality home health care, Dorson Baby Care expanded into Dorson Home Care, Inc., and the Petersons were my first home care case. To help build a client base, I offered the Petersons a reduced fee if they referred me to their friends and family. It is through promotions and incentives like these that got Dorson Home Care, Inc., off the ground. In home health care, the power of referrals is the key to success. Just like in child care, word-of-mouth testimonials proved to be the most successful form of marketing.

In 1995, I relocated the agency from my basement to the inner city, where there was a great need for elderly care services. Furthermore, Dorson Home Care was not just about providing home health care, it was also a community initiative to provide jobs—predominantly to immigrant women, single parents, and inner-city high school graduates.

As an immigrant woman juggling a marriage and three children myself, I found it easy to relate to my home health aides who also struggled to find a work-life balance. Many of my aides would vent to me about their kids hanging out with the wrong crowds and their struggles to keep them out of trouble in the inner city. As a teenager in Harlem, I remember the lack of community resources to help keep children on track and how easy it was for them to be led astray. One morning in 1998, I held a workshop for my home health aides' kids, teaching them what I know best—how to start a business—in an effort to instill a sense of responsibility in them.

Dorson Community Foundation Fills a Need

Every Saturday morning since then, a team of business professionals—including me—teaches a business skills class for kids. This is one of the many featured programs of Dorson Community Foundation, the nonprofit organization I subsequently founded with the mission to provide inner-city youths with a creative outlet and a meaningful alternative lifestyle to one involving drugs and gangs.

Dorson Community Foundation was an instant success because I was able to directly tie it with my home health-care company and use my home health aides as the foundation's ready-made client base. Today, Dorson Community Foundation runs computer classes, dance classes, SAT prep classes, a mentoring program, and an intergenerational program where our participants visit the elderly in nursing homes.

Dorson Vocational Training Institute Fills a Need

In 2005, when Dorson Home Care, Inc., and Dorson Community Foundation were at an all-time high, many of my home health aides were feeling at an all-time low. Home health aide work is one of the lowest-paying health professions, and many of my home health aides craved a career path that would enable them to provide more for themselves and their families.

This recognition led to that memorable morning when I woke up and decided, "I want to open a school." Opening a vocational school without prior experience in education was not an easy feat. But the power of self-education and perseverance is what led me to open the doors. I reached out to the New Jersey Departments of Education and Labor for contacts; I attended every school development seminar out there; and I built mutually beneficial relationships with professionals with similar goals. Together, we exchanged knowledge about the logistics behind opening a school.

Fast-forward to today, and Dorson Vocational Training Institute has offices in two New Jersey locations (East Orange and Jersey City), provides classes in home health aide, patient care technician, medical billing and coding, and many other professional fields in health care. Dorson also specializes in certifying caregivers in Alzheimer care. Since opening the doors of Dorson Vocational Training Institute, I have watched many of my home health aides transition into better-paying, in-demand professions.

Venturing from nanny care to elderly care to nonprofit work to vocational training felt natural and fluid. Through it all, I kept the mission to help my community by providing jobs, opportunities, and quality health services. The conventional wisdom about growing a business is: give your customers what they want and what they need. However, with each new business, I recognized a gap in the market and unmet needs, and went after them. Subsequently, in expanding my business, not only did I grow the Dorson brand by filling needs, but I expanded my outreach to the community.

What needs are you ready to fill?

 Sonia Y. Scott owns and runs three businesses related to the field of health care: Dorson Home Care, Inc., a home health-care agency; Dorson Baby Care, an agency providing in-home child care and baby support; and Dorson Vocational Training Institute, a vocational school specializing in career training for the health-care industry. The Dorson brand also expands into the nonprofit sector with Dorson Community Foundation, an organization providing enrichment programs for inner-city youths. To learn more about the Dorson companies, visit www.dorsonhomecare.com or call 973-951-1371. Sonia can be reached at sonia@dorsonhomecare.com.

Passion and Purpose
Drive Business Success

by Cecile E. Sutherland

As a business owner, you understand passion. Without it, without that burning desire to stay the course, especially during difficult times—you won't make it as a business owner—or anything else you have your heart set on. But passion alone doesn't result in a thriving business or success. After all, you can be passionate about golf or gardening, yet know you can't make a living doing either. In fact, business owners who are passionate about their work do fail.

Of course, there are many reasons why a business fails, but in my opinion, lack of a sense of purpose is a major contributor. Because it's human nature to want meaning from our work, as the leader of your company, you must articulate your purpose—the reason you exist—to your team members, so they share in the vision.

For instance, the primary reason my company exists is my passion for caring for seniors. I have over thirty years experience in the health-care industry and was called upon to help my parents look into home care services for my dad. After researching the industry, it became apparent that our senior population needed advocates to make sure they receive quality services that allow them to age at home. The secondary reason my company exists is to provide employment to individuals who have the passion and compassion to care for seniors.

Sharing my vision with my team has given them a sense of purpose, and because of the high level of services provided by the caregivers, my company has grown from one part-time employee to forty-two employees over a two-year period.

Because our clients are vulnerable—they are ill or are recovering from an injury or illness—everyone must be on the same page. Team members must be caring, compassionate, and have the ability to communicate clearly with our clients and their families. As the leader, it is my job to see that they do. Below are six keys that I use to bring out the passion and purpose in my team members. Use them to do the same for your team.

1. Develop leaders. So much has been written about the qualities of great leaders and leadership style, but the most effective leaders understand the value in cultivating and bringing out the leader in every team member.

This is not about turning every employee into a supervisor or vice president—it's about building self-confidence to unleash the leader within. To do that, every team member must have a clear vision of what needs to be accomplished, personal commitment to the task at hand, and integrity. Naturally, as the company leader, you are the role model. All eyes are on you.

2. Cultivate the leadership relationship. How do you bring out the leader in team members? You must provide the tools—the proper training your team members need to be successful in their work. Most important, *communicate*. Explain why decisions are made. Employees "follow the rules" because they have no choice. When they don't know or understand why they have to follow a specific procedure, there is no purpose in their work. When there is no purpose, there is no passion. Self-motivation takes over when there is open and honest communication because it builds trust and mutual respect. That's how leaders emerge.

3. Expect competence. Regardless of the economy, most business owners will tell you that it is difficult to find the "right" person to fill a position. That's why I look for competence. Skills and knowledge matter, but I want to say "yes" to two key questions: "Is this person qualified?" and "Does this person have the capacity to perform and fulfill the mission?"

Background checks, personality assessments, drug screening, and skills assessments tell me immediately if a job candidate is qualified for a position in my company. The second question is more difficult to determine, but I get a sense of whether or not a candidate is committed to our mission during an interview.

Finally, if you want competence, you must invest in your team members—not only through training—but also through compensation. This is critical to building your business. Remember, it is less costly to pay well to retain a competent employee than it is to let go of an incompetent one.

4. Build commitment and get others to follow. One of the most successful ways to build commitment and get others to follow is through shared values and principles. Cedas Home Care Services' mission is simple, and every team member knows what it is: "To provide *Quality* home care services with *Dignity*, *Compassion*, and *Respect* to the clients we serve." When everyone is on board, you create a positive work environment. As a result, the road you travel will be smoother, and your business will grow at a quicker pace, with fewer bumps to slow the progress.

5. Communicate with clarity. Experience has taught me that good listening, questioning, and writing skills are the keys to clear communication. Because e-mail has replaced the business memo, and for the most part, the phone—writing skills are more important than ever.

Listening and questioning skills are critical, especially in the health-care industry. If a health-care worker is not sure about some aspect of her instructions, she is trained to ask questions. When you deal with people's lives, you must ask questions. The truth is, poor communication skills will cost your company time, energy, and money; so train team members accordingly.

6. Manage the process. Once you build your team, to keep your business running smoothly, you have to manage the process. The best way to do that is to get out of the way. If you don't get out of the way, you can't move forward. Start by empowering people. Trust team members to solve problems and make decisions. This is how you help them build self-confidence and become dedicated employees.

When you build a business, you create a family, so be prepared to deal with conflict. To stop negativity from spreading and infecting everyone, have a procedure in place to resolve conflicts. I use conflict as a teachable opportunity to bring people together to work through their differences. Bringing team members together usually results in a better understanding of how the other person feels and is better for the working relationships.

Remember, as the business owner, you are responsible for shaping your team members into individuals who not only know and understand their purpose, but are proud of their purpose. When people are proud of the work they do, they tend to be passionate about it as well. When you have passion and purpose, nothing can stop you from accomplishing great things.

 **Cecile E. Sutherland, MS, BSN, RN,** is the founder and president of Cedas Home Care Services, LLC, a senior home care company with locations in Montclair and Fairlawn, New Jersey. The company provides Certified Home Health Aides and Certified Nursing Assistants services. Cecile has extensive health-care experience, which includes leadership positions in nursing homes, hospitals, and outpatient surgery centers, and is also acknowledged as an expert in addressing challenging operational and strategic issues that enhance service quality. She holds a bachelor's degree in nursing from Long Island University and a master's degree in healthcare administration from Central Michigan University. Cecile can be reached at csutherland@cedashomecare.com, 973-746-0165, or by visiting: www.cedashomecare.com.

Management

Business Longevity
Is No Accident

by Roberta Ferrara

I became the president of Budd's Auto Body by accident. When my husband, Matthew, died suddenly in 1999, I had to take over the business. I like to tell my customers that "We met by accident." Yet, it's no accident that Budd's has been in business for over fifty years. People are always amazed at how we have survived for so long. But the secret is simple: business longevity is achieved by working at it from the first day you are in business and then focusing on it each and every single day.

Budd's winning formula is a combination of caring customer service, quality work, and a staff of dedicated, skilled employees. These three areas are the keys to maintaining and improving our performance while satisfying our customers beyond their expectations. To forge a valuable bond with our customers, we insist on top-level results as we repair their vehicles.

Take Care of Your Customers

At Budd's, customer service begins the moment customers contact us, whether it is by e-mail, phone, or by walking into our place of business. They have an important need and want us to meet it expeditiously and with a simple process. In this business, our customers may be dealing with an accident, so they are often overwhelmed and do not know what to do next. I always take the time to greet each customer and put him or her at ease by explaining what's going to happen, step by step.

Although I have been through this countless times, I understand the anxiety and stress a customer feels following an accident—especially if it's a first accident—so I try to make the customer feel comfortable and confident that I will make this experience as worry-free and smooth as possible. I do this every day, with every customer.

In most cases, our customers must have a vehicle to use while theirs is in the shop. I don't provide loaners, but I do work with car rental companies and arrange for them to bring their vehicles directly to the customer at Budd's. Our customers can then drop off the rental at the shop when their car is done. It's all part of making the process easy.

Excellent customer service means nothing without quality work. As president, quality assurance is one key area that I do not delegate. No car leaves the shop before I personally inspect it. We supply every car with extra paint. Each car is test driven and thoroughly cleaned inside and out.

Quality assurance is my responsibility, but my team knows that quality is their job too.

Take Care of Your Team

As the owner of Budd's for all of these years, I still find every day challenging, and I know my team feels the same way because we are driven to deliver excellent customer service and to perform quality work. They know that their work is paramount, and they must meet the highest level of expectation—not only for our customers, but for me.

Knowing this, I strive to maintain and improve our service through continuing education. I budget at least one new training course a year for each employee in my company. Whenever possible, I bring in reps from major manufacturers to give in-house training. This keeps everyone up to date—including me—with the newest products, technologies, and techniques. Training not only educates, it motivates employees, cuts costs, and improves customer service. And there is always something new to learn.

So that everyone is on the same page, it's critical to share your vision and priorities of the business with your team. At Budd's, each person knows the priority we put on excellent customer service and the quality of our work—which must be completed by the date we promise a customer. That often means working together to meet the customer's expectations. If a job needs to be completed by closing time, people will team together to get the job done.

Because employees want to be recognized as professionals and to have their expertise appreciated, I show this by guaranteeing the work done at the shop for as long as a customer owns the car. My team knows that I proudly stand behind their work—so when an opportunity arises, I like to show my appreciation to my employees in unexpected ways. For instance, when a vendor selling work boots showed up at the shop one day around the holidays, I bought everyone a new pair of work boots. All of this has helped me achieve close to zero turnover. And I am proud to say that my ten employees average over twenty years of service with me.

Take Care of Business

I did not choose this line of work. I got into it out of necessity during a tough time in my life. This is a man's industry, with a thick glass ceiling. But I needed to succeed. I had to provide for my family, and I had to continue to provide for the families of my employees.

I worked hard at keeping up with the boys—especially with my highly skilled staff—and it paid off. I gained the respect of towing companies, parts distributors, car rental companies, and insurance adjusters. In turn, I respect the suppliers and partners for the work they do and for helping me provide excellent customer service, quality work, and for keeping my employees on top of any changes in the industry.

Through my work, I have learned that cars suffer from serious body breaks. I have also learned that a female who is willing to master skills and knowledge and is committed to making it work can break through the thick glass ceiling in the auto body shop business. I am proud of what I have accomplished, and I am here to stay.

Of course, business longevity brings many rewards beyond financial stability. After fifty years with a history of satisfying customers, I still feel the pride every morning when I open the door, knowing that I am keeping up the quality and legacy on which the business was founded. There is also the comfort that I feel every night when I put my head on the pillow—the comfort in knowing that at the end of the day, I have served my customers well.

 **Roberta Ferrara** is the owner of Budd's Auto Body (www.buddsautobody.com), which celebrated its fiftieth year in business in 2011. Roberta has been involved in the automotive industry for the past twelve years, and continually takes classes so she can provide her customers with the latest, most up-to-date techniques. She has also been recognized by her peers, and has appeared in several automotive industry magazines. Budd's Auto Body is family owned and operated, and its commitment to excellence provides every customer a completely hassle-free experience. In addition to working with and accepting all insurance, Budd's provides a comprehensive written warranty for as long as the customer owns the vehicle. Roberta will be happy to answer any questions relating to the auto body industry. You can reach her at buddsautobody@aol.com, 973-256-4566, or www.facebook.com/buddsautobody.

Let Go to Grow: The Amazing Power of Time and Task Tracking

by Donna Miller

Why did you open your business?

To make more money? Control your destiny? Achieve more work-life balance? I'm sure you didn't plan to work seven days a week, miss your children's activities, or go from feast to famine without any continuity or predictability.

Yes, it's exciting to embark on the entrepreneurial dream. You'll be the next Bill Gates or Rachael Ray, or maybe you'll make a decent living and have some balance in your life—lofty goals for sure.

Well, after eighteen years in business, I must admit that when I walk into my office, I still feel the excitement that I did on day one. Although failure never entered my mind, I never realized how hard it would be.

Did you?

Of course you have a great business plan, but somewhere along the line it creeps out of control. There are so many aspects you aren't prepared for—like working insane hours—yet loving it in a bittersweet kind of way. But no matter how much you love it, running a business is exhausting when it takes over your life. And if you're home based, your business permeates your life in ways you never imagined.

For the most part, successful entrepreneurs and small business owners are risk takers, leaders, multitaskers, and creative problem solvers—a perfect breeding ground for control issues. In my experience working with hundreds of business owners, helping them to establish and achieve business goals, not only are many control freaks, but they also suffer from a lack of focus. And when you think that you're the only one who can do everything it takes to run your business, you don't have a sound business model—unless you're happy with your results.

So how do you get off this merry-go-round?

Here's the plan: For the next two weeks, do some time and task tracking. Create a spreadsheet (or scratch it on napkins) and keep track of what you do on a day-to-day basis. Divide your tasks into the following three categories: (1) Tasks I MUST Delegate, (2) Tasks I SHOULD Delegate, and (3) Tasks I WON'T delegate.

Tasks I MUST Delegate (Category 1)

These are the tasks you'd gladly delegate to a support team (staff or vendors). Typically, these are tasks that waste your talent and time but are safe and easy, so you find yourself gravitating toward them. These tasks include filing, office organizing, database work, travel arrangements, errands, graphic design, and social media updates (a huge time drain). For most business owners, it's easy to identify these tasks and create a list for this category.

Tasks I SHOULD Delegate (Category 2)

This second category of tasks can be more difficult to identify than the first because they require a deeper understanding of the business, which makes them harder to give up, so it may take more time to develop this list. These tasks can include researching competitors, researching new business opportunities, preparing for meetings, managing the calendar, telemarketing, bookkeeping, and handling collections.

Tasks I WON'T Delegate (Category 3)

That leaves the third category—the tasks you are uniquely qualified to do—the tasks that drive the organization and revenue. These tasks could include project management, prospect and client meetings, speaking engagements, cultivating referral sources, and strategic planning.

After separating your tasks into the three categories, your spreadsheet might look like this:

Task	Category 1 (time in hrs)	Category 2 (time in hrs)	Category 3 (time in hrs)
Opened mail, paid bills	0.50		
Worked on website updates		1.5	
Made new business calls			2.0
Entered contacts from networking event into database	1.0		
Worked on project timeline			2.0
Created personalized docs for client project	1.5		
Totals	3.0	1.5	4.0

Now that you know how you spend your time, ask yourself this question: How would my business change if I shift the time I spend on Category 1 and Category 2 tasks to Category 3 tasks? What would the return on investment be if you devote more time to tasks that drive your business and revenue? For example, I know that if I spend three to four-and-a-half hours on driving revenue (Category 3 tasks), my results (hard dollars) far exceed the cost to delegate those tasks.

Add Tasks; Move Tasks

Once you get comfortable delegating tasks, start adding new tasks to your lists. Also keep in mind that when your circumstances change, so will your task lists. In other words, a Category 2 task (SHOULD delegate) could become a Category 1 task (MUST delegate). As your business grows and changes, you'll find yourself moving tasks back and forth from one category to another. Or you might decide that it's more efficient to divide one task into smaller parts, so you put each newly created task into the appropriate category.

Here's the bottom line: Unless you let go of what's in Category 1, you'll continue to be dragged along at a pace you don't set and you don't control. (So much for the theory of control.)

So how do you make the shift? After creating your three task lists, begin by finding the right talent to take over your Category 1 tasks, followed by your Category 2 tasks. You can delegate tasks to employees, outside vendors, or virtual assistants. But take your time in hiring the right team members.

Don't rush in. As a business owner, one of the most expensive mistakes you can make is hiring the wrong contractors or employees. In fact, there isn't a single management skill more critical to your personal and professional success as a business owner than learning to delegate and understanding that delegating work is the cost of doing business.

If you want to become the next Bill Gates or Rachael Ray, you have to build your small business into an organization. (Yes, that's the goal: to grow into an organization.)

Once you start delegating tasks, you'll reach the goals you set out to achieve.

Donna Miller is president and founder of Above & Beyond, Inc. Her company provides support, training, and growth opportunities for small business owners, professionals, and entrepreneurs who are ready to move to the next level, but lack the support staff, training capability, and/or the office space to move forward. Whether you need full- or part-time support staff, daily office rentals, virtual assistance, or virtual receptionist services, Above & Beyond frees you from the daily administrative demands of running a small business, so you can concentrate on more strategic issues, such as serving clients and driving revenue. To learn more about maintaining an image of success while keeping fixed overhead as low as possible for as long as possible, visit Above & Beyond at www.virtualofficestaff.com. Donna can be reached at dmiller@virtualofficestaff.com.

Simple Ways to "Green" Your Business That You Can Implement Now

by Cindy Plantz Malinchak

In this age of sustainability and eco-awareness, a business can no longer afford to overlook the publicity potential, as well as the cost benefit, of being a "green company." And although there are literally hundreds of things a business can do to go green—with a small investment of time and money—you can implement a number of the simple strategies listed below, right now.

Since most businesses still use large amounts of paper in their everyday activities, start with modest recycling measures, but strive for paperless options that are easy to handle online, such as bank statements, billing, and interoffice memos. Dealing with everyday tasks online not only reduces paper use and paper waste—it increases productivity. Still not ready to go paperless? Then follow these steps to reduce paper use and waste:

- Designate a "recycle" area in your office and encourage all employees to participate.

- Place public documents (not confidential or legal) in a recycle bin.

- Use the blank side of printed paper (void of staples and paper clips) to print interoffice documents. This simple trick can reduce paper costs substantially.

- After using both sides of the paper, instead of recycling, consider shredding the paper and donating it to local animal shelters to use as bedding.

- Or, if you have a green thumb, bring the paper home and add it to your mulch bed or worm composting system (a self-contained composting bin). Over time, you will benefit from rich, dark soil.

Go for the Green

Still faxing the old-fashioned way from a fax machine? It's time to consider an electronic fax system such as eFax (www.efax.com) to send and receive faxes. Through your e-mail program, you can send faxes from your office computer, laptop, or smartphone and receive them in your inbox. Besides having a permanent record of your faxed information stored on your computer—and instant access to this information anywhere you have Internet service—you'll save money on paper and toner. And speaking of toner, most ink cartridges can be refilled for a fraction of the cost of purchasing new, keeping used cartridges out of a landfill.

For ambitious recyclers, consider putting a small worm composting system in your break room for employees to recycle their food scraps (excluding meat) to produce a highly fertile soil additive for the office plants. This idea may take some time to get accustomed to (for the most part, it's odorless), but the rewards are well worth it. Check online for companies such as www.compostbins.com that sell small worm composting systems that take up slightly more space than a waste container.

Following the old adage, "One person's trash is another person's treasure," implement a "reuse system" within your company—and with those in your network outside of your company who would like to participate. Through e-mail, you can post office items you no longer need, as well as items you are looking for. For instance, when you upgrade your office furniture, you can find someone who can use what you're replacing. Or, if they're not "ancient," you can donate your older-model computers to a start-up company that will be excited to have them. Once your office reuse system is running smoothly, expand it to include household items as well.

You can also take advantage of organizations such as the Habitat for Humanity ReStore resale outlets (www.habitat.org/restores), which sell reusable and surplus building materials to the public. Green Demolitions (www.greendemolitions.org), with stores in New Jersey and Connecticut, sells luxury commercial surplus and donated kitchens, appliances, home décor, and more from home renovations and demolitions. Other nonprofit organizations such as Waste Match (www.wastematch.org) redistribute gently used items to those who are in need of them.

Go Green with Energy-Saving Techniques

Starting to catch the "green fever"? Then, let's move on to energy-saving techniques that can help save money and the environment.

"Adaptive comfort" is a term I use to explain the temperature an individual has become accustomed to as his or her comfort level. A comfortable temperature for an office is between 69 and 73°F. But slight adjustments to the thermostat can save money and resources. So let everyone know that you are turning the thermostat up a few degrees in the summer and down a few degrees in the winter. I have discovered that a sweater does wonders; so I usually carry one with me so I can be comfortable, regardless of the temperature, in the venues that I find myself.

Another easy solution that helps you control the climate is adding soft shades to windows that receive the afternoon sun. Simply close the shades during the summer to keep the sun out and open them in the winter to allow the warmth of the sun in.

For a small investment, you can install occupancy sensors or motion sensors throughout the office to automatically turn the lights off after a set period with no occupants in a room. This can substantially reduce the amount of electricity you use over the course of the year.

Getting hungry for more? Convert your restroom faucets and your toilet flushers to automatic. The water you save on these two features alone will reduce your overall water consumption.

These techniques—which any small, medium, or large company can implement—are not only simple and cost effective, but result in savings to your bottom line. Obviously, greening your business is a smart strategy to include in your corporate philosophy. But if you are new to this endeavor, go slowly; choose a few green ideas and become comfortable with them before implementing additional measures.

And remember—do not be shy to boast to everyone that you are taking these measures. One of the greatest goodwill messages you can get out to your clients is the effort you are making to help in the global initiative for energy conservation and sustainability. It is good for the environment and your bottom line.

 **Cindy Plantz Malinchak** is the owner of Environmentally Based Green Building, a commercial design build company with offices in New Jersey, New York, and Pennsylvania. She is certified in sustainable design and construction from NYU, and is currently pursuing a Master of Science in Green Technology. Cindy is also an LEED accredited professional. She serves as an instructor for the "Green2Go" course at Rutgers University Small Business Development Center in Newark, New Jersey, and is a seminar speaker for the Columbia Society of Real Estate in New York. To find out how Cindy can help you go green, contact her at 646-765-5410 or cp124m@aol.com, or visit www.ebgbllc.com.

Is Your Retail Business Seasonal?
How to Stay Profitable Year Round

by Lucille Skroce

Whether you are buying an established retail business, starting a new one, or looking for another location, there are key issues to consider before opening your doors. Since retail selling cycles vary greatly from one industry to the next—and are affected by the store's location—research to prepare for the store's distinct merchandise, customer profile, sales trends, and seasonal sales cycles is critical.

Know the Sales History

When purchasing a retail establishment, ask about its sales history and analyze typical sales cycles. Once you factor in seasonal sales, you can create an annual budget based on your sales forecast. For example, a ski shop is likely to have sales heat up during the fall/winter months and cool off during warm weather. In a women's dress shop, customer demand will spike at different times of the year, so budget appropriately to purchase new inventory in advance of those established seasonal sales spikes.

Planning for your business to generate enough revenue during the busy times to carry it during the slow times makes it easier to stick to your operating budget (and ride out the slow periods). However, if your anticipated busy season falls flat, consider making budget revisions and investing in more marketing to boost marketplace awareness and drive sales. Such is the ebb and flow of retail.

Diversify to Build Your Retail Business

The need to market more aggressively could also result in innovation and reinvention that attracts more foot traffic. To better serve your customers, you might decide to relocate your store to position it differently from both a geographic and a branding perspective.

After nine years in business, I relocated my chocolate shop to triple our space and diversify our offerings. The bigger space allowed us to add services such as children's parties and adult chocolate-making classes, and expand our retail lines as well. Offering these extras helped level out the ebbs in our weekly sales volume and made up for slow retail days. We have built our sales steadily, thanks to this diversity. My experience has taught me the following key retail lessons:

Expand your services/merchandise. Services that align well with your business will add value for your customers and a new revenue stream for you. To expand, sell items that complement your core merchandise. A florist, for example, could sell plush toys to accompany arrangements or as stand-alone gifts; a clothing boutique can sell accessories. To drive traffic to your store and acquire new customers, host special events that tie in with your business. Attendees are likely to browse and buy.

Location...location...location. When it comes to real estate, location is king—especially in retail. Because of the many considerations regarding store location—area demographics, availability of parking, foot traffic, square footage, landlord build-out terms, lease versus buy, etc.—working with an experienced real estate agent will help you deal with these issues. Before signing a lease or purchasing a business, keep the following four points in mind:

1. Select a retail location that puts you in your target customers' path.
2. Size matters. In my case, a larger location gave us the space we needed to diversify and increase sales.
3. Parking lots rule, but in many towns, the only available parking is on the street. This can present challenges and frustration for store owners and customers, so carefully consider parking availability.
4. Negotiate with your landlord for maximum build-out money or lower rent in exchange for any cosmetic or capital improvements you make.

Listen to your clients. What do your clients ask for when they come to your store? Chances are it's what they want to buy from you. Accommodate their requests if the goods fit with your overall brand (style, price point, quality, etc.). You'll gain customer loyalty, repeat business, and enthusiastic referrals.

Stay abreast of industry trends. Attend industry trade shows and read trade publications. Educate yourself so you become an expert in your field. You'll also be prepared when customers ask about certain items (know what they are and where you can get them).

Polish your brand. This could mean equipment upgrades, a new line of trendy merchandise, a new or enhanced website, updated packaging—whatever keeps your business current and appeals to your customer base. Always make a great impression: refresh your merchandise, keep shelves stocked, and have the tools on hand to make, wrap, and ring up efficiently.

Market/network/advertise. You can never do too much to stay in front of your customers. Years ago, it took three times to be seen by prospects for them to recognize you. Today it's dozens of times before they decide to purchase from you. So run programs that provide results you can track, such as print ads with a specific offer.

Networking gets you name recognition but is less tangible in terms of sales. However, it gives you the opportunity to get involved with your community or other organizations that may not know about your business. Be creative about how to keep your name in front of the public.

Cut costs to trim the bottom line. Try the following cost-cutting suggestions:

- Hire seasonal help through a temp agency (and keep your year-round staff to the minimum you need to run a smooth operation)—you'll save on your workers' compensation insurance in the short term, and payroll over the long term.

- Evaluate all the products you purchase and make sure you have negotiated the best price. Ask about loyalty or volume discounts; many suppliers will negotiate terms.

- Buy only what you need when you need it.

- Pay all vendors on time to maintain a good credit rating, which helps if you ever need a line of credit or business loan.

- A line of credit is crucial to cash flow for a small business that is seasonal.

Sure, retail hours are long and busy seasons can be tough—but selling merchandise you love, in a business all your own, has many rewards.

Lucille Skroce owns Matisse Chocolatier in Englewood, New Jersey, (www.getfreshchocolate.com); she had been a long-time customer before she and her husband purchased the store from the previous owners in 1995. Matisse specializes in hand-dipped, chocolate-enrobed pretzels, chips, cookies, and fresh fruits, chocolate fruit and nut barks, and molded items. The shop has won repeated first place awards in several readers' choice surveys (*Jewish Standard* and *The Record* newspapers, and *Bergen Health & Life* magazine). Matisse's homemade chocolates were included in the 2011 Daytime Emmy Awards Show gift bags. In December 2011, a second location opened in Orangeburg, New York. Lucille can be reached at 201-568-2288 or Skroce@aol.com.

Recipe for a
Successful Business Partnership

by Christine Spear

What does it take to make a business partnership successful? Typically hatched in an aura of optimism and excitement, the individuals involved often have no idea how rocky their journey might be. To be sure, the odds are stacked against them. In fact, only about one in three partnership ventures succeed according to Karen Katcher of Katcher Associates, LLC, a New Jersey–based strategic and business planning company.

But for those whose partnership gels, the relationship, as well as the business, can grow and prosper. Certainly, many of the seventy-two percent[1] of small business owners who are sole proprietors have wished on more than one occasion that they weren't shouldering all the responsibilities of managing a business alone. There is, after all, something to be said about sharing the ups and downs of running a business.

The Female Dynamic

What if the business partners are women? Does the sex of the partners make a difference in terms of chance for success or failure as entrepreneurs? Not according to a study released in the spring of 2011 by the Kauffman Foundation. *Are Women Entrepreneurs Different Than Men?* concluded that "actually women and men entrepreneurs are very similar in terms of education, a strong desire to build wealth or capitalize on a business idea, access to funding, and they largely agreed on the top issues and challenges facing any entrepreneur."

The study did not specifically address partnerships, however, and I believe that is precisely where the male and female dynamics differ. As a partner in a well-established business, I draw insight from my personal perspectives, as well as observations of many other women-owned and male partnerships.

For women, the journey appears to be as important as the end goal—just as having fun playing a game is as important as winning. Doubles tennis among average, amateur players is a perfect example. Watch a women's match, and you are apt to see competing players compliment one another on a great shot, express support when a player makes an error, and at the end of a match tell one another how much fun they had. Men, on the other hand, tend to be driven more by the competitiveness of the game than the enjoyment.

In recent years, corporations have learned that having women board members can actually improve the bottom line. Why? Because of the different core values women bring to the table. Those values, such as honesty, respect, and trust, are more important to women (whether in corporations or partnerships) than closing a deal no matter what the cost.

Linda Wellbrock, partner and cofounder of Own It Ventures, LLC, could have been speaking for most, if not all, women with partnership businesses when she recently said, "Trust, respect, and valuing what your partner brings to the table are crucial elements to a successful partnership. Having a good sense of humor and a positive attitude always helps as well."

Sharing a Vision

Silk Purse, LLC, is a partnership founded in 1999 by Lorraine LaShell and me. We had both recently retired from successful business careers in the fast-paced environment of advertising and marketing. It didn't take long for both of us to realize that stepping away from the world of business was not for us.

We met informally several times to talk about what type of business we could form that would engage us and be less stressful than what we had done previously, but still be challenging. We also wanted to do something that afforded us the opportunity to make a difference for women. Eventually, we decided to form a publishing business. Our goal was to use the publishing platform to build a community of New Jersey women age forty and older, like us, and provide them with relevant information and resources as they moved into uncharted life territory.

Today's boomer women are not at all like our mothers. Our generation has a longer life span in which to accomplish life ambitions. The flip side is because we live longer, we are more likely to care for aging parents and spouses and, sometimes, grandchildren. Because we have few role models from an earlier generation, we need to learn from our peers.

Fast-forward twelve years. Silk Purse stands among the thirty-three percent of women-owned businesses in the United States.[2] Our partnership remains intact, as does our friendship. Lorraine and I recently talked about this, and I want to share the following reasons why we believe our relationship has endured:

1. **Maturity.** We don't mean age, but rather the experience that comes from having been in business for a good number of years. We understand that one crisis, or a differing of opinions, is not the end of the world, and that always keeping the big picture in focus is key.

2. **Aligned goals.** It is important that both partners have similar objectives for the business, or they will be working counterproductively. Using Silk Purse as an example, the overarching goal has been to be a reliable go-to source as we build our community of women. Had one of us focused all of her energy into driving profits higher, we would have diluted our primary goal.

3. **Mutual respect.** If two people are going to work together, then respect for the unique capabilities each brings to the business is critical. Understanding and respecting the strengths of each partner's contributions allows for complementary skill sets to be maximized, and also minimizes duplication of effort.

4. **Sense of humor.** Life is way too short to build a business based on drudgery. If you make a conscious effort, then you'll find humor everywhere—in just about every situation you face.

Owning a small business today is probably tougher than it has ever been. But for those with that special entrepreneurial spirit, it can be extremely rewarding. And sharing the journey with a partner doubles the rewards.

References

1. Darrell Zahorsky, About.com Small Business Information.

2. Rutgers Institute for Women's Leadership, based on the 2002 economic census.

Christine Spear is president and editor in chief of Silk Purse, LLC. She is responsible for editorial content of all *Silk Purse Women* media outlets, including print, website, blog, and e-newsletters. *Silk Purse* has represented the pulse of women over forty in New Jersey since 1999, and has gained a reputation as a respected resource for timely and trusted information. Visit *Silk Purse* at www.silkpursewomen.com to learn more and to watch Christine's television interview with Steve Adubato. Christine can be reached at chris@silkpursewomen.com or 973-689-4751.

Marketing: Branding

A Brand-Building Checklist:
Simple Strategies to Keep Your Brand Current

by Adriana O'Toole

Your "brand" is your identity; it speaks volumes about you and your business. It represents your values, your mission, and your personality. And just as you grow, change, and mature, so does your brand. To make sure your brand truly reflects who you are and what you do, use the following checklist of strategies that I have used for more than 37 years as a Realtor®, including seven as the broker/owner of Montclair Realty, to keep your brand current and upmost in the minds of your customers and clients:

Your brand is your face. Is it time for a makeover? With the speed of change in the twenty-first century, it's easy to get left behind. So make sure your face—your image—reflects who you are today. In addition to your values, mission, and personality, your image should reflect your products and services, and the problems they solve.

To reveal who you are today, start by writing a list of words that describe you, your business, and the results of using your products and services. To help you visualize your new look, think about well-known brands such as Nike, McDonalds, and Apple, and how the logos represent these companies. Also, think about the universal messages from signs such as "Deer Crossing," "One Way," and "Exit." Perhaps you can create a message in that manner.

Of course, color is a key component when it comes to representing your brand, so consider color carefully. Because your brand should incorporate as much of your personality as possible, it's best to work with a professional graphic designer. Graphic designers can help create your image and prepare several options for you to choose from. And make sure your website and blog are consistent with your brand.

Get your message out. Once you have created your message, get it on *everything*—business cards, ads, mailings, website, a QR code (quick response code)—and make sure it links to other avenues of information. Make your phone message a part of your brand, too. Consider using your tagline in your voice mail message, or leaving a tip of the month.

Identify your customers/clients. This sounds obvious, but it is often neglected. There are 80 million boomers (born 1946–1964), 46 million Generation Xers (1965–1979), and 78 million Generation Y/Millennials (1980–2000). These are age groups labeled by marketers, and each has a different view of what they buy, sell, and use. How well do you know them? How will you attract them? Do some Web research to see which of their needs you can tap when preparing your story.

Know your competition. It's easier than ever to keep tabs on the competition. Simply check their websites, blogs, and social media platforms to see what they are doing that might be more attractive to one of your potential customers, and adapt it to suit your personality. This is not about stealing—especially content, which is protected by copyright law.

Start a blog. Blogging regularly helps drive traffic to your website, and it will boost your reputation if you provide valuable information such as resources, expert advice, and what is new and changing in your industry. On your business blog, keep personal information to a minimum. Several blog platforms, including WordPress and Blogger, are free.

Be active on social media sites. Facebook, Twitter, and LinkedIn are the big three. Before you jump in, have a plan for how you want to use them (you don't have to be active on every platform), otherwise you will be overwhelmed). Also, consider Yelp, Foursquare, and HootSuite, which give you the ability to stay in touch and keep consumers engaged. Regardless of how you feel about social media, today's buyers are there.

Stay up-to-date in your industry/profession. Join local business organizations, such as your community chamber of commerce, and networking groups, such as LeTip and BNI®. Become a member of the national organization for your industry to keep current and to share information. After you join, volunteer to work on committees as a way to showcase your leadership skills. Consider starting a networking group if there are none in your community.

Join a nonprofit organization. Whatever you have an interest in, such as Red Cross, museums, Rotary, Lions, hospitals, etc., get involved. It's another way to let people see firsthand who you are and what you do. Remember, people who don't know you, don't know how they can use you.

Promote your business with a giveaway. I give things to customers with my name, e-mail, and phone numbers on the items: pot holders, silver-polishing cloths, calendars, pens, pencils, magnets, etc. For instance, I've given away liquid and dry measures for cooking that say *O'Toole measures up to good service*, and a jar opener that says *One good turn deserves another*. Although these are corny, people use them and remember whose name is on them. Consider e-mailing useful information to your customer base (with your logo and tagline). I send current market information related to real estate because people want to know what's happening.

Promote your successes: awards, honors, achievements. If you receive an award or honor, share it with the world. You're not bragging when it's a fact. Send a press release. Post it to your website. Blog about it. Share your good news on social media platforms. We get enough bad news—your good news will put smiles on the faces of your colleagues, clients, family, and friends.

Connect through shared interests. Your hobby or special interests, such as bird watching, opera, singing, hiking, football, gardening, travel, etc., can be links to others who share your interests because it creates a connection and builds friendships. Although I would never recommend sharing the intimate details of your personal life on a business blog, an occasional post about your hobby and how it relates to business can capture the interest of like-minded prospects and customers.

Naturally, make sure you do a good job for your customers and clients because word of mouth is the epitome of advertising. And remember that your brand will keep evolving—so refer to this brand-building checklist often to keep your audience buzzing about you and your business.

 **Adriana O'Toole, CRB, CRS, CIPS, ABR, SRES, CDPE** (to find out what those letters mean, visit Adriana's website), realtor since 1975 in the Essex and Passaic County areas of New Jersey, but with referral capabilities across the United States and internationally, has completed the National Association of Realtors programs and courses to provide referral abilities to professional realtors anywhere. Adriana is an expert in advising seniors in getting ready to make a move, whether downsizing or relocating, and how to prepare their properties for quick results (watch her video on this topic at www.AdrianaOtoole.com). A graduate of Douglass College, she holds an MBA from NYU. Adriana is a broker associate at the Re/Max Village Square office in Montclair. For more information, visit her website or contact Adriana at aot@adrianaotoole.com, or by phone at 973-509-2222 ext. 105 or 973-650-6039, or connect with her on Facebook, Twitter, and LinkedIn.

The Truth about Your Brand: It Is Not Your Logo (but Your Logo Should Be Smashing)

by Raquel Bonassisa

Have you ever heard of a "smashable logo"?

The best way to explain it is when a brand becomes so recognizable—such as your favorite cola—that if you saw a smashed can and could only make out a few of the letters or part of the logo, you would still know the company. That's brand awareness for sure—the type that most business owners would love to achieve.

Brand awareness is more than a logo, which many business owners fail to understand. In fact, many believe that a brand consists of a logo and a catchy slogan, but it's way more than that. So let's start thinking about a brand with this statement: A graphic designer cannot "make" a brand—the target audience does. A designer, however, helps form the foundation of the brand. In other words, designers set the stage for the premiere of your products and services.

Your brand is your image, so everything it does, owns, and produces must carry through the same value and consistency. Now try this little test with your own brand: Close your eyes and take away your company's logo; visualize your fonts, your colors, your graphics, your packaging, and your products. Do they still convey your brand's identity? They should. If they don't, think about a brand redesign. Your logo should not be the only thing that represents your brand.

The Graphic Designer's Role

When you hire a graphic designer for your brand, that person will need to know and understand your company as intimately as you do. I call this "getting to know your company's DNA." You need to share the *who, what, where,* and *why* of your company before the designer can put ink to paper (now, mouse to screen). As a client, you must communicate the characteristics of your brand to your designer in the following ways: attributes, benefits, values, culture, personality, and the target market.

The identity or image of your company is made up of several elements. These elements are logo, stationery, marketing collateral, products, packaging, and signage. (Usually, there are guidelines for how the elements look and work, which your designer will implement.) All of these make up your identity and play a supporting role in your brand as a whole. The logo is just the pretty mark that identifies your company—not your brand—in the simplest form.

Creating Brand Awareness

When creating brand awareness, three things come into play: emotional image, support materials, and logo.

- Brand is the perceived emotional image as a whole.

- Identity is comprised of the support materials that form the overall brand.

- Logo identifies your business by a mark or text, or in some cases, both.

You could only hope that through the collaboration process of client and graphic designer that your brand shoots to the top of the branding pyramid, which is referred to as top-of-mind awareness. This is where your brand pops instantly into the customer's mind. (Think Apple, eBay, Volkswagen.) It's the most desired positioning you could ask for. Brand recall, such as the smashing logo, is not a bad place to be in, either.

Engagement—the emotional association with a brand—is the new frontier. As brands aspire to create deeper connections with distracted consumers, your print materials are only part of the big picture. So be sure to carry your brand through to other media as well: video, website, and social media outlets—and be consistent with your efforts. We live in an ever-changing, modern, digital world, and as we change as a society, your methods for creating increased awareness must also change.

Five Tips for Hiring a "Smashing" Graphic Designer

How do you find a graphic designer who can capture and create the feel, the passion, and the message of your brand? The following five tips will help.

1. **Ask for a referral:** Look to your social network; chances are that someone has used a professional designer.

2. **Look for experience and education:** Professional designers have earned a degree in graphic design. Most will have a website that includes a bio and that showcases samples of their work. Beware of "crowdsourcing" websites that list hundreds of designers who tend to be amateurs with no understanding of design basics.

3. **Check the portfolio:** Look for a designer whose portfolio samples are in the same industry as your business. Designers will often specialize, and you may come across a portfolio of work that you feel could translate easily into the type of design you have in mind for your business.

4. **Look for one that offers outstanding customer service:** Communication is key. Your designer should be available by appointment, phone, or e-mail.

5. **Look for one that provides pricing/cost information:** A good designer will work on an hourly rate or a flat fee to fit your budget. Give the designer a brief on your project and ask for a quote.

Note: If you want to learn more about graphic design, visit the following websites: AIGA (http://www.aiga.org), the professional association for graphic design; the Graphic Arts Guild (www.graphicartistsguild.org); and the *Art Directors Club* (http://www.adcglobal.org).

When building your brand, work with a graphic designer and go for the smashable logo—the brand that stands out in the crowd because it is recognized for the loyalty it creates and the passion it instills in those who purchase your products and services.

 Raquel Bonassisa, a sought-after, New York City design veteran and Parsons School of Design graduate, owns Hit Designs, a graphic design boutique. After working in many sectors, designing for high-profile clients such as Pepsi, Colgate, Budweiser, Miramax Films, and the NBA, Bonassisa opened her boutique design studio in 2002. As creative director, she leads a team of designers, photographers, and interactive artists to create stunning designs, including in print, online, and mobile. She is also an entrepreneur, having created two successful brands, Pup'n'Pak for the pet industry and Tap and Track Rentals for the real estate market. Based in New Jersey, Hit Designs strives to provide the best resources the big city has to offer. A free, creative brief sample can be downloaded from the Hit Designs website at www.hitdesigns.com/creativebrief.pdf. To reach Raquel, visit www.hitdesigns.com.

Four Printing Tips That Will Save You Time and Money—and Enhance Your Image

by Holly Kaplansky

You might not think about turning to a printer for image enhancement, but your printer can help make you look very, very good. In fact, your business cards, letterhead, and marketing materials make a strong statement about you and your business, so you want to choose the paper, ink, and design that best represents your brand—and a printer can help.

Of course, there are many components to a printing job, but the following four are key:

1. Paper isn't the biggest cost, but it sure is important. Having been in printing and printing-related businesses for over thirty years, I find that the price of paper typically is a major concern when business owners need printed material. In fact, most believe that paper is the biggest price driver and think that choosing a lighter weight paper will save them money.

Well, unless you use superthick stock or pick an unusual paper, this just isn't the case. Paper is usually a small cost of a printing job—about thirty percent. However, paper is still important because it represents your business and your brand and can make you stand out from your competition. Coated stock (usually gloss) is especially good for photos and crispness. Linen or laid can make you stand out in your letterhead and envelopes. Color paper, such as Baronial Ivory, can also make a statement (lawyers and accountants use this type of paper).

Keep in mind that if your graphic designer designates a specific paper type, you (or your designer) should discuss the selection with your printer. If it is an unusual type of paper, there is a good chance your printer can recommend something similar that is stocked in house or is readily available—and will be less expensive. If you do go with the original recommendation, you will understand the cost implication. Not only will you pay more for the paper now, but think in terms of *each* time you place your order and calculate for the full impact over time…not just for a one-time order. So think ahead—especially if you purchase something unique for your letterhead, envelopes, and business cards. What seems like a reasonable price quote today might be more than you budget for next year.

2. To bleed, or not to bleed—that is the question. My customers often don't know what a bleed is. Bleed is when the ink goes to the very edge of the finished product. The job is printed on an oversize sheet (larger than the finished printed sheet) that is cut to size. To picture a bleed, think of a photo without a border. It's common and usually not a problem to bleed flyers and brochures. On the other hand, printing short runs—anything under 500 digitally (more on digital printing later)—can be costly because trimming and folding for short runs create a large fixed cost when you consider the price per piece. For normal offset runs—usually 1,000 or more—the cost is minimal.

However, this is not true for letterhead and envelopes. To bleed letterhead will add cost since it will be printed on oversize sheets (9 × 12) and trimmed down to size (8.5 × 11). Bleeds on envelopes typically have to be printed on a flat sheet of paper and *converted* into envelopes (die cut, glued, and folded to make envelopes). This is much more expensive than purchasing envelopes and printing on them. Talk to your printer for advice on the most cost-effective and good-looking way to proceed.

3. Digital versus offset: this is a *biggie*. People want a better understanding of the difference between digital printing and regular (offset or other type of press) printing. As a general rule, printers will use digital for short runs and offset for long runs.

Digital printing is done by sending a file directly to a very expensive, high-quality digital printer (which looks like a copier machine on steroids). The difference between making a "digital print" and making a "copy" is whether you send the file directly from computer to printer—as opposed to lifting up a lid, putting an original down on glass, and "copying" it. The more you copy, the more you diminish the quality of the copy from the original. The best quality is achieved when you print directly from the electronic file.

So, is it digital or offset? Three things to consider that truly separate them and come into play are speed, number of copies, and cost. One key distinction between digital and offset is speed. Offset printing requires ink. The press has to be set up, plates have to be cut, and there's "make ready" involved. Then the ink has to dry before folding or cutting, and this can take days. On the other hand, digital printing is fast. There's little or no "make ready," toner doesn't have to dry, and the time required to complete the job is for the actual run. Run it, and you're ready to go!

Another factor is length of run. If you've got a long run (5,000 or more), in order to hold quality and color constant throughout the run, you should go to a press. A press will hold the consistency of the images and color better than a digital printer. Cost, of course, is always a consideration—and the benefits of digital printing (speed) come with a cost: digital printing costs more than offset printing.

4. One color... two color... three color... four. In the past, two-color printing was less expensive than full four-color printing. However, with technological advances, that's no longer true. The least expensive printing is either one color (black especially), followed by four-color (also known as full color) printing, then two color, followed by three color. Why use two- or three-color printing if it's more expensive than full color?

Companies that want to control the color from the beginning of the print run to the end, and from a run that was done in January to exactly match the reprint in April, will use two- or three-color (or more) printing. These are done using PMS colors (also known as the Pantone system) where the ink is matched exactly to a Pantone color.

The next time you need printing services, use these tips to save time and money. And if you want your print material to look very, very good, the most important tip I can give you is to work with a printer you like and trust—and to bring that person into the process as early as possible.

 Holly Kaplansky is the owner of Minuteman Press of Newark, a high-quality printer known for exceptional service, fast turnaround, and reasonable pricing. Holly purchased the business in 2005 after a thirty-year career in corporate America holding upper-management positions, including product manager for Doubleday Book Clubs, brand manager for Kraft Foods, global marketing director for Ovid Technologies, and chief operating officer for Russ Candy Bears. Having this extensive management and marketing background at their disposal gives Holly's clients the added advantage of having a brand and marketing advisor on every job. So the next time you need printing, call Holly at 973-624-6907 or, for more information, visit www.mmpnewark.com. Minuteman Press of Newark is a registered Minority/Women Business Enterprise (M/WBE).

The Power of the T-Shirt:
Create a Walking Billboard to
Boost and Brand Your Business

by Angelica Aguirre

Not too long ago, the T-shirt was considered an undergarment. The only time you would see one in public was on a clothesline or in a corner of a department store. With time, the T-shirt gained acceptance as casual clothing. Now, millions of T-shirts are sold every year. In fact, the T-shirt has emerged as a powerful tool of expression for social, political, and business purposes.

Business owners who underestimate the power of a T-shirt miss opportunities to market, promote, and publicize their business. First and foremost, the T-shirt is a highly visible, hardworking communication tool. It is used to express feelings, to make a statement, and—for business owners and entrepreneurs—to promote their company. Using the power of the T-shirt (and other branded apparel), I'm going to show you how to take your business from the back of the store to the front of the line. And to help you understand how to use this power to your advantage, I'm going to show you how a T-shirt—when used as a human billboard—creates excitement and attracts more business.

To effectively use a T-shirt as a human billboard, you must answer three key questions. What message do you want people to see? How are you going to get people to read the message? And, finally, how comfortable (physically and emotionally) will the people (or pet—they make great T-shirt mascots and walking billboards as well!) wearing your walking billboard feel? To help create a message/image people will wear proudly, and to catch the eye of onlookers, use this checklist:

- Before choosing the apparel's colors and styles, identify your walking billboard—the type of person who will wear it. To assure they will wear it often, showcasing your company name to everyone they come in contact with, the T-shirt must appeal to them.
- Consider the printing area on the shirt. For example, instead of printing on the typical front or back areas, you can brand the bottom front, bottom back, sleeves, etc. This will have a double effect: It will attract more eyes to the shirt, forcing people to read your message, and it will make it more appealing to the person wearing the printed apparel.

- Decide on the color combination, which is a key component to accomplishing your goals. You can combine ink colors with the T-shirt color to reflect your business, but always keep in mind who will be wearing the T-shirt. Make it fun for that person; however, be aware that although a bright, neon-pink color will draw eyes to your message, if you give one to the football coach, I assure you the shirt will *not* end up on the coach—and it will not fulfill your walking-billboard goals.

- Keep your message clear and consistent—and short and sweet. If the name or logo of your business does not say what your business does, include this information on the T-shirt by using your tagline or a phrase associated with your business, similar to Nike's "Just do it."

Be sure to include your contact information (website, phone number) so people will know how to reach you when they are moved by your message.

Benefits of Branded Apparel

There are a number of benefits for using printed apparel for your business: It reaches audiences that typical publicity (a story in a community publication, for instance) does not; it creates goodwill; it exposes your business to potential customers. For example, if you sponsor a local sports team and donate the T-shirts, you create friendly, positive feelings for your business. Whenever "your" team has a game or a practice, your name is exposed to people from a variety of backgrounds—and all of these people have needs and connections. Best of all, it doesn't cost much, so sponsoring a team with your business name/logo on the T-shirt is a smart investment.

Using the power of the T-shirt, a local business can create a marketing campaign to attract new customers. Let's see how a walking-billboard T-shirt drives customers to Rosie's Ice Cream Shop. Rosie creates a printed T-shirt with her logo on the front and a coupon on the back that says something like this: "Every time I wear this T-shirt I get a free ice cream at Rosie's Ice Cream Shop." Most likely, whoever wears this shirt won't go to Rosie's alone to claim the free ice cream. Besides, the message encourages people to wear the T-shirt all day, turning each person who wears one into a human billboard for her business.

Because Rosie is offering free ice cream to those who wear her T-shirt, people will start talking. You can be sure they'll want one of these precious T-shirts with the free coupon for themselves—which they have to earn by purchasing a certain amount of ice-cream cones first. And if Rosie puts an expiration date on the T-shirt, she can repeat the campaign every year. Using the power of the T-shirt, Rosie attracts new customers, reaches more places than she normally would have with other marketing campaigns, and increases brand recognition for her business.

Sponsoring a team and using a coupon are just two ways in which customers, who wear your T-shirt, become a walking billboard for your business and help boost your brand. There is, however, another side to the brand apparel coin—your employees. When your employees wear branded apparel, it creates professionalism and uniformity, builds team spirit, and keeps your company/brand name in front of people. When you are looking for an inexpensive, effective way to build brand recognition, get your message out, and reach a wider audience—why not wear it?

 **Angelica Aguirre** is the owner and president of Monster INK, which specializes in branded apparel for business, schools, team sports, clubs, and organizations. Monster INK emerged as a true American dream of Angelica, who started this business in 2006 after realizing she wanted more than just a job. The company specializes in screen printing, embroidering, and imprinting a name, logo, tag line, or any message for promotional purposes. Aguirre offers the unique capability to print in very small quantities from her own in-house equipment, which guarantees quick turnaround and low or no minimum quantities required—something not available anywhere else. For lasting brand awareness, Monster INK can print anything on just about everything. You can reach Angelica at angelica@printmonsterink.com or learn more about how she can help you by visiting www.printmonsterink.com.

Sales

The New Science of Excellent Customer Service: Common Sense

by Elsa Reinhardt

How's this for memorable customer service? You're at the supermarket or department store checkout while two cashiers are chatting away, ignoring you. Or perhaps they're texting, so heads are down and thumbs are flying. Neither cashier looks up to acknowledge you. When you clear your throat to grab their attention without being rude, one says, "Hold on a minute." They continue to text. You continue to wait (and fume). Yes, this is an example of memorable customer service—the kind you remember because you feel forgotten.

As a business owner, you're probably thinking, "I'd fire those two. They wouldn't last more than a day with my company." Which leads to the customer service your business delivers. Think you're good? Think you're great? What do your customers say about you? Which leads to the *big* question: What is excellent customer service? Although a number of ingredients go into the mix, it's not rocket science. Excellent customer service boils down to common sense. To turn your customers (and prospects) into frequent buyers, you need to serve them a slice of scrumptious, customer service cake—so irresistible that they'll beg for more.

Below are the key, commonsense ingredients for creating a prize-winning, customer service cake. Do you use them? Are you missing any? Let's see.

Smile. I'm sure you've heard the saying, "A smile goes a long way." When you smile at someone, you get a smile in return. Smiles make people feel comfortable—and when they're comfortable, they're more likely to open up and be more accepting of you and what your business has to offer. If you want your customers to feel good about their experience with you—so good that they share it with the people in their circle of influence—*smile* (even when you don't feel like it).

Call the customer by name. Nothing is sweeter than the sound of your name. Are you greeted by name and with a smile when you walk into the deli, coffee shop, pharmacy, restaurant, etc., you frequent? If so, hearing your name makes you feel important—it makes you feel connected to the business and the people who work there. The same is true for *your* customers. So make it a habit to use names. When meeting for the first time, say the customer's name repeatedly. Use it during your conversation, then commit the name to memory. People love to be recognized. And from a business perspective, using names is a simple and smart strategy.

Find common ground. Instead of starting the conversation about what your product or service can do for your customer or prospect, ask about their family or family pet. Your goal is to make your customer feel comfortable, so he or she will open up. (Remember to smile!) As you talk, you're likely to find something that you have in common. Perhaps you are alumni of the same college, root for the same team, or enjoy hiking. When you find common ground and capitalize on it, you set the stage for a lasting relationship.

Listen with interest. When you are networking and trying to meet potential clients, instead of shoving your business card in their hands, strike up a conversation. Get prospects to talk by asking about their business, family, hobbies, etc. Listen carefully and respond with genuine concern. Before you leave, you can exchange business cards. I guarantee you will be remembered, and your prospects will be more inclined to call you when your services are needed because you listened and made your new acquaintances feel important.

Focus on the phone conversation. With e-mail, texting, and social media, people are spending less time talking face-to-face and on the phone. As a result, phone etiquette has fallen by the wayside. When you are on a phone call with a customer, give them your full attention. Don't read your e-mail, surf the Web, or check your Facebook page.

And watch your tone—it says more than your words. If you sound annoyed because of the "phone interruption," your customer will pick that up. So smile; your customer will pick that up too. Of course, when you are meeting with a customer and get a phone call, let the message go to your voice mail. If you have to answer, tell the caller you are with a customer and will call back. Taking the call sends a message that you don't care enough about the customer you are with.

E-Mail: The Icing on the Customer Service Cake

I don't know what happens to people when they send e-mail. Judging from mine, it seems most have forgotten how to write sentences that make sense, create paragraphs to break up the copy, and punctuate and format to make the message flow smoothly. In one e-mail, the sender typed "RE" in the subject line, but nothing in the body. But I did receive a message?—yes, that I wasn't worth the time it would take to type a few sentences or paragraphs.

Since e-mail is a primary way businesspeople communicate, here are some tasty e-mail tips that are sure to sweeten your commonsense customer-service cake:

- Keep your e-mail message short—about three paragraphs—and keep paragraphs to about three or four sentences.

- Include the specifics: who, what, when, where, and how. To help compose your message, put yourself in your reader's shoes, and keep your tone upbeat and positive.

- When you get a request that you can take care of quickly—*do it*. Your fast response will surprise your customer and show off your great customer service.

- When you can't fulfill a request quickly, acknowledge the e-mail with an estimate of when you can. However, if you can do it in half the time you promised, your customer will be impressed—another demonstration of you and your savory customer service.

As you can see, these are time-tested, common sense ingredients. No secret ingredients are needed to make your customers feel important and appreciated—just genuine attention and interest in helping them. The next time you interact with a customer or prospect, serve them a slice of your most irresistible customer service cake so they clamor for more. All it takes is some common sense—deceptively simple and sure to please.

In 1990, after being a banker for thirty years, **Elsa Reinhardt** founded Elsa Reinhardt Enterprises, a business support company. After a bout of cancer in 2006, she downsized to bookkeeping work for a few clients, including the New Jersey Association of Women Business Owners (NJAWBO). As a firm believer in giving back, Elsa is a trustee of the New World Montessori School in Hasbrouck Heights, New Jersey, a member of the Hackensack Chamber of Commerce, and president and a managing trustee of the Women's Entrepreneurial Foundation. She has also acted as an Angel Investor in several women-owned businesses within NJAWBO. Elsa can be reached at njawbo@optonline.net.

Sales as Living Theatre—Your Business as the Star

by Linda Santangelo-Mosley

Are you having a "sales affair"—better known as an event—with your business? If not, you should.

Why is this important to you as a business owner? Because it's human nature to be attracted to knockout events in stunning venues. But can an event really connect you and your business to your target audience? Do events result in more sales? I know they can, and I'm going to show you how you can use an event to promote your business and boost sales. But first, let's identify the five dimensions of connection—which set the stage for producing a memorable event.

You are probably familiar with the first three because they are about you, while the last two—which are client focused—are often overlooked:

1. Shaking hands creates a physical connection.

2. Your posture creates a visual connection.

3. Your tone creates a verbal connection.

4. An emotional connection is tied to beliefs and outlook.

5. An experiential connection calls on past experiences, memory, and a shared moment or activity.

When you give your clients something to see, hear, smell, taste, or touch, they're bound to remember your company, your marketing message, and your event. For example, the Rainforest Cafe® restaurants create sensory-filled experiences for their customers. As you enter a restaurant, you hear "sss-sss-zzz," and then you "see and feel a cool mist and smell the tropical essence." These sensory connections result in a memorable experience—a shared moment that increases sales. Naturally, most business owners can't create an environment like the Rainforest Cafe®; however, most business owners can create a memorable event that I call "sales as living theatre."

Sales as Living Theatre

Sales as living theatre combines the emotional and experiential connection in an event. By weaving-in the personal story of your business, your event becomes distinctive and establishes an emotional connection to your client and your sale.

One of my favorite stories using sales as living theatre occurred during my years as a senior sales representative for a manufacturer of architectural materials. I noticed during my sales calls to architectural and design firms that some employees at these firms also owned their own businesses designing and selling beautifully crafted handmade jewelry. Here were a group of talented people with dual roles: employee and business owner.

They were employees because they did not have the opportunity, finances, time, venue, or connections to promote and grow their own small businesses. I realized this was an opportunity to help my clients expand their jewelry businesses while they helped me bring new clients to our showroom and grow our manufacturing business. Here's how it played out:

- I created a sales-and-marketing event using my employer's website to promote the event and my employer's showroom as the event venue to sell the designers' jewelry.

- The results were outstanding. Close to 500 people attended this event, where they could both learn about the products I represented and become our new clients.

- The jewelry designers used their own websites and social media to promote the event and added their comments, as well as those of their friends and family, after the event.

- The jewelry designers had a venue to showcase and sell their products, so they promoted this event to colleagues at the firms where they worked.

- This strengthened my relationships with the architectural and design firms whose employees showcased their jewelry.

- To further market their small businesses, the jewelry designers invited their friends and family to the event, which brought more traffic to our showroom.

- I added a charity component to the event: I invited a charity to join us to raise money and awareness for their cause and give back to the community.

- In lieu of a fee, I asked the jewelry designers to donate a portion of their sales to the charity.

- The charity promoted our event to their volunteers, friends, and family—bringing a new client base to our showroom.

- My employer's website was used to promote the designers prior to the event.

- After the event, we used our website to post personal and memorable stories.

Emotions and Experience Create Connections

Every participant had a memorable experience that culminated in a positive connection. After this event, the word spread, and as I traveled my territory, my clients always asked how soon I would be hosting the next event. With the success of this premier event, I promoted and hosted the event for my employer for two more years, showcasing a new group of designers each year. Now that I own my own business, I look forward to hosting similar events in the future.

Here's something I learned early in my career: helping others succeed is the best path to your own personal and financial success. Being your authentic self—and connecting people to one another and to situations that will benefit them—always benefits you. It will make you as memorable as your events. As a result, people will be eager to do business with you, be loyal to you, and think of you first as a referral when a business opportunity presents itself because they know you will do the right thing.

Yes, it takes quite a bit of time to create and promote an event, but doing so made me feel magical, and it made everyone who participated in the event feel valued. And shared, memorable experiences increase sales opportunities for everyone. Finally, when you follow up with those who attended your event, you will be reminding them of that shared activity: *sales as living theatre.*

Linda Santangelo-Mosley, the founder of Santangelo Consulting, LLC, is a consultant, author, and adjunct instructor with over 20 years of experience as a leader in business development, sales management, corporate events, and new business ventures. Held in high regard by her clients, she is recognized for energizing corporate meetings and events, and fostering client connections with successful sales growth strategies while "having a sales affair." Linda, who is an Accredited Staging Professional (ASP), uses her professional training in staging to enhance her creative sales strategies and to stage memorable events. The winner of numerous awards for sales leadership and community service, she was recently awarded the Student Leader of the Year award by Meeting Professionals International for her work with the County College of Morris in New Jersey. She holds an MBA and a BA, and sits on the boards of several charitable organizations.

Building Customer Loyalty to Drive Big-Ticket Sales

by Judith Schumacher-Tilton

Households face many buying decisions far beyond food, clothing, furniture, or cleaning products. When it comes to high-ticket items or hard goods such as large appliances or automobiles, men and women have definite (and differing) opinions about the product—which is based on their needs and goes far beyond sticker price. How does it look? Will it be easy to operate or maintain? Does it satisfy my family's needs?

Selling these big-ticket items is often less about the product's features than about building a trusted relationship between salesperson and customer. It's about finding those touch points where the proverbial rubber meets the road in terms of strong customer loyalty that moves higher-priced inventory and earns repeat business.

Customer Service: The Be-All and End-All of Any Sale

Whether a large-scale purchase is considered a luxury or a necessity is highly subjective. Just remember that the person interested in buying it came to you because of a need (make home life easier, get to work safely, provide recreation, deliver the wow factor), and it's your job to meet that need through every step of the sales cycle.

However, it is no longer enough to simply answer questions or make a follow-up call. In today's competitive marketplace, making the big sale is all about delivering superior customer service. The savvy salesperson will uncover the customer's needs or desires, and address them with a level of service that's unsurpassed by the competition. Those who do so create a customer for life.

Developing a customer-centered culture should be an integral part of your frontline marketing efforts that flows directly from you, the business owner, down to each employee who comes in contact with your customers— from the receptionist to the salespeople to the service representatives—and back to you. Each employee should feel invested in delivering what customers want from your company. There is tremendous value in this level of customer care, especially when people are spending large amounts with you.

The following are some methods and tips that have worked well for my company to drive big-ticket sales:

Deliver an exemplary customer experience. Differentiate yourself from your competition and go the extra mile to earn a customer's trust and respect. Make sure every employee comes to work with a positive, can-do attitude. (No negative baggage allowed!) It only takes one snide remark to ruin a transaction. At our dealerships, we treat our customers as we treat our own family members, and we monitor our customer-employee interaction in each department to ensure they're giving our customers personal and respectful service. We have weekly meetings with managers and sales and service personnel, and on-site training to keep everyone at the top of his customer service game.

Build up your customer service department. Buyers have an increasing number of choices in terms of brands and places to buy. Therefore, it is never a good time to downsize this crucial area of your business. You need qualified, well-trained employees who are prepared to deliver a quality customer experience no matter what you are selling. It's a vital part of sales cycle marketing, and if you sell a product that requires routine maintenance and repeat visits, that sales cycle continues long after the item has been purchased.

Recognize what the buyer wants. This is not always so easy, especially if you are dealing with a couple who appears to want different things. Spend the time to talk and really listen to your customers so you get to know them. Find out why they are interested in buying your product—personal or commercial need, convenience, safety, special features, a gift, a personal status symbol. Take all their concerns and questions into consideration and match them with the best item for their needs. Become their trusted adviser as they make their way through the first transaction, and you'll do repeat business with them.

Be on site, visible, and available. The business owner is the face of the company and sets the stage for a great customer experience by being there and taking an interest in each sale, so get out on the floor and meet your customers. Today's buyers want that personal relationship with the business owner. They want to feel connected to the person at the top, especially with a large-scale purchase that they will likely have for a long time. They are spending a lot of money and will be returning for service or, if you've all done your job well, for another purchase in the future. You want your customers to feel comfortable with the company and the company owner they are buying from.

Stock inventory that's priced right for your target customer. This is crucial for marketing big-ticket items, where customers are particularly sensitive to pricing. Make sure your pricing is in line with their budgets. Don't try to sell them what they cannot afford or what they don't need—and don't fill the selling floor with merchandise you won't be able to move (and lose money). Customers will trust you if you demonstrate that you can work within their price range and have options that fit their budgets.

If you sell to women, consider becoming Women Certified®. Businesses and brands that meet a higher standard of customer experience among women are awarded the Women's Choice Award from WomenCertified (www.womencertified.com). These companies are acknowledged for providing a better customer experience for women, in part, by recognizing that selling to women is a different process from selling to men.

From glittering jewels to a new car to a high-definition, widescreen TV—in the end, the customer experience is what really sells your product and keeps customers coming back for more, and recommending you to others.

 **Judith Schumacher-Tilton** is the president of Tilton Automotive Group, which owns Schumacher Chevrolet and Gearhart Chevrolet, two of New Jersey's highest-volume Chevrolet dealers. She is the vice chairman of the General Motors Women's Retail Network, and serves on the General Motors Minority Women's Council. Her dealerships have won the Genuine Leader Award from GM and she was awarded GM's Women's Retail Network Performance Award in 2009 (northeast region). Judith was nominated as 2012 TIME Dealer of the Year—New Jersey's first-ever female to compete for this very prestigious award. In recognition of her dealerships' performance and her extensive community service, she won the title of Northeast Regional TIME Dealer of the Year and was among the four finalists for the national title. She is also the winner of the 2012 Women's Choice Award by Women Certified for Outstanding Female Friendly Service and the recipient of the 2012 Shirley Chisholm Award for magnanimous achievements in entrepreneurship. She can be reached at 973-256-1065 or judychevy@aol.com.

When Networking,
The Secret to More Sales is Giving, Not Getting

by Judy Bennett

At Grove Baskets and Gifts, we like to recommend someone we know and can rely on. We want to be sure that the recommendation will be useful and rewarding—and that's where networking comes in. Networking is less about "getting the sale" and more about "giving of yourself." If you want business referrals during networking gatherings, here are eight ways to both give, and build a reliable reputation, which can end up in amazing sales.

1. Share contacts. While exploring the nature of someone's business, I start thinking about other businesses that could align perfectly. I think about people I know who could help this business owner become more successful. I ask probing questions to better understand the company's client base, and ask if there is anyone specific he or she would like to meet. Helping someone else succeed makes you successful.

Example: A casual business friendship has turned a prospect into one of my top clients. She will be the first to tell you that I am responsible for creating her success, and recommends me to everyone she meets. Although I'm not a hundred percent responsible, I am flattered that she recognizes that I was instrumental in introducing her to people who helped her grow her business. Sharing your valuable networking contacts to help grow someone's business will make you a superstar.

2. Make a referral. If you know someone who is looking for a service or a product, act immediately.

Example: Having a referral available when someone else needs one keeps you top of mind as the person who made the connection. That's why my phone is indispensable, especially at networking events. It contains information about my clients such as where and when we met, and what I know about the business that will help make a referral. I also store contact details including phone, fax, e-mail, address, company name, etc. (and always back up the data on a secure server or database). This is essential to making that on-the-spot referral.

3. Offer advice. But avoid giving *unsolicited* advice. However, be honest and personal when asked, and share what you know based on your experiences. Talk about what has and hasn't worked for your business.

Example: When I give advice about marketing, which can be a huge part of a business budget, I suggest spending resources on networking because I have found that it pays for itself. Nearly eighty-five percent of my new business comes from targeted networking, so that's the advice I share when asked.

4. Help. Is there something you can offer business owners that will help them succeed? Sometimes it is as simple as sitting at the computer, and showing how to create an effective PowerPoint presentation. It doesn't take much time to lend a hand.

Example: While chatting with a client, I learned that we use the same bookkeeping software. I also learned that he had lost his assistant and was in a bind because he was behind in his billing. So, two afternoons a week for eight weeks, my daughter, Stacia, (who is my business partner) helped him catch up. Besides getting back on track with the billing, he learned the ins and outs of the software program and discovered he could manage the bookkeeping himself. We now have a client who is indebted to us, and have made a friend forever. The best part is that he refers us to many of his clients.

5. Be reliable. Have you ever worked with unreliable people? Perhaps they're great individuals, but you have to think twice about recommending them for fear they won't show up or follow through. Do what you say you'll do. You always have the option of delegating, but when *you* show up, people know you are someone they can count on. I want to be recommended. Don't you?

Example: We have clients who call and say, "Just do what you do best; I know I'll be impressed." A history of trusting service allows these clients to leave the order to us. If you have tried to work with businesses that never call back when you need their service or product, you move on, looking for someone you trust. If you want recommendations, be reliable.

6. Get Involved. If you want to exhibit your skills, abilities, expertise, and passion—get involved.

Example: Joining an organization is more about getting involved than just getting your name on the membership roster. When people see you in action, they learn to trust you. My business grew because I got involved, and people could see me in action. By working alongside me, they knew they could recommend me and trust me to deliver. They also learned much more about me than they ever would have by exchanging pleasantries at a meeting. So get involved.

7. Donate. We often donate gift baskets to organizations that have relationships with our customers and our business because it further strengthens a strong relationship.

Example: We like to support the charity event with the best exposure, so we ask how many guests typically attend, who the market is, how the event is marketed, and if there is an event brochure. We also ask to be listed on the marketing materials or introduced at the event and to serve on the planning committee. As a result, our business has grown because people get to know us, and we can showcase what we do best at Grove Baskets and Gifts.

8. Make an impression. You want to be remembered. You want your business to be remembered. To make a lasting impression, give your best to build and maintain trust.

Example: Often, our clients do not see the gift baskets they order by phone. They trust us to do a superior job and that the baskets will impress their customers—so that our clients make a lasting impression. When the recipient of a basket thanks my client, it's a testimonial to our business and the work we do. When my clients make an impression on their customers and business partners—my business makes an impression.

Now you have eight ways to increase sales by giving, instead of getting—but I'm sure you can come up with more. What could you be giving?

 **Judy Bennett**, partner at Grove Baskets and Gifts, has more than two decades of experience working as a professional home care nurse liaison. Through her experiences, she saw first-hand how families showed their gratitude and appreciation by sending impressive gifts. In 1998, Judy launched Grove Baskets and Gifts. Her daughter, Stacia Lupinacci, joined the business in 2005. Grove Baskets and Gifts serves local and national clients from their online website at http://grovebaskets.com. For your entire, custom, gift-giving needs, and to discuss how Grove Baskets and Gifts can help you make an impression, contact Judy at 973-226-4430 or judy@grovebaskets.com.

How Pricing Strategies and Customer Experience Create a Sales Frenzy

by Hazel Fraser

No matter what business you are in, you must focus on sales. Equally important is the quality of the products and the services you offer. When the quality is poor, it's easy for consumers to move on—all it takes is the click of a mouse or the touch of a smartphone button.

In my fashion and accessories mobile pop-up and online retail stores, www.ShopJonic.com, we have built a loyal customer base and constantly work to attract new customers. I took my product-based business from less than nothing to six-figure sales in just the first year by offering innovative, good quality products at the right price, and by working every day to improve our customers' shopping experience. This combined strategy translates to increased sales and reduces the loss of sales opportunities.

How ShopJonic Creates Loyal Customers

1. Our customers enjoy being rewarded and appreciated. To show our appreciation, we offer one or a combination of the following: free gifts with a purchase, discount coupons for future purchases, flexible payment plans, and free shipping with $100 purchase.

2. We present the new fashion trends of the season and show our customers how to wear them. These "invisible" benefits keep them coming back and buying more.

3. We have a team with a common goal and guiding principles to ensure that every step leads to the company's ultimate goal, which is customer satisfaction and loyalty. Our staff is educated and keeps current about our products and offers. They always suggest coordinating products to shoppers, and are trained to help the buyer make a purchase. They are not afraid to entertain new and different ways of doing business or to check with management if they're unsure about a customer's request.

Let me share with you how valuable your staff is with a good example of a bad loss. I was at a salon when a customer walked in, eager to buy twelve gift certificates for her office staff. The clerk quoted the price, and as the customer pulled out her credit card, she asked the clerk, "Do I get a discount because I'm buying twelve?" When the clerk told her there was no discount, the customer said, "Well, I've changed my mind. I'm sure another salon will give me a discount for buying twelve," and walked out.

As an observer to this loss, I asked the clerk why she did not offer a discount. The clerk said, "I'm not the boss, so I can't give discounts."

I questioned her further. "That was a large sale," I said. "Why didn't you call the boss for approval?" She grumbled something, took a phone call, and did not answer my question. Not only did this clerk lose a large sale, but she created a bad feeling for the customers who witnessed such an abrupt dismissal of a potential customer!

The Best Price for You and Your Customers

Figuring out the right pricing strategy is a skill that all business owners must develop. When buying wholesale, manufacturing products, or selling services, the costs are usually based on what is called economies of scale. In other words, the more you buy, the less it costs. Buying at the right price can put you ahead of the game, so we use multiple product sources and *always* negotiate prices. If you don't ask for a discount, in most cases, you won't get one. And a discount doesn't always mean getting a less expensive price; it can mean free shipping or an earlier delivery, which allows you to make profits sooner than anticipated.

When pricing products, markups, in most instances, are determined once you have figured out the total cost of a product—including incidentals. For example, if we import an item from Europe, we add duties and shipping costs. For products from California, we add trucking or UPS costs. Depending on the product, you generally mark up two or three times the total cost. Some businesses may have a clientele that allows them to apply even greater margins. You must understand your customer base, and calculate prices accordingly.

If you're selling a service, know the going rate, be it hourly or priced per project. Determining the right price is based on the quality of your expertise, years in business, nature of business, and the clientele you are serving.

I always recommend bundling services (if appropriate) by offering multiple options with savings attached as opposed to offering one service at a fixed price. This method shows the customer you care. For example, my sister Lana at Hot Homes Realty recently had a client who listed her home for sale. Lana packaged a deal by offering to also find a new home for the client. As a result of handling both transactions, the client received a better commission rate. This was a win for both Hot Homes Realty and the client.

Consumers talk to their circle of social influence about how much they saved and how helpful your company was during their shopping experience. This spreads the *good* word about your business. It is social interaction— word of mouth at its best!

Create an Incredible Customer Experience

New forms of marketing and advertising can be implemented without significant, increased costs. Be creative—don't be afraid to experiment and find your own unique ways to present your products and services to make an impact with consumers. For example, we had a dress that was not selling well until our sales staff became our models and wore the dress. Once our customers saw how great the dress looked, sales increased dramatically.

Whether you sell to businesses or consumers, it's important to have a good understanding of your customers' needs and give more than what the customer expects. Price will not be an issue when you add value to the customer's buying experience, which will earn you a loyal customer. It's critical to retain and grow your list of "loyals," so listen to their ideas and suggestions, and apply them when appropriate. There's no wrong way to do the right thing!

The best advice I can offer business owners is something my son Nicolas (Boss Major Salute) taught me: "Value your customers more than you value their money. Money comes and goes, but your customers will come and stay."

Hazel Fraser, the owner and founder of www.ShopJonic.com, a fashion and accessories company, is a twenty-plus–year veteran of the apparel industry with a focus on import and domestic fashion manufacturing as well as merchandising, product, sales, and brand development. She has initiated private-label programs for the likes of Louis Vuitton, Calvin Klein, Tommy Hilfiger, DKNY, JC Penney, Sears, QVC, Macy's, Banana Republic, and Express stores. Fraser is widely credited as the creator of Latina-inspired clothing with her brand "Chula" for Macy's Federated Store Group, "Azucar de Bella" for the Sears stores, and "Candela" for JC Penney. Fraser has been recognized for her talents by *Women's Wear Daily*, *The New York Times*, *El Diario* newspaper, *Latina* magazine, and has showcased her fashions on *CBS, NBC, WB11*, and *Telemundo TV*. Contact Hazel at Hazel@ShopJonic.com or 646-919-8167.

SALES STRATEGY

CHAPTER 32

Three Great Sales Strategies
for "The New Era"

by Cecelia Inwentarz

How can you and your business become great in "The New Era" when you're not great at sales?

It's easier when you know that the best sales strategies come from deeply knowing and understanding yourself. After a lifetime as a professionally trained, highly successful businessperson, I've identified three keys to strategic sales that are better suited to the ever-changing business environment of The New Era. And the process begins within *you*: the quality of your heart, the intensity of your passion, and actively engaging your heart-mind connection.

When I left the corporate world to start my own business, the hardest thing for me to do was to ask people for money—especially when the money was for my consulting services. Naturally, I took courses to help me overcome any obstacle that would prevent me from being successful in sales. In fact, it's fair to say that no method of selling exists that I haven't studied. But the end result was that I just didn't love selling.

Fortunately, I never had any difficulty investing money by spending business budgets. In fact, as a Fortune 500 food-brand marketer with "P&L" responsibility, I was rewarded for nothing more than the efficient and effective investment of my brand's multimillion-dollar advertising and promotional budget. I created the sales strategy that the sales team used to "push" the brand onto supermarket shelves, and I created the marketing belief that would "pull" those brands off.

In fact, it was a snap to create belief because I hired from top-notch creative vendors who lined up to pitch their best advertising and promotional ideas from their brightest selling talent to win my approval. But, as I found when I started my own business, selling is hard work, even when you're creative. And yet selling is at the heart of every business. If there were no sales—even for one day—the business world would come to a jarring halt!

Why does great selling have to be so hard? It doesn't—when you infuse your best self into following these three keys as your sales strategy: consultative selling, collaborative sales, and empowered choice.

Strategic Key 1
Consultative Sales: Your Heartfelt Strategy

In consultative selling, you have a true interest in the other person's well-being—not your own. Successful salespeople don't manipulate clients to suit their own purposes to make the sale. They serve clients by consulting—by using their creativity to solve their clients' problems. That takes what I call "a natural salesperson"—or any person, who by being strongly connected to his or her own heart, has the insight and compassion to empathize with a client.

Consultative selling is about finding your unique way to be of service and provide a solution. It's about giving before you receive—about developing a relationship of trust by placing yourself in service.

When clients are ready to buy, they choose from consultative sellers first, who are actively engaging their heart-mind connection. What do you give your clients and prospects?

Strategic Key 2
Collaborative Sales: Your Unique Serving Strategy

Just because you're the business owner doesn't mean you should sell. Even if you do it well, maybe selling is not your passion. So don't let anyone sell you on becoming a salesperson if you're not so inclined—no matter how many tricks and techniques you can learn. If selling is not at the top of your list, there are options such as collaborative sales that help you develop your unique serving strategy (USS).

Collaborative selling creates partnerships and opens the doors to opportunities you might not be able to open on your own. And it does the same for your collaborative business partners. You create a USS not only for your clients and prospects, but for your business partners—especially when they are heartfelt.

Now, instead of worrying about selling, you can spend more of your time on what you do best. In fact, your best strategy for growth could come from collaborating with another compassionate, consultative business owner who will passionately support or represent you. For instance, to sell my brand of leadership training, I collaborate only with high-energy designers to facilitate group business events and webinars to develop higher-performing corporate teams and leaders.

Not only do I serve my clients, but I serve the business partners I collaborate with. What do you have to offer a potential partner so you can collaborate, create your USS, and increase sales?

Strategic Key 3
Empowered Choice: Your Inner Sales Strategy

There is power in choice—in your decisions where to focus your time and energy. The greatest power to achieve comes from your choice that stems from positive beliefs. Empowering beliefs should form the basis of your motivation for all of your choices. Always ask yourself: What is motivating my choices?

Negative choices are motivated by fear, and we all have fears. But I define FEAR as useless, negative worry or "false events appearing real." Fears grow from negative thinking and produce powerless outcomes, especially when it comes to money. So look within to overcome any fearful sales energies tied to needing money. And pay attention to your thoughts so you are aware of the underlying basis for your choices—your motivations.

Some people say, "When I see it, I'll believe it." But that is not how choice operates. Powerful sales strategies are set by choice, based on belief, and your best sales strategies come from higher motivations. So I say, "When you believe it, then—and only then—will you see it." This is ultimate selling. This is the essence of a positive "pull" strategy, the universal law of energetic attraction versus the negative "push" strategy, which is an outmoded, competitive sales model.

Once I eliminated my old, energetic thoughts and feelings about sales and how I truly connect with people, I saw that these three key strategies— my choices, consultative selling, and collaborative sales—resulted in greater sales success. I encourage you to use the three keys to set your business and sales strategies from your own higher motivations by choice. Once you activate your inner passions, your sales will soar, too!

Cecelia Inwentarz, MBA, is a marketing brand executive and leadership development consultant with over 25 years experience working with Fortune 500 companies to develop strategic marketing plans, sales growth strategies, and new business entrepreneurial ventures. Her experience with IBM, Best Foods, and Zone Nutrition, and her insights managing such brands as Hellmann's, Mazola, and Domino, led her to be recognized as one of the most prominent food marketing executives in New Jersey. As an author, speaker, and consultant, she is widely known for her perspective on increasing leadership brand value with "consultative energy" and generating profitable, high-performing business teams with "collaborative energy." Learn more at www.CeceliaInwentarz.com. Contact CeCe at 973-285-7590 or CeCe@CHiConsultant.com.

Ask for Referrals:
It's Not as Hard as You Think

by Debra Knapp

One of the biggest challenges small business owners face is finding new clients to grow their business. For many, this is a time-consuming, costly process that leaves less time for income-producing work. What you may not realize is the golden opportunity to market your business—and it's right in front of you.

If you have a private practice like my business partner and I do (The Hearing Group), your current clients represent a group of credible advocates and a low-cost, high-return method of marketing your business. In our case, we accomplish this by asking our patients for referrals.

In fact, implementing a plan for maintaining and increasing your referrals should be a key part of your overall strategy to capture new clients and grow your business. If you have never asked your clients for referrals—or tried but failed to gain new business—pay attention to the four key action steps I learned about referrals, and use them to grow your company:

1. Transform your thinking. If you want referrals, the bottom line is that you have to ask for them. Many business people are uncomfortable asking for referrals because they don't want to come off as "sales-y" or appear desperate for work.

Our patients come to us with their own concerns and needs, none of which have to do with growing a business or getting more clients for us. But assuming they are happy with our services, it is not that they don't want to help us—rather, the thought hasn't crossed their minds unless we ask. Requesting a referral doesn't guarantee an opportunity to help someone else; however, not asking guarantees that you will help fewer people.

2. Implement a plan. One way to get into the habit of asking for a referral is to develop a script. Your script should fit your personality and be modified to fit each staff member's personality as well. By working with your staff so everyone in the practice knows how and when to ask for referrals, you can be assured that your practice is making the most of the referral network without being too pushy or aggressive. Ultimately, the request for referrals will become second nature, and a normal part of your daily routine.

In our practice, we developed "who cards" that we give to our patients to facilitate asking for a referral. The cards say: "Who would you like us to help hear again?" The cards have a place for a name, address, and phone number. When we hand them to our patients as they check out of our office, we say, "I am so happy we were able to help you with your hearing needs. The greatest compliment you can give us is a referral of a friend or family member who may also benefit from our services. Do you know of anyone we may be able to help the way we have helped you?"

We use promotional items, too. Giving out promotional items is a way to show your appreciation and remind the patient to think of your business and send you referrals. We place pens, magnets, and note pads with our logo where our patients check out. In addition, giving a few business cards to every client who walks through your door is effective. This makes it easy for them to pass your name and contact information to someone else.

3. Thank patients or clients for referrals. When patients or clients send you referrals, take the time to let them know how much you appreciate their thoughtfulness and how much it means to your business. Most people enjoy being recognized for something they have done—and there are easy, inexpensive ways to thank your patients. In our practice, we send a thank-you note with a handwritten message expressing our appreciation.

You can also start an "Ambassador's Club" for people who send you multiple referrals. Offer people in the club a discount or free service for every referral. Hold a patient appreciation day with refreshments for those in the club. People will feel good about the impact they are having on your work and be motivated to look for more opportunities to send business your way.

4. Ask and you shall receive. It's true: the more referrals you ask for, the more referrals you will get. We aim for a referral ask rate of eighty percent and track our referrals daily. We keep a record of our referrals on a large bulletin board in our office so all the staff can see it. We also offer our staff a bonus when we maintain our referral rate every month.

Most important, don't wait until business is slow before implementing a referral plan. To have a consistent flow of business, make sure your referral plan is part of your overall marketing strategy. And don't let your fear of asking for referrals get in your way.

Develop a referral plan that fits your office style and your staff, so your business can start capturing referrals today. Above all, you must believe in your commitment and in your ability to provide exemplary service—and ask *everyone* to help you.

Treat every client or patient like the most important person of the day. Let them know their business is appreciated, and more than likely, your efforts will be rewarded with a never-ending stream of referrals.

 **Debra Knapp, Au.D., CCC-A**, is a Doctor of Audiology and a partner in The Hearing Group, located in West Orange, New Jersey. Her practice provides hearing solutions to people of all ages. She is there to help you every step of the way, from identifying hearing loss to dispensing the hearing aids to helping you hear better. To find out how Dr. Knapp and The Hearing Group can help you, contact Debra at 973-243-8860 or hearinggroup@comcast.net or visit www.thehearinggroupusa.com.

Growing Your Business with Body Doubles

by LuAnn Nigara

Do you want your business to be more profitable this year? Do you want to be more profitable more efficiently? Do you want to grow your business?

I'm going to share with you how to do the following:

- Reach consumers outside of your usual sphere of influence
- Multiply your number of quality leads
- Increase your close ratio
- Develop satisfying relationships that consistently bring you new business

Sound interesting? Naturally, there are the traditional methods for growing your business. These include increasing your advertising, hiring additional staff, or adding another location. All are valid ways to increase your sales, and they have their place in your efforts to increase business. However, all of these tactics require capital.

So, how do you increase your sales without this outlay of capital?

Find business body doubles.

Imagine business body doubles out on the streets every day, talking to people about you, your business, and your products or services. Also imagine that whenever these business body doubles find someone who needs your products, they call you to arrange the meeting. Further imagine that by the time you have this meeting, your business body double has already sold the new client for you.

How do you do this? You look within your industry for businesses that provide the same service as, or a similar service to, yours—but to a slightly different end user or consumer.

How Partnering Helps Window Works Grow

At Window Works, we specialize in custom window treatments and awnings. We realized that our products are frequently a single component of a consumer's much larger design project—a project often managed by an interior designer. In this case, by someone who provides a similar product and service to ours, but to a different market—a more exclusive, prequalified market.

Recognizing this, we approached designers in our area offering to partner with them on their projects. We provide them with technical and design expertise, as well as professional measuring and installation of all window treatments. Additionally, we relieve them of the entire ordering process—which is detailed, complicated, and time consuming. The designer is then free to oversee the other details involved in the design project—and comfortable in knowing that the very expensive aspect of window treatments and awnings is expertly handled by our company.

Here are four top benefits of having business body doubles and how this strategy has helped (and continues to help) Window Works grow.

1. Through the designers, we access a consumer base that would normally not cross our path. Many people will not attempt a home remodel or a design task without the counsel of a professional interior designer. No matter how well we are positioned in our field, these are almost exclusively clients we never would have had the opportunity to pitch our products and services to because they have entered the window treatment and awning market through "trade" channels rather than "retail" channels. They are normally out of our sphere of influence. But not anymore.

To be clear, we never overstep the designer relationship by soliciting their clients in any way. However, the satisfied consumers we meet through the designers have their own network of family and friends. And when a happy consumer shares her satisfaction with Window Works, it has a reverberating effect through the marketplace.

2. We have dramatically increased the number of quality leads with no additional money spent on advertising. With dozens of design professionals partnering with Window Works, every lead of theirs is a lead of ours. On any given day—by e-mail, phone, or fax—new leads, new jobs, and new requests for project budgets come to us. And all are generated by each designer's advertising and marketing efforts—not ours.

3. The close ratio for these leads is nearly a hundred percent. Why? When the designer calls us, he or she has a client who has signed a contract. The designer considers us part of the team, and calls us to handle and complete our part of the project.

4. Through this alliance, we build lasting, meaningful relationships with our esteemed designer colleagues. This association is gratifying, both professionally and personally. Together, we work to grow our businesses by referring and recommending each other because we both benefit when we both prosper. After many years of cultivating relationships with dozens of designers, we have created business body doubles who sell our products every day to hundreds of consumers.

The most extraordinary benefit is that this sales force is not on our payroll. We do not hire, train, or pay any salaries or benefits. They are business owners who we have partnered with to create new revenue for our company without incurring more expense or more overhead.

How to Create Your Business Body Double

So, who is your business body double?

If you are specialists like us, consider larger businesses that offer your products within their portfolios. What can you offer them? Expertise, resources, services?

If you are a larger business, explore aspects of your projects that you can outsource to others, which allows you to be more effective and more profitable. Or, find a business that complements your products or services and adds value to yours.

There are examples of this everywhere you look—from small start-up companies to Fortune 500 companies. Have you noticed a Starbucks inside your grocery store, or a pet grooming salon inside a Petco store? The key is to explore ways you can work in tandem or through other professionals by looking for the benefits for both of you. If you want your partnership to be successful, it must be a win-win arrangement.

After you identify your business body double, outline the advantages each partner gains through the alliance. Of course, don't forget to include the responsibilities. Finally, approach your new partner with your proposal, and you are on your way to growing your business.

To jump-start your thinking about business body doubles, here are some suggestions for potential business partnerships: professional home stagers and realtors, florists and restaurants, decorative artists and interior designers, wallpaper/painters and general contractors, massage therapists and hair and nail salons, makeup artists, and portrait photographers. You get the idea. So be creative when considering business body doubles—the possibilities are endless.

LuAnn Nigara owns Window Works in Livingston, New Jersey, along with her husband, Vincent Nigara, and their cousin Bill Campesi. Together they have been servicing the New York Metro area since 1982. Window Works specializes in custom window treatments and awnings, catering to both the direct retail consumer and the professional design trade. LuAnn is responsible for sales development and the maintenance of their professional trade clients. You can reach her at 973-535-5860, or visit Window Works on the Web at www.windowworks-nj.com.

Marketing: Relationship

Put Your Business Blog to Work

by Laurie A. Hauptman

Marketing is the lifeblood of any business. If you don't have customers coming through the door, you won't be able to provide your great services or products—not to mention pay the bills that keep your doors open to support your family. But when you are a small business, chances are you have a small marketing budget. And because maximizing your time and money is so important, I believe that blogging is one of the best ways to get your marketing message out to the masses for little money. But before I share with you how my business has benefited from blogging, let me tell you about the business.

My husband and I have our own law practice, concentrating in elder law and disability planning. It is a very specialized area—and often difficult to explain. We guide seniors and their families through the various stages of long-term care. We coordinate the maze of laws and benefits that can provide them with home, assisted-living, and nursing home–level care. Most people avoid dealing with long-term care until they are in complete crisis mode, and then often are stressed or depressed because they waited too long to seek help.

As you can imagine, it is not easy to reach our target market, educate them about our services, or be there at the exact moment they are ready to act. Much of our business is referral based—received from other legal, financial, and health-care professionals, as well as former clients. We have to consistently stay in front of this network, which takes persistence, repetition, and time—and usually lots of money—until we started to blog.

How Businesses Benefit from Blogging

After blogging consistently for nearly four years, we learned the following:

- Blogging allows your prospects to get to know you and what you are about before they do business with you. For instance, by educating our market, we have been able to reduce time-consuming and unnecessary phone calls.
- Blogging helps level the playing field. In our instance, blogging allows us to compete with bigger law firms with much bigger budgets than ours.

- Blogging helps you stay "top of mind" with your network of customers, affiliates, and referral sources. It distinguishes your business from the competition and personalizes your message.
- Blogging can drive traffic to your website and increase your search engine rankings, but by itself, that isn't enough. You must capture your visitors' contact information and continue to market to them until they are ready to buy from you.
- Well-written blog posts can help you handle the common objections from your prospects and educate them about your product or service before they walk through your doors.

Blogging can help maintain and strengthen your business relationships and make the sales process much easier because your audience feels they know you and your business—even when you haven't met face to face.

If You Blog—Will They Come?

If you're thinking about blogging as a marketing tool, or you want to see better results from an existing blog, consider the following:

Your blog. Unless you are tech savvy, it's best to talk to a Web developer to help you get your blog up and running. On the other hand, if you or a staff member is capable, using a free platform, such as WordPress, makes the cost minimal if you choose to set up the blog yourself. Setup is a once-and-done process.

Your content. Decide who will be responsible for creating the content and how often you will post to your blog. It must be someone who knows your business well. Of course, posting regularly is key to growing and maintaining your audience. My husband writes most of our posts, which appear every Monday morning without fail.

To keep your readers interested, post entertaining and educational stories. We are all conditioned from childhood to learn through stories, so use stories to show how your product or service changes people and makes their lives better. Some of our best posts—ones for which we have received the most feedback—are the "horror" stories of "do-it-yourselfers." For example, these are often people who tried to qualify for government benefits to help pay for long-term care without seeking proper legal advice—and miscalculated. Some of the stories end with us helping to fix the problem. In other instances, it was too late, but the story is an illustration of what not to do.

Your list. Once you've written and posted to your blog, you must get people to read it. Just because it's on the Internet doesn't mean they'll see it. You've got to have a delivery system, and that's where automation comes in. Customer relationship management (CRM) software allows you to send an e-mail message to your list of readers announcing a new post. There are many options available, such as Constant Contact, iContact, and Blue Orchid. We use Infusionsoft, which not only automates the delivery, but gives us very detailed statistics and information about who we are reaching and what our readers are interested in. This valuable information allows us to laser focus our marketing message.

Your audience. We send out a teaser e-mail with a catchy headline to raise curiosity so the reader will open it. There are many "classic" headlines that can be used in any business. Examples are: "How to _____" (fill in the blank as it pertains to your product or service); "The Right Way and the Wrong Way to _____"; and "The One Mistake _____ Made—Don't Let It Be Yours." The body of the e-mail is the first paragraph of the post, which is designed to draw the readers in. If they want to read "the rest of the story," they can click through to our website.

In the past, when prospects raised a hand and requested information from us, it occasionally resulted in an immediate sale; however, that was not typical. Why? Because they weren't ready to commit, or they didn't realize they needed our services, or they truly didn't need our services—yet.

Our challenge was getting prospects to remember us when they were ready to move forward—whether it was in a few weeks, months, or even years. Blogging has helped us overcome that challenge. Blogging allows us to stay in touch with our audience, so when they do reach out—they reach out to us—not a competitor. In many instances, the reason they contact us is because of something they read on our blog that made them realize they must do business with us.

Laurie A. Hauptman, Esq., has been a practicing attorney for over twenty years, the past fourteen with her husband, Yale, in their elder law and disability planning law firm in Livingston, New Jersey. In addition to growing a successful law practice, she is an active member of her community in both civic and religious organizations and the proud mother of three teenage children. Laurie's firm and its blog can be found at www.hauptmanlaw.com, and she can be reached at laurie@hauptmanlaw.com.

Seven Biggest Mistakes Business Owners Make When Following Up with Prospects, and How to Avoid Them

by Kelly Lynn Adams

How many connections or "touches" do you make with potential customers or clients before you stop reaching out to them? Most experts agree that it takes between five to seven touches to finalize eighty percent of sales. Yet, the majority of business owners follow up two or three times, and never reach out to the prospect again. Without a follow-up strategy in place, you are leaving money on the table.

Following up with prospects also builds relationships because people like to buy from someone they have a connection with. It's a widely accepted sales principle that people do business with people they know, like, and trust. So cultivating and managing the relationship with your prospect is vitally important for future success—and you do that when you follow up.

To avoid losing your prospects to your competition, pay attention to the seven biggest mistakes you want to stay clear of when implementing a follow-up strategy:

1. Not following up immediately. It is critical to take action immediately while you are foremost in the prospect's mind. Prospects actually expect you to follow up with them because it shows professionalism on your part and helps to increase the good feelings from a meeting, whether the meeting was virtual or in person.

2. Providing fluff and no valuable content. Adding value to your prospects' lives is key. On the other hand, if every follow-up is to sell something, you could be labeled a pest and ignored in the future. Your goal is to provide value every time you communicate with your prospects with information that helps make their lives easier, helps them make money, helps them solve a problem, or introduces them to valuable connections. You do this by sharing content-rich articles and videos that you or others created via a blog or e-mail, or by inviting your prospects to a networking, charity, or social event.

3. Being inconsistent. Once you establish and cultivate relationships with your prospects, be consistent in your follow-up. Because your prospects are not always thinking about you, maintain a system that makes it easy for them to remember you when they (or people they know) need your products or services. For example, you can create an Excel spreadsheet or a specific database of past, current, and future clients. Include their name, date of follow-up, and how you plan to follow up.

So you don't become a "follow-up stalker," communicate to your prospects when they can expect to hear from you. At the end of a phone conversation or an in-person meeting, always ask when would be the best time to follow up with them. You build trust and lasting relationships when you manage your prospects' expectations and communicate with them.

4. Staying off all social media platforms. Today, there are so many social media sites to join that it can become overwhelming. But if you are not on at least one of the most popular platforms (Facebook, Twitter, LinkedIn, YouTube), you are leaving more money on the table. Think of social media as a marketing avenue that can give you "free" advertising, marketing, and visibility. Choose one platform, and have a marketing plan in place. You also want to apply the eighty/twenty rule when trying to engage and gain potential clients: eighty percent of your content provides valuable information, and twenty percent of your content promotes and sells your products or services.

5. Never sending anything by snail mail. Since the social media craze, people are drowning in e-mail and virtual coupons. Business owners tend to forget about how marketing and advertising were done in the past and the effectiveness of good, old-fashioned snail mail. Think about how you feel when a thank-you note or a birthday card shows up in your mailbox. Sending a thank-you note, a birthday card, an article with helpful business tips, an invitation to an event you are attending, or a VIP coupon for your products or services is a necessary part of developing successful strong relationships with your customers.

6. Not asking for a referral. Always ask for a referral. I personally know an entrepreneur whose entire business is referral based. She started out with ten clients, and from there grew (and continues to grow) her business on referrals. Referrals are often excited to hear what you have to offer because someone they trust recommended you. Another benefit of getting a referral is that they usually pay your fee with no questions asked. Referrals can become the cash cow of your business, and the first step in receiving one is to ask.

7. Not scheduling your follow-up time. Like anything in business, if something is not scheduled or written down, there's a good chance it will not get done. Many business owners are guilty of skipping this step and do not schedule follow-up time. To make sure you follow up with your prospects, note the time in your calendar. It doesn't matter if you block out one to two hours a week or four hours a month, as long as you are consistent. What matters is that you schedule the follow-up activities and take action. As with any strategy you plan for your business, implementing and taking action are the keys to success and a sure way to generate more profit.

Now that you know the pitfalls of failing to follow up—it's time to get going—it's time to follow up.

 **Kelly Lynn Adams** is a certified business and energy leadership coach, motivational speaker, and multi-passionate entrepreneur. Her content has appeared on Forbes.com, as well as many other online magazines and media outlets. Kelly Lynn helps passionate women entrepreneurs start lucrative businesses they love. She also helps entrepreneurs who want to give back to their communities. Kelly Lynn is helping to empower and positively impact one woman, one business, and one community at a time. To get motivated by Kelly Lynn, please visit www.KellyLynnAdams.com to receive her free, downloadable e-book, *10 Powerful Tools That Will Transform Your Life & Your Business*. Follow Kelly Lynn Adams on Twitter @KellyLynnAdams, Facebook: Kelly Lynn Adams, and on LinkedIn under Kelly Adams.

Growing Your Business by Reaching Out and Touching Someone

by Deborah Gussoff

No doubt you've heard the saying that all things being equal, people choose to do business with people they know, like, and trust. I would amend that phrase to, "…know, like, trust, and remember." Just because you went to a networking event nine months ago and had a lovely conversation with someone you met, if you haven't stayed in touch over the past three-quarters of the year, she may not remember or think of you when she needs the services you provide. The key is to meet someone, stay in touch, and build a long-term relationship with that individual.

So How Do You Do That?

As soon as you get home from an event, you should enter the person's contact information into your contact management system. Be sure to note where and when you met. You may even want to include some notes (long blonde hair, son plays soccer, husband is a pharmacist) that will help jog your memory when you pull up the contact in the future.

Within two days of meeting a person, send an e-mail or a card saying, "It was nice to meet you." Follow up with a phone call, suggesting you meet for coffee. Sitting down in person for a half hour or so provides an opportunity to learn more about each other—from business offerings to personal life to goals and dreams. The better you know someone—and the better she knows you—the easier it is to refer business to each other.

After your coffee, enter a reminder in your contact manager to "touch" this person in another month. Touches can take the form of a phone call, e-mail, or greeting card. And then do it again the following month or quarter. The key is to keep the momentum going and continue to build, maintain, nurture, and sustain that relationship over time.

Your annual marketing plan should include a strategy and specific tactics for staying in touch with clients, prospects, and referral sources. After all, you never know when someone you've met will need the products or services you offer, or have the opportunity to refer you to others. Consequently, you want to be sure to remain "top of mind." Your goals, and time and budget constraints, as well as the type of business you have, will shape your relationship-marketing strategy. As you are thinking about your strategy, ask yourself the following questions:

- Do I have the time to sit down and call my clients monthly? If so, do I have something relevant to say?
- Do I have the skill set to write (or the funds to hire someone else to write) a monthly or quarterly newsletter?
- Do I want to commit to writing a blog or an e-mail "tip of the day"?
- Does my targeted client base have time to read a newsletter? Do I want to stay in touch by snail mail or electronically?
- Is my communication adding value and keeping me top of mind, or am I annoying someone by filling his in-box?
- Can I hold informational seminars or courses a few times a year to help educate my clients and prospects?
- Do I have the time and budget to take my clients out for lunch or dinner on a periodic basis?

Whatever form your plan takes, be sure you have a way to track and measure results so you know what is working, and you can calculate your return on investment.

I Remember You—Will You Remember Me?

Let me share with you three examples of relationship marketing from the automotive industry. After reading each example, you decide if the strategy helped strengthen the relationship between the customer and the car dealer.

Example 1

Years ago, my mom bought a new car. For the first three years she owned the car, each year on the anniversary of the date she took delivery, her car received a birthday card. My mom displayed this card on her fireplace mantle as proudly as she would display a card to her from one of her children, and she put it in her purse to show her friends what her car dealer sent her. When she had to replace her car, guess what dealer she went to first?

Example 2

Approximately seven years ago, I leased a car from an area car dealer. Three years later, I returned the car at the end of the lease. However, several times a year, to this day, I get a letter from the dealer, telling me they want to buy back the car I no longer have. They also send e-mails stating the same thing. At this point, I automatically delete any e-mails from this dealer. My perception is that they are not on top of things.

Example 3

This example involves a car salesman named Joe Girard who, for more than a dozen years, was the best-selling new car and truck salesman in the world—and has *The Guinness Book of World Records* title to prove it. Girard built his business on word-of-mouth marketing. He sent a thank-you card to everyone who came into the dealership—including those who didn't make a purchase. He also sent a card to everyone he spoke with. And, if someone purchased a car, the owner received a monthly card. In the years leading up to his retirement, Girard was mailing 13,000 cards monthly; each of those months he sold an average of seventy-two cars.

The overall key to successful relationship marketing is consistency. Pick one or more methods to stay in touch, and make sure you do it on a scheduled, ongoing basis. Your relationships will flourish, and your business will prosper as a result.

 **Deborah Gussoff** refers to herself as an appreciation marketing guru and networking maven, and is always looking for reasons to reach out and touch people in her life. She has been an independent distributor with SendOutCards® since June 2007 and uses this high-tech card and gifting service to build better relationships, one card at a time. She holds an MBA in marketing and loves to help business owners brainstorm ways to uniquely use SendOutCards to market their business. Deborah has been known to send cards for unusual holidays, such as Penguin Awareness Day and No Socks Day. E-mail deborah@sendcardsplus.com, call 973-334-3477, or visit www.sendoutcards.com/deborah and www.sendoutcards.biz/deborah to find out how she can help you with your relationship marketing.

Gift Programs:
How to Make an Impression,
Show Appreciation, and Get More Referrals
than Your Business Can Handle

by Stacia Lupinacci

If you understood how showing customer appreciation would help you gain or retain customers and get referrals, would you add that to your marketing plan? Then get ready to add gift programs and start rewriting. Gift programs are an effective marketing tool for strengthening business relationships and increasing sales because they provide an opportunity to make a lasting impression. And in the gift-basket industry, we practice this mantra: It's all about impression!

My company (which I co-own with my mother, Judy Bennett), Grove Baskets and Gifts, customizes the "impression" of the companies we serve with attention-getting, one-of-a- kind gift baskets. Because the gift you give is meant to show your appreciation, you want it to be memorable—so memorable that people will talk about your gift and remember it for years to come. In fact, the impression your gift leaves on your client will strengthen your business relationship more than the actual value of the gift.

Most business gift programs use a tier structure that is based on sales, and assign a percentage value to each tier based on their marketing budget. If there are two or three value levels, for example, top clients (those who generate the most revenue and refer your business) might receive a $150 gift, middle revenue–producing clients a $75 gift, and small revenue–producing clients a $50 gift. Businesses with more aggressive marketing programs will send their sales team to visit prospective clients with a gift in hand. Often, that little, extra something will do more than get you in the door—it will keep you top of mind in the prospect's thoughts. And this is where the reciprocity begins.

A business owner doing business with you sends a gift to say "thank you for your business." This stimulates the business gifting back to you with more business because people love to be thanked. (Don't you?) In fact, they notice when they're not thanked, remember when they are, and will talk about you when you do thank them. If you want your clients to remember you and talk about you for years to come, follow these tips before you send your next gift.

Customize: When creating your customer-appreciation gift list, do your homework. You need to understand your client and the value the client brings to your business. Because the gift needs to be appropriate, which takes special attention, customization is the answer. For example, if you know your client loves sports, consider including a sports magazine as part of the gift. If your customer loves to cook, include a cookie mix and a kitchen gadget. If your gift is going to an office for a morning meeting, muffins, breakfast cakes, and coffee would be the perfect solution.

Research: Some industries have regulations about accepting gifts, and some companies have a "no gift" policy, so do your research. If the company policy restricts individual gift giving, perhaps you can send something that everyone in the office can share. Others have gift price limitations such as under $100 or $50. Don't put yourself, your client, and the company receiving the gift in an embarrassing situation by having to pick up a gift you sent because it was over the dollar limitation. Check with the Human Resources department to find out about gift-giving policies.

Differentiate: When to send your gift is also important. The December holidays are the perfect time to show client appreciation, but everyone is thinking the same, so your gift could get lost in a sea of sweets and savory delights. How do you increase the impact of the impression you wish to make? How about sending your gift before everyone else?

At Grove Baskets, we think Thanksgiving represents the sentiment that a "gift of thanks" embodies. Your gift arrives early in the season, and can be enjoyed independently of the holiday gifts that arrive in December. Keep in mind other opportunities to show your appreciation: Administrative Professional's Day, Mother's Day, and No Socks Day are in May. They're all good days to send a gift that will set you apart from the December crowd. Some industries, such as health care, have their own holidays: Nurse's Day, Doctor's Day, Social Service's Week, Case Management Week, and more.

Timing: It's important to be sure that no matter when you decide to send the gift, you order early enough so your gift arrives before the holiday begins. Will your recipient be away or will the business close for the holiday? If you have a fairly large list, be sure you talk with your gift vendor early enough to be able to take advantage of early-buy programs and ensure stock availability. A three-month head start is not too early, especially for the fourth-quarter holiday season. It's also less costly when your order isn't marked "rush."

Pitfalls: There are common pitfalls when implementing your gift program, so be careful and mindful. Be sure to check the spelling of everyone's name. Since you are trying to make a good impression, this is crucial. You don't want to be remembered for misspellings—especially names. Also, get the address right to avoid extra delivery charges and ensure a timely delivery. Of course, consider religious or cultural beliefs. Wine could be a poor choice for some clients, while kosher foods might be in order for others. You want to make sure your gift is business appropriate, so don't give bath bubbles to a CEO. Best advice: Refrain from items too personal in nature.

Impact: If you have sales reps, we suggest that the basket be hand delivered by them for a more personal and impressive delivery. Do that whenever possible. It solidifies the relationship between you and your client and has the most impact. Besides, the element of surprise at the office when the gift arrives adds to the excitement, and everyone will ask who sent the gift.

You can personalize the gift with your business information or a promotional item that carries your logo. This keepsake will remain long after the last scrumptious snack in the basket is enjoyed. To ensure the perfect gift that shows your appreciation and reflects your business, work closely with your vendors.

Remember, it is all about the impression. The positive feedback you receive will last forever and will increase your bottom line with a return far greater than what you were expecting.

Stacia Lupinacci is a partner at Grove Baskets and Gifts with her mother, Judy Bennett. She holds a bachelor's degree in business marketing and has valuable international corporate experience. Stacia specializes in corporate and personal gift gifting. To create your custom gifts, contact Stacia by phone at 973-226-4430, visit www.grovebaskets.com, and connect with Grove Baskets on Facebook to keep up with the latest trends in gift giving and how you can impress your clients and prospects.

E-Mail Marketing
Made Easy

by Suzanne Buggé

In this age of social media you may wonder: Why e-mail marketing? The trendier alternatives seem to get all the attention. Some people would even have you believe that e-mail marketing is dead. Not true. E-mail marketing remains an effective way to communicate with your clients. E-mail marketing is different from social media because it comes to you. It is the most direct line of communication and the easiest way to move the reader from conversation to action.

Nearly everybody has an e-mail address. You send an e-mail and it lands in your recipients' in-box where they see it. But the trick with e-mail marketing is to get your readers to *open* them on a consistent basis. We get so much e-mail that we delete all but the most compelling. So, how do you create a compelling e-mail? Start by focusing on what's in it for your readers, follow a few basic guidelines, and you should get a good open rate—one of the measures of the success of an e-mail. Open rates vary by industry, but generally range from fifteen to twenty-five percent. (A good e-mail should beat the industry average.) The amount of business your e-mail generates is, in part, relative to the open rate.

Grab Attention

Start by creating an intriguing subject line that will make a reader open your e-mail. Don't send a generic monthly health newsletter, even if it actually *is* your monthly health newsletter. Select a topic from the newsletter and create the subject line around that topic, such as "7 Foods to Reduce Cholesterol" or "Restless Leg Syndrome: Fact or Fiction?" You want to peak interest so the reader is moved to open the e-mail to read the rest.

For instance, an e-mail from a health/lifestyle publication said: "What Your Hair Color Says about You.[1]" As a woman who colors her hair, you can bet I opened that one! But the subject line might not work for male recipients. To increase your open rate, create two subject lines for the same e-mail. Send the newsletter with one subject line to half of your readers, and another subject line to the other half, and compare the open rates for each. This will help you get an idea of what motivates your readers to click and open.

One technique for getting your readers to open your e-mail is to write a subject line with a sense of urgency, such as "Last Day to Register for Next Week's Lecture" or "3-Day Sale—Coupon Attached." Putting a number in your subject line also increases open rates because it lets readers know exactly what to expect and makes the content seem manageable.

Build Brand Recognition

Now that the e-mail is opened, let's talk about the look. It's important to maintain brand consistency across channels, and an e-newsletter is an opportunity to expand your brand recognition. Include your logo and a head shot. Use color accents that support your logo or brand. Once you get your look together, *stick to it.* Consistency is important, so the look should not change from newsletter to newsletter. Many e-mail programs have a preview pane; the top section of your e-mail will show up there. Create the e-mail so your logo or masthead appears in the preview pane.

Your e-mail should be easy to read, simply designed, and professional looking. Limit the number of fonts to two or three, and be sure they are legible. Easy-to-read fonts include Calibri, Arial, and Tahoma. Use a single style and size for headlines. If you are using Arial for the body, then Arial Narrow makes a good headline font. For the headline, go up about two or three font sizes from the text. Include white space to create breaks between sections. Balance text and images. Use images to support a topic, but since many people open e-mail on devices that don't download images, make sure your newsletter communicates equally well without them.

Your e-mail should convey not only your business expertise, but also who you are. There are lots of accountants out there—what makes you different? Let your personality shine through your writing style and the topics you choose. Include some tangential information, such as did you just complete an advanced degree or are you doing a workshop? Introduce your staff. These are opportunities to let your readers know more about you and your business.

Connect with Content

Most of your newsletter should contain informational content that helps and benefits your readers, so focus on what's in it for them. If your readers don't find value in your e-mail, they won't open the next one. Your clients already come to you for goods and services, so share your expertise. Whether it's health advice or makeup tips—share what you know. The more they learn from you, the more they will perceive you as the expert, and the more they will rely on you and your product.

Content does not always have to be something you've written. If you come across a helpful article by someone else, write an introduction about why you like it, and provide the link to the original source. This technique has two benefits: First, it will help keep your newsletter shorter, and second, you can see how interested your readers are in any given subject by monitoring the click-throughs. If you get a high click-through rate on a particular topic, you can expand on it in future newsletters.

As you set out an e-mail marketing plan, it is important to decide on the type of e-mail you want to send and the frequency. It can be helpful to think about e-mail in two categories, namely, e-newsletters and the more pared-down e-blast. Newsletters often have several different content blocks, while blasts are a single subject—but there's any variation in between.

In general, the longer the e-mail, the less frequently it is sent. It can be a balancing act between too frequent and risking spamming complaints (seriously, no one wants to hear from you every day) and not frequent enough and missing business. A good rule of thumb is to do newsletters once or twice a month, and blasts two to four times a month. Start with what you are sure you can manage. You can add to the schedule later, but random, infrequent e-mails will leave your readers confused and can send a negative message about the organization of your business as a whole.

E-mail marketing is an easy, inexpensive way to maintain contact with your readers, build brand loyalty, and increase business. It's an opportunity to get in front of your clients on a regular basis with new ideas, deals, and information. It is one marketing tool that should be in every business owner's toolbox.

References

1. What Your Hair Color Says about You, www.lifescript.com/HA/424652_61892054_101333_1.htm; date accessed: February 27, 2012.

Suzanne Buggé has extensive experience in sales and marketing. She worked in promotional programs and new product initiatives with national retail chains before moving on to build her own sales and marketing business, A Focused Advantage. To find out what a focused plan can do for your business, visit www.AFocusedAdvantage.com or contact Suzanne at Suzanne@AFocusedAdvantage.com or 973-951-6258.

Personnel and
Professional Development

Training and Development: How Smart Business Owners Invest in Their Employees

by Lilie Donahue

So, you've started a business, and you're wearing *all* the hats. Eventually, you will need employees. For most business owners, this is a significant and scary moment—a sign that "I'm doing well and growing." But how will employees be able to do the things you do? After all, no one can do it better than you can!

It's time to take a deep breath and implement a formal training and professional development plan for your one employee (or hundreds of employees), so your business will thrive. Investing in your employees—your most valuable asset—is of utmost importance. Unfortunately, many entrepreneurs see employee training and development as an optional expense instead of an essential investment. This thinking can be costly to both short-term profits and long-term growth. In today's economy and competitive landscape, if your business isn't learning, you're going to fall behind. A business learns and grows as its people learn and grow.

Five Reasons Employee Training and Development Are Essential

1. When an employee joins your company, new-hire training sets your expectations and assimilates and prepares employees to tackle their responsibilities in a focused and productive manner. Training reduces the risks of errors, poor quality, and poor customer satisfaction.

2. Extraordinary technological advancements have revolutionized the marketplace, creating significantly more competition and higher consumer demand. To keep up with these changes, routine technology training is a must, or you risk losing opportunities to your competitors.

3. The pace, complexity, and timing of today's regulatory changes are unprecedented. "Missing the boat" or "being in the dark" on some regulatory issues come with costly consequences. Timely training for industry-related changes is crucial.

4. Technical skills are important to the quality of your product or service. Continuing education in your field of expertise keeps you current on topics that are important in your industry or market, and it reduces or eliminates potential problems. Don't forget soft-skills training, such as

communication skills, conflict resolution, and personal development. In some professions, soft skills are more important than occupational skills.

5. Incorporating training as a standard in your policies shows your commitment to a learning culture. Education and the emphasis on its importance give you a competitive edge. Fresh knowledge builds a new frame of reference for your employees, allowing them to develop better problem-solving skills and to generate new ideas, which increase overall productivity, effectiveness, and innovation.

Six Ways to Get the Most Out of Training

Training is available in many forms. To make the best choices and get the most out of the training for your employees and company, consider the following:

1. **Prepare for training.** When you're ready to develop your program, be clear about your company's mission, values, and goals, and align them with your employee-training plan. Next, create a list of what training areas are most important for your company, industry, and each employee. Professional development plans for an employee should be a collaborative effort. When you allow employees to achieve their personal goals, you set the stage for satisfaction and positive morale in the workplace.

2. **Assess training options.** Who will do the training? Many professional associations and organizations offer training; so, look for training and development programs within your industry. These organizations might also provide a forum to exchange ideas with other professionals. You can also consult with training organizations such as the American Management Association or with local colleges. With training available in person, online, and via live Webinar, determine the best option for your company. To reduce employee travel costs, consider onsite training via Webinar. Another option is to send one participant to the training and have that person teach other employees. This provides an excellent opportunity for the attendee to share and reinforce what was learned and to develop teaching skills.

3. **Set the stage for employees.** For more teaching opportunities, allow employees to select a topic that is new to them. Then, have them research the topic and do a presentation. If the presentation is well received, have your employee teach the topic to your clients by hosting a client-education class. When you share your knowledge and expertise, you show your clients your commitment to them. This value-added service will set you apart from your competitors. You could expand the program further by working with your local library or college and share the knowledge with your community, thereby creating visibility and goodwill.

4. **Provide "lunch and learn" sessions.** By creating a training session with a company-provided lunch, employees learn in a casual environment and limit disruptions to their daily workload and responsibilities.

5. **Implement mentoring/cross-training programs.** You could implement a mentoring program where each employee has a "partner in learning." When one shadows the other on the job, you create cross-training opportunities so staff can learn skills beyond their own job duties and are prepared to be a potential backup in case of emergencies.

6. **Hold roundtable meetings.** I especially enjoy our company's roundtable meetings. We set aside time on a regular basis for a "meeting of the minds." All employees come to the meeting with something new they have learned or an issue they are struggling with. An open dialogue allows them to teach one another and offer solutions and knowledge to the rest of the team.

Invest and Gain

Employee training and professional development are extremely important. Business owners should consider them must-have investments in their employees. Educating, cross training, and mentoring your employees will set you apart from your competitors. In addition, well-trained, happy employees bring new ideas, solve problems, provide added value to clients, and deliver superior services and products. Of course, happy employees also tend to thrive and become more creative, effective, and productive. Your training efforts will result in higher visibility and goodwill for your company—and over time, your investment will yield greater benefits and returns.

Mary Kay Ash said, "People are definitely a company's greatest asset. It doesn't make any difference whether the product is cars or cosmetics. A company is only as good as the people it keeps." To that I add, "...and the training and knowledge they have received."

Lilie Donahue, CPA, is the president of Payroll Architechs and several affiliate companies that provide business services throughout the United States in the area of payroll, benefits, human resources, tax, accounting, business administration, and paperless office. With more than sixteen years of public accounting experience in "Big Six" firms and as the chief operating officer for a regional accounting firm, Lilie has tremendous insight into the inner workings of many businesses. Her passion for best practices ignited her interest to provide services in a way that increased client efficiencies, compliance, and profitability. She is a member of several organizations, including the American Institute of CPAs and the American Payroll Association. For a free consultation to discuss how Lilie and her team can support your business, call 888-700-8154, e-mail Lilie@payrollplus.us, or visit www.PayrollArchitechs.com

Are You Prepared to Become an Employer?

Two Checklists to Help You Assess Your Readiness to Hire and Manage Staff

by Abby Duncan

When your business grows to the point where you can no longer "do it all" yourself, hiring employees is an important next step. Besides hiring the "right" people for the positions you are creating, there are legal, financial, and management issues to deal with.

Unfortunately, the majority of small business owners think hiring and managing employees is a simple process, when in fact, it isn't. Besides bringing one or more "outsiders"—new employees—into your business, there are a number of things you need to be aware of.

To prepare yourself for this next big step, use the following two checklists as your guide. Besides opening your eyes to a host of new responsibilities you'll face and things you need to know, these two checklists can prevent you from making costly and time-consuming mistakes.

Checklist 1: Legal and Financial Matters

For the legal and financial matters, it's wise to consult with your lawyer and accountant. They will guide you and answer your questions. But even when you get professional advice, when you're planning to hire, you must do the following:

- **Familiarize** yourself with the kinds of taxes that are withheld for W-2 employees, such as temporary disability and family medical leave insurance. Make sure you have an EIN (employer identification number) to use on tax documents.

- **Calculate** the total cost of hiring employees, not just the salary. Equipment, benefits, training, and the hiring process itself should be offset by the contributions expected by the addition of staff. Can your business handle the extra overhead on an ongoing basis?

- **Understand** the legal requirements of hiring W-2, 1099, and full-time and part-time employees.

- **Register** with the state Department of Labor and get the appropriate posters that must be displayed prominently to notify employees of their rights. You can obtain these for free at

  http://lwd.dol.state.nj.us/labor/employer/content/employerpacketforms.html

  For posters required by the Federal government, go to

  http://www.dol.gov/osbp/sbrefa/poster/matrix.htm

  Also, get the forms you need to report immigration status.

- **Obtain** workers compensation insurance. Proof of this insurance coverage must be posted. Make sure that appropriate measures are in place to provide a safe workplace.

- **Set up** personnel files—one for each employee—to house applications, employment offer letters, IRS W-4 form, benefits sign-up forms, and performance evaluations. Create a second file for each employee for I-9 immigration status forms and another for medical records. Keep these files securely locked away.

- **Create** an employee policy manual to prevent confusion about company rules and to avoid frivolous lawsuits.

Checklist 2: Management Skills

For the most part, the legal and financial issues are straightforward. Yet, if you think that's all there is to expanding your company, you're in for a rude awakening.

From previous good experiences working for others, you might already possess some of the skills needed to manage employees. However, management is more than simply giving orders—and more often than not, management skills have to be learned.

To help you assess these, answer the following questions before finalizing your decision to bring on employees:

- Do you understand how to hire effectively? Do you know…
  - o what to post in an ad?
  - o how to initially screen responses?
  - o how to construct interview questions to compare "apples to apples"?
  - o what to never ask an applicant?
  - o how to negotiate with the finalists?
- Are you prepared to be the "motivator in chief"? Do you assume that employees will care as much about your business as you do—especially

when you are reluctant to share any of the key aspects of the business with them and just want them to focus on specific tasks?

- Do you recognize that the addition of each new employee changes the dynamics of your organization, in much the same way as adding a new child or puppy does to your family?
- Do you assume that employees will understand your expectations of what their jobs entail…
  - without a clearly defined structure of how each job relates to the others?
  - without clear job descriptions? (Do you know how to create these?)
  - without training or follow-up?
  - without regular, objective performance evaluations?
- Do you understand how to set boundaries between you and your employees?
- Have you stated the firm's professional norms in your employee handbook?
  - Are you prepared to model the behavior you expect from your employees?
  - Do you know how to enforce policies and procedures evenhandedly?
- Are you prepared to handle inevitable conflicts between employees?
- To what resources can you turn to help you with management issues?

Hiring and managing employees are important steps for a growing company. They allow the owner(s) to focus more on vision and strategy while delegating some of the tasks of implementation to others. However, that decision should be the result of careful forethought. Are you prepared for the challenges involved?

Abby Duncan is a seasoned human resources consultant. She takes a "teach a person to fish" approach by helping owners of small businesses hire, manage, train, and retain their employees. Rather than relieve them of these tasks, she educates and empowers entrepreneurs to be better managers and to make informed decisions relative to outsourcing any part of human resources. For more information about how Abby can help your growing business, visit www.duncanresources.com, call 973-256-8443, or e-mail her at aduncan@duncanresources.com.

Massage Therapy:
A Surprisingly Simple Way to Increase Profits

by Pamela Olsen

Business owners know that rising health-care costs are hurting profitability. Sick days, loss of productivity, and medical expenses caused by the stress of work-life pressures are strangling American businesses. You can help curtail those costs by providing massage therapy treatments for your employees. Massage therapy administered by a licensed, medical massage professional reduces stress levels, leading to a whole host of positive health effects. To see how stress reduction, offered through employer-sponsored massage therapy, can help reduce your company's health-care expenses, we will examine the following:

1. When combined with other cutting-edge employee benefits, stress reduction via massage therapy can help create a healthy company culture.
2. When combined with good nutrition and exercise, stress reduction can help alleviate the long-term effects of this country's most costly diseases.

Let us see how both of these can greatly increase your company's overall wellness—and your bottom line.

The quest for a high level of company culture is a new benchmark for modern business success. Corporations listed in *FORTUNE* magazine's *2012 100 Best Companies to Work For*[1] are organizations that place the quality of their company culture as a top priority. Zappos is number eleven on the list. In his book *Delivering Happiness*, Zappos CEO and founder Tony Hsieh describes in detail the domino effect that results from creating a positive, engaging working environment at Zappos and how this eventually led to multimillion-dollar profits.[2]

Here is a brief overview of the sequence of events leading to Zappos' cultural and financial success. Hsieh's first step was to work with his employees to make their working environment more supportive and appealing, which greatly reduced stress levels, increased employee retention rates, and increased productivity. (Massage therapy is an employee benefit at Zappos.) Working with less stress and anxiety reduced the amount of sick time and workers' compensation used. This reduced the company's health-care costs.

Less pressure on the job created happier employees at Zappos. These happier workers became more productive and great advocates for their company. (They have a say in how the business is run, which gives them a sense of ownership in the organization). These happier employees have benefited personally and are better at creating interpersonal relationships—both within their organization and outside with customers and vendors. Better relationships have, in effect, created more loyal clients and business partners/vendors. It is obvious how this type of loyalty has brought in higher profit margins at Zappos.

So, how does the application of massage therapy fit in with this cause and effect? Massage therapy is proven to reduce stress levels. Three big indicators of stress, namely, blood pressure, blood sugar, and stress hormones, are significantly reduced when massage therapy is regularly administered.[3] Controlling work-related stress is the first and foremost factor in creating a high level of corporate culture. Reducing workplace stress increases productivity and retention rates, while reducing health-care costs, which makes massage therapy an obvious choice for taking care of your employees.[4]

Top Causes of Death Linked to Stress

The Centers for Disease Control and Prevention report that the top causes of death in the United States are directly linked to stress (although stress is not the only factor involved). For example, in 2010, the following were top killers:

- Heart disease: 616,067 mortalities—for which stress is a known factor.[5]
- Cancer: 562,875 deaths—stress reduction greatly improves conditions for cancer patients.[6]
- Stroke (cerebrovascular diseases): 135,952—atherosclerosis is greatly reduced by controlling stress.[7]
- Diabetes: 71,382—glycolic levels are better controlled with reduced stress levels.[8]

Stress is certainly not the only cause for these diseases, but untreated stress is a strong, negative factor that can be avoided. The costs for employer-sponsored massage therapy treatments or any preventive care are far less than the price employers are paying for treating major diseases.

Although massage therapy is not known to cure major diseases, it is specifically proven to help reduce the effects of anxiety, back pain, headache, sciatica, and arthritis. Massage enhances immunity, helps improve athletic ability, decreases repetitive motion injuries such as carpel tunnel syndrome, increases flexibility, improves circulation, and helps reduce dependency on medications.[9,10]

The Mayo Clinic now has a Complementary and Integrative Medicine program that has conducted a number of studies showing the effectiveness of massage therapy for many medical conditions. For example, massage therapy is a major part of Mayo's complementary treatment for oncology patients. Oncology massage is comfort based and safe for most cancer patients. It helps alleviate symptoms of nausea, sleeplessness, and general discomfort, enabling patients to continue their traditional treatments without costly delays, and with less stress.[11]

In a recent video, Brent Bauer, M.D., describes how Mayo's evidence-based approach has proven that alternative therapies, when combined with traditional medicine, greatly improve healing.[12] In fact, healing time, pain, anxiety, and post-op medications have been reduced since massage therapy was introduced at the Mayo Clinic. Giving massage therapy to post-op cardio patients was the first step toward this discovery, according to Dr. Bauer. Because patients recovered quicker than usual and experienced less post-op pain, they used fewer pain medications.

Therefore, the use of massage therapy greatly reduced the overall costs for post-op care. Now, many other departments in the hospital are using massage therapy as a regular part of patient care.[13]

As an entrepreneur, you are well aware of the need to reduce health-care expenses. Raising the level of your corporate culture and reducing the probability of your employees suffering the effects of long-term stress are two promising alternatives you can implement to increase your long-term profitability. Massage therapy is an inexpensive method of caring for and retaining your employees, which complements traditional Western medical practices. Why not incorporate massage therapy into your health and wellness plans for the future of your organization?

References

1. 2012 FORTUNE magazine's 100 best companies to work for, *FORTUNE*, Feb 6, 2012; http://money.cnn.com/magazines/fortune/best-companies/2012/full_list/; date accessed: April 5, 2012.
2. Hsieh, A., *Delivering Happiness: A Path to Profits, Passion, and Purpose*, Business Plus, New York, 2010.
3. Field, T. M., Massage therapy effects, *Am. Psychol.*, 53(12), 1270–1281, 1998.
4. Ives, J., Massage is in business, reduces health costs, reduces stress & improves productivity, *Massage Therapy J.*, Spring, 57–63, 2004.
5. Dimsdale, J. E., Psychological stress and cardiovascular disease, *J. Am. Col. Cardiol.*, 51, 1234–1246, 2008.
6. Carlson, L. E., Speca, M., Patel, K. D., and Goodey, E., Mindfulness-based stress reduction in relation to quality of life, mood, symptoms of stress, and immune parameters in breast and prostate cancer outpatients, *Psychosom. Med. J. Biobehav. Med.*, 65, 571–581, 2003.
7. Castillo-Richmond, A., Schneider, R. H., Alexander, C. N., Cook, R., Myers, H., Nidich, S., Haney, C., Rainforth, M., Salerno, J., Effects of stress reduction on carotid atherosclerosis in hypertensive African Americans, *Stroke*, 31, 568–573, 2000.
8. Rosenzweig, S., Reibel, D. K., Greeson, J. M., Edman, J. S., Jasser, S. A., McMearty, K. D., Goldstein, B. J., Mindfulness-based stress reduction is associated with improved glycemic control in type 2 diabetes mellitus: A pilot study, *Altern. Therapies Health Med.*, 13(5), 36–38, 2007.
9. Associated Bodywork and Massage Professionals Website, Benefits of massage, http://www.massagetherapy.com/learnmore/benefits.php; date accessed: April 5, 2012.
10. For more information on scholarly studies indicating the efficacy of massage therapy, see the National Center for Complementary and Alternative Medicine. http://nccam.nih.gov/health/massage/massageintroduction.htm; date accessed: April 5, 2012.
11. Bergstrom, L., Hudak, B., Costello, Doraly, R. N, Pettiti, R., Mayo Clinic Oncology Massage Program, Nov. 21, 2011; You Tube Video, http://www.youtube.com/watch?v=R_wr-ru7pqg; date accessed: April 5, 2012.
12. Bauer, B., Alternative medicine overview—Mayo Clinic, Mar. 20, 2009; You Tube Video, http://www.youtube.com/watch?v=zkHS3hMq0E8&feature=relmfu; date accessed: April 5, 2012.
13. Bauer, B., Massage therapy—Mayo Clinic, Mar. 20, 2009; You Tube Video, http://www.youtube.com/watch?v=LiQHBwEhXvk&feature=relmfu; date accessed: April 5, 2012.

Pamela Olsen, MM, LMT, NCBTMB, is the founder and sole proprietor of Olsen Shiatsu & Massage. She is licensed in New York, board certified in New Jersey, and nationally certified as a Massage and Shiatsu Therapist. Pamela received her training at the Swedish Institute, Manhattan (the Harvard of massage schools), and has studied with Professor Jeffery Yuen, learning classical Chinese medical concepts, which she applies to her treatments. Pamela is an expert at dealing with issues such as stress reduction, muscle issues such as tendonitis, strains, and sprains, and energy-balance problems. She has served several corporate organizations including Goldman Sachs. To find out more about reducing stress in your workplace, contact Pamela at info@pamelaolsen.com or visit http://pamelaolsen.com.

Payroll: Not "Just Overhead"

by Colleen S. Flores

In 2011, in honor of National Payroll Week—which recognizes American wage earners and the payroll professionals who pay them—the American Payroll Association said this about wage earners and payroll professionals: "Together, through the payroll withholding system, they contribute, collect, report, and deposit approximately $1.7 trillion or 71.9 percent of the annual revenue of the U.S. Treasury."[1] What a revenue maker!

Without a doubt, the payroll department is at the focal point of ensuring that your business is in compliance with federal, state, local, and Department of Labor regulations. Failure to be in compliance can initiate audits from these agencies. The consequences? Possible monetary penalties and subsequent audits.

An audit typically causes stress and worry—and has a busy business owner spending more time thinking about past action than on the future of the business. Unfortunately, an audit often puts a stop to any forward progress, and can delay or damage growth—resulting in missed opportunities and lost revenue.

Therefore, it is critical (and wise) to have a knowledgeable payroll professional—not merely someone to ensure that your employees are paid correctly, but someone who is aware of the continuous changes in the payroll laws on the federal and state levels, and is able to follow through on the implementation of these changes.

The Mysterious Payroll Professional

A payroll professional's career does not start as an actual "career." One falls into it. I never heard anyone say, "I want to grow up to be a payroll professional." In fact, there is no degree for this profession. It is a career that requires knowledge of the IRS and government laws. And in case you're wondering: there is no interpretation in IRS and government laws. It is black and white—yet, there are those who think there are gray areas. Gray areas will turn into audits if you are not careful.

Payroll is generally learned through on-the-job training for the regular day-to-day operations such as data entry, pay information, and other general payroll duties. However, outside of the day-to-day operations, compliance knowledge is obtained through networking, payroll instruction classes provided by the American Payroll Association (APA), and other outside sources. To become a "payroll expert," an exam is offered by the APA so payroll professionals can be certified (Certified Payroll Professional, CPP). The exam is four hours long and covers a variety of topics from 401(k) plans to gross-to-net paycheck calculations. Now that the veil of mystery has been lifted, you can clearly see the important role the payroll professional plays in a company.

However, if you still doubt the value payroll professionals bring to a business, read on. Payroll professionals do the following:

- **Protect your business.** Continuous changes to the law keep payroll departments up and running to conform to any changes, as well as attempt to anticipate future changes that will affect your business.

- **Assist with budgets to build your business.** The payroll department is instrumental in assisting with a company's budget since it keeps a company informed of state unemployment rate changes, Social Security rate changes and limits, federal unemployment rate changes, and many other changes that can affect a company's bottom line.

- **Offer fact-based advice to benefit your business.** A company can have a payroll department that just "processes" payroll and is viewed as nothing more than "overhead." A company can also have a payroll department that is an integral part of the business operation that not only processes payroll, but offers suggestions for cutting costs, building processes, and streamlining payroll duties.

- **Keep employees focused on their job responsibilities.** One of the responsibilities a payroll department has is ensuring that employees are paid accurately and on time. One of my favorite sayings is, "An accurately paid employee is a productive employee." If an employee is preoccupied with an incorrect paycheck, he is not focusing on his job responsibilities, which is not productive for the company. It takes many people to work together to ensure that the payroll is processed accurately.

- **Are, without a doubt, team players.** Payroll must work closely with upper management, line supervisors, and other staff to obtain the information they need to process a payroll successfully. Even with the best and latest electronic timekeeping and computerized systems in place, there is still a challenge to process successfully because the human element comes into play. So the data is only as good as what is put in.

Payroll is always a team effort in conjunction with human resources and benefits. Years ago, the norm was to have Payroll report to Finance. More and more, the trend is Payroll working hand in hand with Human Resources. I have always found this combination a great partnership because these two areas are more integrated than one would think. Both departments must be aware of the employment laws (although sometimes different areas). But most important, they must work together to ensure that proper employee information is processed accurately and is in compliance with U.S. laws.

Still, Payroll and Human Resources do have their own set of conflicts. Payroll tends to see regulations in "black and white," while Human Resources tends to see regulations in "gray." This usually leads to some discussion between the two disciplines. However, it is a great way to validate the final decision based on two opposing schools of thought.

As you can see, payroll is just not overhead. Payroll professionals are dedicated to making sure your company is in compliance with ever-changing laws and regulations. They guide you and keep your business operating smoothly, so you can make informed decisions as you plan to expand and grow your business.

References

1. http://www.nationalpayrollweek.com; date accessed: January 26, 2012.

Colleen S. Flores, CPP, vice president of Donahue & Flores Consulting, LLC, has been a payroll professional for over twenty-five years. Colleen brings expertise and knowledge that keeps her clients in compliance with U.S. national and local legislative regulations. Not only can Colleen provide compliance advice, she is diverse enough to be able to assist you with processing payrolls in an emergency. To find out how Colleen can turn your payroll department into a world-class operation, e-mail her at colleen@df-consulting.net or call 908-510-6695.

What Are You Afraid Of?

by Rita Williams-Bogar

What are you afraid of? Why?

Sometimes in life, we are presented with opportunities that require a "leap of faith" to execute. If we let our "fear factors" get in the way, we stand to potentially lose out on wonderful benefits that life has to offer.

Imagine, if you will, a corporate executive with twenty-five years invested in her career. She was responsible for a large department, a multimillion dollar budget, a territory covering eight states, and she had the flexibility to make decisions that impacted hundreds of employees and hundreds of thousands of clients. Many would think: "Wow! She's got it made." And, they would be right.

However, this same person knew she was capable of doing more—of reaching greater heights. The desire for entrepreneurship was a spark burning deep inside of her for years. She knew she needed to have greater control over her own destiny. At last, she decided that it is time to take that leap of faith and leave the relative security of a corporate career and pursue her dreams.

That woman was me.

Since leaving the corporate world, a question I've been asked frequently is "Weren't you afraid?"

This got me thinking: "Should I have been afraid?" After all, when I left corporate America, I did not walk into another career opportunity. Although I had a plan, I did not know what specific path I would follow to create a business. However, as I worked my plan, things began to crystallize, I discovered my path, and have moved forward ever since.

What about you? What fears are stopping you from moving forward? I hope that by sharing my story, and how I overcame my fears, you will be inspired to face your own fear factors to find success.

Fear Factor 1: *Everyone is telling me to do something else or that my idea won't fly. Can I pursue my goals despite this advice?*

Before moving forward, answer these questions: How confident are you in your objectives? Have you created a plan?

Before leaving corporate, I devised a strategic plan to ensure that my financial needs would be met. Set aside savings, create a cushion, and protect your retirement fund, for example. Develop an outline of the business you wish to create. Know your own skills and abilities. Use tools such as the Myers-Briggs Type Indicator® (MBTI) or DISC® Profile to uncover your strengths and preferences.

Fear Factor 2: *I don't know if there's a market for my product or service.*

How carefully have you analyzed the marketplace? I knew I enjoyed helping people grow. For me, training and development came naturally. After all, I had proven that in my corporate life. So I connected with women who owned their own training and development firms and volunteered my services to them. It was through this effort that I learned about the needs in the marketplace for corporate talent development. Where can you dedicate your time? To whom can you align yourself to create opportunities?

Fear Factor 3: *I'm going to be all alone as I develop my company.*

Empower yourself. Explore networking opportunities to build a support network. Create an advisory board against which you may bounce ideas. Within a couple of months of forming my business, Personal Development Solutions, LLC, I created a four-member advisory board comprised of people whose knowledge and skills complemented mine. One member worked in corporate at a director's level; another worked in corporate from a project management perspective; the third was a professional coach; the fourth was a marketing expert. We met regularly during the early phases of my business. As my business grew and changed, so did my board.

Fear Factor 4: *Is anyone really going to pay for my product or service? How can I determine the right price?*

This is an issue, especially for women business owners who may not value themselves or their businesses as highly as they should. As a result, there is a tendency to leave money on the table. In the early stages of my business, my only reference point was what I was paid as a subcontractor, so that's what I charged for a speaking engagement. When the prospective client jumped at the price, I knew it was too low. People value what they pay for. If your price is too low, then so is your perceived value.

When determining your fee, it is important to answer the following:

- *How much is my time worth?* Build in the cost of preparing your product or service.
- *How much do my raw materials cost?* When presenting a workshop, I need to consider the cost of printing handouts. This cost may change, depending upon how fancy the bindings are.
- *Is travel involved?* If you drive, calculate the mileage. Consider air, hotel, and destination travel costs.

- *Should I charge per person for an engagement?* I highly recommend you do not charge per hour or per head; the client may attempt to cut the costs by cutting people or hours.

- *How do I present this?* Language is powerful. Instead of presenting it as a fee to clients, consider presenting an "all-inclusive investment" from their perspective. I work with employers who are investing in their staff's development. When they see my costs, it is directly related to the investment in their people.

Fear Factor 5: *I'm just afraid to "get out there."*

My recommendation here is to do something personal that will increase your confidence. For example, I decided to pursue a quest of identifying and facing fears. The personal activities I undertook included parasailing, riding in a hot air balloon, and traveling to Hong Kong alone. Last, I decided the culmination would be to visit the Grand Canyon Skywalk and "walk the sky" 4,000 feet above the Colorado River. I am happy to say I accomplished the Skywalk objective despite the fears. Now I feel there's nothing I cannot do as a result of demonstrating that courage within.

This brings us back to the original question: "What are you afraid of?" I hope this journey helps you create your plan to empower yourself to conquer those fears, create prosperity, and ensure your legacy.

 **Rita Williams-Bogar, MBA, CPCU, ChFC,** is the founder of Personal Development Solutions, LLC, and PDS Institute, LLC. She is recognized by *NJBIZ* as one of New Jersey's 2011 Best 50 Women in Business and by the SBA as the Region II and NJ 2011 Minority Small Business Champion of the Year. Rita provides consultative services to businesses and individuals in the areas of leadership development, team building, emotional intelligence, diversity, and insurance technical education. She is a keynote speaker and conference presenter. Her mission is to share proven strategies to better leverage individuals' talents and skills to reach their full potential. To bring Rita to your organization or for a complimentary copy of *Rita's Dozen: Criteria for Leadership Success*, contact her at 201-404-7960 or info@PersonalDevelopmentSolutionsLLC.com, or visit her website at www.PersonalDevelopmentSolutionsLLC.com.

Photo Credit: Christina Mazza/NJBIZ

Marketing:
Public Relations

How to Get Free Publicity for Your Business in an Increasingly Crowded World

by Caryn Starr-Gates

As advertising budgets for many small- and medium-size business owners shrink, the lure of getting visibility for your business through free publicity grows more attractive. Although it's not impossible to get mentioned through "earned media"—generated by you to promote your business through media channels—there are a few tips to remember.

As opposed to paid media, such as advertising, earned media is the free publicity a company gets when it is mentioned in a journalist's story, a respected blogger's entry, or virally through social networks (where everyone can be a citizen journalist—so beware of the writer's quality and the message). By virtue of what you did or what you said, you and your company may earn placement in a newspaper article—perhaps as the feature subject. Or you might be quoted as an industry expert, be included in a radio or TV interview about your line of work, or get mentioned somewhere online (in a positive light, of course).

Attention is usually drawn to the company/product/service through press releases, media advisories, and story pitches, as well as social media updates. Bear in mind that reporters and editors are not interested in promoting your business. They are interested in delivering news, products, and events that will have value to their readers, viewers, or listeners.

Here are three proven ways, which include a number of strategies, to boost your marketplace exposure and get free publicity for your company:

1. **Share your expertise for free**. Free is good, especially if you are trying to grow your audience while also getting your news release placed.

   - If you are a skilled public speaker and enjoy talking about your field or related topics, hold a free seminar or webinar at no charge—then publicize it. You can also host a speaker at your place of business and promote the free event. Free events often earn media placement and cast your business in a positive light.

   - Write a white paper or an e-book on your area of expertise and offer it as a free download. Promote it online through your social network contacts or by e-mail to your list.

2. **Do something good and spread the news**. Perform community service, sponsor a community outreach program, volunteer your services, or

collect goods for a worthy cause. Local newspapers favor feel-good community stories over business promotion (they'd rather have your paid ad). Take clear, posed photos, identify the people in them, and send one or two out with a short press release. If relevant, be sure to note the charitable cause or organization that benefited from the effort or results of the drive. If your office is holding a donation drive, send a press release to the local newspapers about it, inviting area residents and businesses to pitch in. This promotes goodwill about your company.

3. **Become a source of knowledge, insight, and helpful tips.** Position yourself as a go-to expert in your field. Over time, this can generate buzz about your business. Here are a few routes to take:

- Respond to social network discussions or comment on blog posts that are related to your business. Explain why you are responding if appropriate (e.g., you work in that field). Don't overtly promote your own company; it's a turnoff to readers. Simply respond to the post respectfully from the standpoint of an expert or helpful, interested reader. Over time, you'll develop positive relationships with others in your field, area of interest, or shared online groups. Other members in your groups, circles, forums, or blog communities will start to recognize you, and connections can develop as online conversations begin.

- Post information to your social networks that helps others. Update your status with links to articles of interest, industry facts, and commentaries by other experts.

- Become a contributor. Write an expert article for a trade or organization publication, or pitch an editor about writing a column in a newspaper or magazine about your field. If you follow a blogger who invites subscribers to contribute tips—tip away!

- Pitch a feature story to a business editor about a trend in your industry, or tie an industry-related topic to current events. Keep it short (one page) and targeted, and explain why you are making the pitch (expert in your field, or a company that offers that service). If there is relevance to news that's already happening, or if your pitch resonates with the editor as a potential story of interest to the media outlet's audience, you might get a call for an interview.

- Start writing a blog about your area of expertise. Make sure to post a link to your new entries on your social networks. NOTE: Do not blog if you cannot maintain it with fresh posts on a regular basis. It's bad marketing to host a seemingly abandoned or neglected blog.

- Sign up to receive e-mails from the journalist crowdsourcing outlets. These aggregator sites inform subscribers about stories that writers are working on and who seek information or quotes from industry experts. Three popular sites are *Help a Reporter Out*, *Pitch Rate*, and *Reporter Connection*. By responding, you might end up being interviewed on their radio or TV shows or be quoted in their articles—with valuable links you can post on your website or social media accounts.

- Join online business communities that share public relations opportunities with members locally and nationwide, and respond to queries.

Before you go out there with your marketing shotgun, consider taking on one or two of these methods that you and your team are comfortable with, and see how it goes. If you need help, a marketing consultant can create the framework for your publicity-minded activities to keep your efforts organized and manageable.

Of course, make sure all of your marketing and publicity materials are well written and a good reflection of you and your company. If the message is a good one, appropriate for your intended audience, and well crafted, you'll soon add earned media to your marketing achievements.

Caryn Starr-Gates owner of StarrGates Business Communications (www.starrgates.com) is a freelance promotional copywriter in Fair Lawn, New Jersey. She helps small businesses and soloprenuers market their messages across all media platforms—print, broadcast, digital—in the fields of advertising, marketing, and public relations. Caryn has over 30 years of experience writing copy for marketing materials, SEO website content, press releases and story pitches, expert byline articles, ads, and advertorials across a diverse range of industries for B2B and consumer accounts. She can be reached at caryn@starrgates.com or 201-791-4694.

Ten Hip Tips to Create Buzz for Your Business

by Maria Cucciniello

Whether your business has been around for five decades, five years, or five minutes, there's never a bad time to drum up ways to get noticed.

But unlike yesterday's clients, to draw them into a place of business or to get them to purchase a product or service, today's consumers require much more attention from the companies that court them. They typically ask, "What's in it for me?" and typically think, "Why should I care about what you do?" They yearn for personal connections to what they do, where they go, and what they purchase. To win them over, businesses must have a clear and swift response.

The key to connecting with modern-day consumers lies in developing a strong relationship with them, not only in your place of business—but also in their local communities and in the media channels they frequent. Does it seem a bit overwhelming? Well, don't fret. Follow these ten hip tips, and your business will be buzzing in no time.

1. It's my party and I'll buzz if I want to: plan an event around a product, place, or service. Whether you're opening your business, launching a new product, or celebrating decades of service, it's never a bad time to invite people to experience what you offer. By giving prospects and customers a little taste, they are more likely to spread the word to others— including how much they enjoyed the atmosphere of your business.

2. Buzz for a cause: tie in charities to special events. Charity tie-ins offer potential attendees a comfortable way to spend money on services or products they would normally not consider. These special events not only bring increased exposure for your business, but they also provide a positive reputation boost in your neighborhood—even reaching those that couldn't attend. This is a great way to give to a worthy organization that your customers support and to bring your business local media coverage for its goodwill.

3. Star sighting: invite local celebrities to your event. Love them or hate them, local celebrities can bring a huge boost to your company's level of exposure. Since each celebrity comes with a built-in fan base, the key is to find the celebrity who uses products or services similar to yours and whose status will bring in the type of clientele you want. Remember, to stay in the public consciousness, local celebrities need you as much as you need them.

4. Say it loud and proud: write a press release or media alert to promote your business. Write one about your newest product, acquisition, or upcoming event. Post it on your website and link to it on Facebook and Twitter. E-mail your press release to your local paper and magazine editors. You never know who will see it and contact you as a result.

Keep in mind that if you want the press to write a story from your press release or media alert, make sure it is concise and free of fluff. In other words, don't tell the media how great you, your business, and your products or services are. When you stick to the facts and include surprising and newsworthy information, the event, product, or news you are sharing will speak for itself.

5. Play nice in the sandbox: create strategic partnerships with businesses in your area. Strategic partners are not only a great resource for filling in potential gaps—like vendor connections or press relationships—in your business or event, but they can also help improve the success of your business. A mutually beneficial partner will share clients and contacts, and become another hub to increase your business's reach. Of course, this works both ways.

6. Feel the love: collect names and e-mail addresses from attendees and follow up after an event. Word of mouth starts with a dedicated few. These people were kind enough to attend your event, so next time, invite them as VIPs, and they will become brand ambassadors for your business. Add to your list whenever you can and watch your business grow.

7. Be a social butterfly: maintain a presence on Facebook, Twitter, and YouTube. If you're going to pick three social networks to dabble in, make it Facebook, Twitter, and YouTube. They offer businesses the opportunity to connect and communicate directly with prospects and customers. Hundreds of millions of people use social media platforms every day, so make sure your business has a presence and is easy to find. To become a reliable source and build meaningful relationships, share industry tips, trends, and insider information through these platforms.

8. Shout it from the rooftops: build buzz for an event using viral social networks. Post event details and invites on social networks that can be shared easily. Don't be afraid to tell followers and confirmed guests to pass along the event details to their friends as well. Keep in mind that followers and guests do not use every social network at the same time and in the same way. Make sure to post on all platforms when the greatest number of people will see your messages. The day and time matter.

9. Extra! Extra! read all about it: send a newsletter each month. Use the contact information you collect from events and turn it into positive growth by creating and sending a monthly e-mail–based newsletter. E-mail newsletters are easy to create and easy to share with others—the perfect ammo to fuel your word-of-mouth campaign. Include upcoming events or appearances, some interesting information about your industry and company, and links to your company's blog and social media platforms—and don't forget to include a media recap of your last event or business activity.

10. Keep an open hand: network and maintain relationships with industry professionals and local journalists. Think strategic partnerships here. You want to reach out to industry professionals and journalists who provide opportunities for free press or promotions. Mix, mingle, and play nice. Include these select individuals on your VIP event list, stay in touch, and never burn bridges.

 **Maria Cucciniello** is founder of The Hip Event, a full-service public relations, lifestyle marketing, and special events firm that creates successful campaigns for clients in the fashion, beauty, hospitality, retail, and entertainment industries. Whether it's a nationally recognized brand or a local business, The Hip Event creates targeted strategies to sustain brand and business growth. Since 2007, Maria Cucciniello and The Hip Event have helped dozens of clients reach far beyond their goals and experience unprecedented numbers of new customers, product placements, and press exposure. Visit TheHipEvent.com or call 973-707-7125 for more information about how to get your business buzzing.

Use Public Relations to Drive Sales (and Stop Confusing It with Marketing and Advertising)

by Amy Delman

What is so confusing about public relations (PR) that people lump it together with marketing and advertising, and expect the three to function interchangeably? More important, why is the word "sales"—which is the ultimate goal of any business—rarely mentioned when attempting to define what each does?

Public relations does sound glamorous, and most think of it as a way with words—a press release touting a product or service or a speech written for a client or senior executive. Unfortunately, many business owners—especially small business owners—treat public relations like the step-sibling to marketing and advertising practices. That's a big mistake.

Public relations is a low-cost, highly effective way to accomplish business goals. It is an invaluable tool in creating favorable public opinion and increased name recognition. It differs from advertising in that it is an unpaid, third-party endorsement of a company, a person, a product, or a service. A third-party endorsement is when a newspaper writes a story about you or your business, or a radio or television station mentions the name of your company during a broadcast—and that alone creates tremendous credibility for your business or brand. So anytime you are mentioned in broadcast or in print, it is an unpaid, unbiased, third-party endorsement.

If you doubt the value of public relations, consider the June 2006 webinar hosted by *PRWeek* in which Hans Bender, Ph.D., of Proctor & Gamble, discussed P&G's "Statistical Modeling Efforts to Determine the ROI of Public Relations." Surprisingly, P&G found that PR does the following:

- Drives sales, often on a par with advertising.
- Delivers stellar returns on investment (ROIs), much greater than advertising.
- Provides a halo effect over other marketing tactics.
- Overall, P&G found about a 275 percent ROI for public relations.[1]
- Delivers ROI on relatively low levels of spending.

End the PR Confusion

Now that you know the magic public relations delivers, why is it so often confused with or cobbled together with marketing and advertising? To answer that question fully, you must understand what marketing and advertising are.

Marketing is everything and anything strategically done to promote a business. Business cards, stationary, the way the phone is answered, networking, relationship building, and selling should all be defined in a comprehensive marketing plan. This plan serves as a road map, and helps identify the customer and the best tactics to make that customer aware of—and impressed by—what the company can deliver.

Advertising is a paid endorsement of a company, a product, or a service, with the goal of bringing that product or service to a targeted audience. Advertising is on display in magazines, on billboards, television, radio spots, and in brochures. What separates advertising from public relations is that advertising is owned and paid for by the creator, and the message is company crafted.

Sales, of course, are the ultimate goal of marketing, advertising, and public relations. For the most bang for the buck, marketing integrates both advertising and public relations into its plan. Marketing identifies the target audience or "market," public relations pursues third-party endorsements (which builds credibility in the public arena), and advertising reinforces the paid message or brand.

Of these three strategies or plans, public relations is burdened with a reputation for being the one least likely to drive sales. Why? In the past, it was almost impossible to measure public relations, and as a result, it was reduced to fluff when examining where potential leads come from. But modern-day public relations shows this is no longer true. For instance, a search engine–optimized (SEO) press release includes keywords, as well as links (backlinks) to a company's website, which helps it rank high in the search engines. The hits on the website can be traced, measured, and quantified. Additionally, an article that appears on the Internet most often comes with links back to the client company's website, which can also be measured.

PR Builds Relationships

At its very core, public relations is about relationship building with clients, potential clients, referral sources, vendors, employees, and the media. Business owners are often surprised to learn that growing a company and generating awareness does not require big marketing dollars. You can work with a public relations agency or an independent public relations practitioner. Large corporations tend to have an in-house public relations team within their marketing department.

A major benefit of using public relations is to make the salesperson's job easier—whether he or she is visiting an established client or going on a cold sales call. By searching the Internet, the salesperson can find out if the client company has been mentioned by the media. Or, the salesperson can ask his or her public relations department to create a list of where the client company has been mentioned. Now, when the salesperson walks into the appointment with a trade publication or newspaper that mentions the client's company, the client feels important and a trusting relationship starts to blossom.

With an established client, any time the company is mentioned in the news, the salesperson can call or send a congratulatory e-mail. It's a powerful way to "touch" the client without discussing sales. When sales and public relations work hand in hand, it's a productive one-two punch. The goal of the public relations team is to create an atmosphere where sales are a natural byproduct of a solid relationship.

As recently as ten years ago, public relations relied solely on press releases, articles, speaking engagements, special event planning, and community/civic activities to create a positive awareness of a company, product, or service. However, with the increasing use of social media, public relations practitioners have a host of online tools at their disposal. The use of video, for instance, has revolutionized the way companies can get their message out to the public, and at the same time, raise their Google rankings on the Internet.

Public relations is not about how many fans a company has or how many followers pursue a brand, it's about creating an environment where sales can take place. When put that way, the goal of public relations hasn't really changed.

References

1. http://metricsman.wordpress.com/2006/06/15/roi-is-statistical-modeling-the-answer-depends-on-the-question/; date accessed: June 2006.

 **Amy Wachtel Delman** has been involved in public relations, marketing, and branding for over two decades. Her expertise lies in using media exposure to raise awareness and increase revenues in companies where she has worked in-house or as a consultant. She has been mentioned in *Inc.* magazine and the *National Journal of Public Relations*. To find out how Amy can help your company grow, contact her by phone at 201-563-4614 or e-mail at amydelmanpr@verizon.net, connect with her on Facebook (Amy Delman Public Relations, LLC) and LinkedIn, and follow her on Twitter @amydelmanpr.

Would Your Business Benefit from Working with a Professional Marketing Consultant?

by Maria Paladino-Fitz

Many business owners seem to struggle with the idea of whether or not they really need to hire a professional media buyer or consultant to help with marketing and public relations. In the long run, those are generally the same businesses that end up spending more on advertising and gaining less return on their investment. When their results are less than stellar, business owners typically do one of the following: less marketing or hire an experienced professional to help.

However, savvy business owners understand the overall importance and cost savings when working with a professional who can offer expertise in delivering well-thought-out, cost-effective strategies that are much more likely to deliver consistent and qualified results. Among the many benefits of hiring a professional, consider the following top two:

1. Professional consultants are trained to implement smart marketing solutions to help grow your business by first identifying your competitors and then consulting on the needed strategies to protect your market share footprint.

2. They will package well-rounded media plans that are personally tailored to your business and your budget. Recommended marketing options may include in-person networking, targeted professional press release distributions, and impact-driven, well-thought-out print campaigns using media products that have been researched and identified as the best value and most cost-effective reach for you.

As a marketing consultant for over twenty years, I am also a firm believer that digital and Web marketing, social media, video, and cable TV advertising have carved a permanent niche in smart marketing campaigns and should always be a consideration.

If you do decide to work with an expert, take your time in the search to find that special person who gels with you. Look for someone who shares your goals, passion, and commitment and can demonstrate a structured plan of action to jump-start your connections. If you never worked with a media consultant, reach out to your business network for a recommendation. You can also use social networking sites such as LinkedIn to find a qualified candidate. They should have a proven track record and be able to provide references, testimonials, and success stories from other businesses that use their service. This brings an important point to mind: in-person relationships are a necessary component when building a network of potential customers who in turn will provide long-term, qualified referrals.

This is just one of the perks of working with an experienced marketing consultant who has spent years cultivating relationships, and who will happily make those appropriate introductions happen for you.

And because of long-term media relations, they are able to leverage their ability to distribute your news release into the right hands and will also help generate a series of ideas to stimulate interest in your unique product or service. Many times, they are privy to low-cost (sometimes no-cost) editorial opportunities that can directly benefit you.

Do-It-Yourself Marketing

Yes, you can absolutely do it yourself, but consider the following advice to maximize your return on investment and achieve the best success:

Create a plan. Of utmost importance is developing a plan of action with the right message, frequency, and branding strategy.

Create a budget. The first challenge is to develop a formal budget (generally three percent of annual gross sales is a good place to start), and then implement a marketing campaign strategy to include a series of advertising media that make the most sense for your type of service or industry.

Create a message. Keep your advertisement clear and concise (few words and large impact), and remember the message you put forward determines how your business is perceived by the world. Tap into emotion as much as possible, and above all, maintain a strong call-to-action response to your message. A good example might be a pain management specialist or a physical therapist using a headline that says something like this:

Has Pain Been Interfering with Your Quality of Life?

Let Us Help You Start Living Again…

Come to Our FREE Seminar on Wednesday Evening to Learn More!

Here, you have connected emotionally with a need, and created a direct call-to-action response.

Repeat the message. Frequency is extremely important. And remember that the size of the ad doesn't necessarily matter—it is the repeat branding that will help your business become a more recognized name and ultimately a household word.

Review, rework, repeat. Finally, review your strategy (at least quarterly) to identify which media performed best and rework your future budget accordingly.

Many successful business owners have found it to be a small, but very smart, investment to work with a professional consultant when it comes to separating their business from the competition and rising above the field of play. Sometimes, business owners are much better served by freeing up time to concentrate on what they do best—focus on running the business—and leave the marketing to the professionals.

 **Maria Paladino-Fitz** is the CEO of Media Consultants, LLC (www.mymediaconsultants.com), a full-service marketing solutions provider and public relations firm in North Jersey. Media Consultants provides well-thought-out, creative business strategies that deliver maximum results through the use of innovative marketing solutions and a combination of good messaging, frequency, medium selection, and targeted demographics. With over twenty years experience as a marketing consultant, Maria guides her clients in all areas of advertising, marketing, and public relations. Her approach is unique, her passion is contagious, and with her strong network of strategic business partnerships, Maria is able to deliver a solid marketing plan every time. Maria also serves as vice president of the Suburban Essex Chamber of Commerce. You can reach Maria at 973-931-4111 or maria@mymediaconsultants.com.

Niche

Diversity and Inclusion—The Hard Truth about a "Soft" Competency: A Guide to Creating and Sustaining Collaborative Business Partnerships

by Willa A. Edgerton-Chisler

Diversity is a reality in every aspect of our communities and our businesses—from entrepreneur to corporate entities. Diverse lifestyles, shifting demographics, and rapidly evolving technology are just a few contributors that constantly impact and influence our lives socially and professionally. By having only homogeneous interactions and a siloed, ethnocentric perspective, we limit business growth and block powerful dialogue.

Being a business in a multicultural, global community necessitates an awareness and understanding not only of yourself as a business leader, but of your customers, your employees, and the community where you live and conduct business. Yes, people are people—and yes, we are all members of the human race. However, based on many dimensions (race, ethnicity, gender, values, etc.) and experiences, we have our own perspective through which we see the world. It shapes the way we think things should and should not be—and influences our decisions.

To have a successful business, you need to recognize and acknowledge the factors that sway a person to work for you and why a customer buys from you. Whether you are a solopreneur or you employ many, when you have diversity and inclusion competency, you recognize that every voice is an important voice. Strengthening this competency creates economic inclusion, which increases your competitive advantage.

What is Diversity and Inclusion?

Let's begin with the hard truth—with a few diversity and inclusion points.

Diversity defined. First, a definition. One dictionary defines diversity as the state of being diverse; variety. The condition of having or being composed of differing elements or qualities. To expand on that definition, it means understanding that individuals are unique, for example, in their dimensions of race, ethnicity, gender, sexual orientation, socioeconomic status, age, physical abilities, religious beliefs, political beliefs, and other experiences. Think of diversity as an onion with many layers. Each layer presents an opportunity to discuss and learn—to gain understanding and mutual respect.

Diversity and inclusion as a singular competency. Both diversity and inclusion are only effective when worked in tandem—as valued and of equal importance. Inclusion refers to engaging behaviors that make each person feel appreciated and valued. Think of a time when you were in a business setting where you didn't feel included, regardless of the diversity.

- Diversity and inclusion are not equal opportunity, affirmative action, or tolerance.
- Diversity and inclusion lead to engagement and collaboration.
- Diversity and inclusion create a business advantage with the power to maximize innovation.
- Diversity and inclusion spark customer activism, which has a significant impact on businesses, driving accountability and behavior that speak to trust, diversity, and social responsibility— both locally and globally.

Differences make a difference. The bottom line is simple: Diversity is you and you are diversity. Your business can't afford to ignore diversity and inclusion as part of its business strategy.

Diversity Dimensions (a Few) that Impact Your Business

Generational diversity: People from every generation have launched and continue to launch their own businesses. Each generation has grown up in a world very different from the previous one. And each generation has an impact—exerting influence and adding value to the sustainability and growth of your business. In fact, your customers/clients probably come from a range of generations, such as the radio generation (before 1946), the baby boomers (1946–1964), Gen X (1965–1978), and the Millennials (1979–1997). What generation do you, your partners, and your customers represent—and do you know their expectations?

Supplier diversity: A corporate supplier diversity commitment is a win-win situation for corporations and business owners. It helps companies build their corporate brand while increasing spending with certified minority-, women-, disabled-, and veteran-owned enterprises (MWDVBEs) by opening doors to business opportunities. In addition, more corporations are creating an agreement clause requiring prime contractors to engage and report their tier 2 diverse subcontractors. Are you a certified MDVBE business pursuing growth through supplier diversity? Who can you build an alliance with to diversify your product offerings and expand your geographic reach?

How to Capitalize on Diversity and Inclusion Competency

Diversity and inclusion business competency is a competitive necessity. It doesn't happen by accident and without effort. So, where do you start?

Awaken your diversity hot buttons. The journey begins by awakening the understanding of your own diversity hot buttons and discovering how—and perhaps why—we behave the way we do in order to gain insight about our own values, beliefs, and biases. It's an inside job: you move away from the familiar and comfortable to develop relationships with individuals who are different.

Ask questions. During your diversity and inclusion competency journey, pay attention to your thoughts, habits, and practices—then answer the following: What can I do as a business leader to better understand the diverse business landscape? What do I need to be aware of that may be compromising my business relationships? What are my diversity blind spots, biases, and assumptions? How can I become an employer of choice, and how do I interpret the behaviors of my employees? How can I create and maintain an open workplace environment that draws on the talents of all our employees? Who is my target market? What are its diverse segments? Do I know my target market's buying pattern and expectations? Does our business speak to their expectations?

The road to diversity and inclusion leads to partnerships. Diversity and inclusion create and sustain collaborative partnerships, but it takes work and education. For an empowering journey, use the following tips to guide you:

Dialogue—Build new perspectives one conversation at a time. Step out of your comfort zone and widen and connect with diverse business leaders who bring different business perspectives.

Individual—Maintain authenticity and integrity by increasing your awareness of other perspectives. Keep an open attitude and an open mind.

Vision—Look for new perspectives. Cross mentor. Each generation brings wisdom, expertise, and new approaches to business.

Experience—Get involved in organizations whose members are representative of the group with whom you wish to do business.

Relationships—Intentionally build different relationships with a wide array of people.

Synergy—Collaborate with diverse businesses.

Inclusive—Weave diversity and inclusion into every business aspect.

Transformational—What if ...?

You—Are Diversity.

Diversity and inclusion are more than a return on investment (ROI). Simply put—it's your *Return on Influence.*

 Willa Edgerton-Chisler, PCC, is a consultant/coach developing strategies on leadership, career transition planning, brand congruency, and diversity and inclusion. She has been named one of the NJBIZ 2012 Best 50 Women in Business, and recognized in 2011 Garden State Woman of the Year-Diversity, 2008 U.S. SBA Region II & NJ Minority Business Champion, and the State of NJ Senate and General Assembly Joint Legislative Resolution for her body of work and contributions. She is a certified professional coach and a member of the International Coach Federation, SHRM, and the International Society of Diversity and Inclusion Professionals. Willa can be reached at Willa@symphonycoaching.com or 862-23-WILLA (862-239-4552).

Imagine What You Could Write without Putting Pen to Paper: How to Work with a Ghostwriter

by Lisa Romeo

You want to write a book. You've been invited to contribute an article to a publication or website. You need to give a speech. You started a business blog (or were invited to write a guest post). Perhaps you've even decided to pen a memoir.

You roll up your sleeves and sit at the keyboard, but after the first page or two, banged out in a flush of enthusiasm, you find yourself struggling to transfer your intelligent thoughts and ideas onto the page in cogent sentences and paragraphs. Before long, you start to wonder how anyone manages to write well and still get anything else done. Worse, you see that putting in the hours necessary to write something good means sacrificing time that may be more profitably spent at your core business. Finally, you begin to realize that while most sensible professionals can write a decent memo or report, there are some jobs best left to a professional writer.

Rather than forgo the project, why not consider hiring a ghostwriter? You don't have to be a celebrity or have a superstar's budget either, and your project doesn't have to be a full-length book destined for the bestseller lists to justify adding a ghostwriter to your team of service professionals.

Ghostwriters work for all sorts of people—on all sorts of projects. Relying on one to help you produce the best possible piece of work is smart, not silly. You wouldn't blink about hiring the right professionals to handle taxes, plumbing, Web design, construction, or a dozen other specialties, so why take on a part-time job as a writer when you can form a partnership with a ghostwriter?

Notice that I've described the relationship with a ghostwriter as a *partnership*. Unlike hiring an editor, whose expertise is to revise and refine what you have already written, a ghostwriter creates from the ground up.

A good ghostwriter can enter a project before you've jotted down a list of ideas, and is also comfortable taking on any portion of a project—from a few paragraphs up to the entire thing. Most ghostwriters will need to interview the client. This can be done in person, via e-mail, by telephone—or a combination of the three. The writer will also want any notes, drafts, or lists you already have. The two of you will discuss your vision and goals, the intended audience, and what style and tone you have in mind. For example, is it going to be a casual piece of work with a folksy personal voice or will it take a more formal, prescriptive approach.

Ghostwriters Boost
Credibility and Visibility

The ghostwriter's goal is to make you look good on the page, the lecture stage, or the Web. It's your name on the final product, so if the ghost has performed well, he or she remains invisible. A ghostwriter's ultimate accolade is hearing clients say that the words on the page sound like their own. On a major project, such as a book, you may elect to share author credit with the ghostwriter (for example, by "Your Name" with "Gabby Ghost"), although seasoned ghostwriters do not expect it.

To find a ghostwriter, ask for referrals from anyone you know who has used one, and reach out to any writers or editors already in your circle. Not every writer or editor is interested in ghostwriting gigs or has the skill set of an experienced ghostwriter, although most ghostwriters tend to be competent editors. Branch out further by contacting writers' organizations and directories, such as the Authors Guild or Publishers Marketplace, and working through connections via LinkedIn and other professional networks. Be sure to read some of the ghost's work (only a small number of ghostwriters must sign nondisclosure agreements prohibiting them from revealing their clients—others are happy to show you samples). If possible, talk to a former client, and ask if the ghostwriter will first work on a smaller project to see if the fit is right.

Comfort and Collaboration

Once you have decided on a ghostwriter, come up with a clear action plan together by setting out deadlines and meetings (or phone/e-mail time). The ghostwriter's job should not be complicated by a schedule that doesn't allow you to work together. Give the ghost access to outlines, documents, research materials, places, and other people to help him or her develop the story.

While a ghostwriter is a professional, an extra level of comfort and rapport is ideal—you want to like your ghostwriter enough to openly discuss thoughts, experiences, and ideas. But remember ghosts are invisible, not silent. A good ghostwriter will be firm about what will or will not work on the page. It's probably wise to listen.

Ghostwriters can work by word count, page, hour, or flat project fee, and while there may be room for negotiation, be prepared to pay one-third to one-half in advance. Agree on how revisions will be handled. Usually, one revision is included in the initial fee, but a total rewrite is not. You will retain the copyright to the material, but a ghostwriter is not your employee, so try not to ask for constant updates— let the ghost write!

 **Lisa Romeo** is an experienced ghostwriter, editor, freelance writer, and writing coach. While she is mum about her ghostwriting clients, her own work has appeared in *The New York Times*; *O, The Oprah Magazine*; and dozens of other print and online venues. In a "previous life," Lisa had a twelve-year career in public relations and worked as a journalist covering equestrian sports. Lisa teaches creative writing privately online and in the Rutgers University Writing Program Extension, and publishes a blog (http://LisaRomeo.blogspot.com) offering writing advice and commentary about writing. Located in Cedar Grove, New Jersey, Lisa can be reached at LisaRomeoWrites@gmail.com or via her website at http://LisaRomeo.net.

Six Tips to Embrace Change—or Risk Being Left Behind

by Andrea Nemeth

Change is inevitable. Business owners, especially, understand that their fortunes ride on their ability to adapt and change, especially in our technology-driven culture where change seems to occur in the blink of an eye. Yet, even when you anticipate change, it is human nature to resist it, and difficult to learn how to cope with it.

Like many affected by the economic downturn, I faced unemployment in 2009. I admit that I had my share of downer days, but overall I was excited about my future and believed something bigger and brighter was out there for me. My fear of going back to corporate America led me to explore the franchise concept. After researching and soul-searching, I decided a Synergy HomeCare franchise was a perfect fit for me. Instead of going into a tailspin, I turned frightening change into an opportunity.

> *There is nothing more certain and unchanging*
> *than uncertainty and change.*
>
> John Fitzgerald Kennedy

To use change as an opportunity to grow your business, apply these six tips—the things I learned after finding myself out of a corporate job, and the joy I found in reinventing myself as the owner of a Synergy HomeCare franchise.

1. Understand you have choices. You make choices every day: how to react to a situation, how you see your life, and who you associate with. When change is difficult, the one thing you can change is your attitude. Your attitude will make a difference in how you react to a rainy day, to sitting in traffic, to handling a difficult client, etc.

I work with families who have to make difficult decisions, especially when they're worried about the well-being of an aging parent. I remind them that they have choices. To help them make the best choices, I answer questions such as: How do I care for my aging parents? What options are available? What is the cost? How do I ensure my loved one will get the best care?

To deal with change, answer the question "How does this change impact me and my business?" Your answers will reveal choices. When you realize you have choices, change is less stressful.

2. Seek help. When dealing with change, don't be afraid to ask for help. Find a mentor or a local group at www.meetup.com for emotional support and friendship during difficult times.

When I faced unemployment, I used the outplacement service provided by my former employer. I also picked the brains of my fraternity brothers (I belong to Alpha Kappa Psi Fraternity, a coed professional business fraternity) who own businesses. After purchasing my Synergy HomeCare franchise, I joined NJAWBO (www.njawbo.org) because surrounding myself with women business owners energizes and inspires me.

In my work, I know that our aging population and their families need help to deal with lifestyle changes, so I often recommend community agencies that support and help seniors.

To deal with change, create a list of organizations and people that can answer your questions and recommend additional resources. For instance, SCORE (www.score.org) offers free business counseling—or hire an experienced business consultant or coach.

3. Educate, then adjust. Education is powerful. My years of work experience in corporate America and as a volunteer on Alpha Kappa Psi's management team helped me transition from an employee to a business owner.

When I became a Synergy HomeCare franchise owner, it was clear that families are desperate for information. I educate families by letting them know what options are available, so they are comfortable making adjustments as their situation changes. For example, homecare may be a viable option at first, but a family might consider an assisted-living facility or nursing home for their loved one later on.

To deal with change, stay on top of industry trends. Not only will you find it easier to adjust, but you'll position yourself as a respected industry thought leader.

4. Identify your safety net. Surround yourself with people who have a positive influence on your life. You gain self-confidence from those who respect you, trust you, love you, and support you.

I have been blessed with a mother who loves me unconditionally and provides emotional support. When my husband and I decided to buy our franchise, she provided an additional cushion when she offered to assist us financially if we needed it. My husband has been my greatest supporter, believing in my abilities and having faith in trying something we had never done before.

As a Synergy HomeCare franchise owner, I know that family caregivers need support, so I am part of their safety net. No matter what illness a loved one is dealing with, I provide resources, education, and support.

To deal with change, identify your support network. They might not always agree with you, but they will always support you.

5. Go forward. Although you cannot change the past, you can learn from it.

Learning from my past has made me a better person, a better leader, and a better business owner. I use life's lessons to make smarter choices for my future.

In my business, I know how important it is for families to make decisions based on their situation at a specific moment in time. But conditions change, situations change, and finances change. All these factors affect decisions families make in caring for their loved ones. So that they don't risk further complicating a difficult decision, I use my expertise to help families move forward.

To deal with change, focus on the future of your business. Identify what works, and let go of what doesn't—then move forward with confidence.

6. Energize yourself. To keep a positive attitude, I take care of myself. I go to the gym with my husband. I visit the chiropractor. I travel with my husband, spend time with my mom, my sister, and my girlfriends. I make "me time" a priority.

As a Synergy HomeCare franchise owner, I learned that the family caregivers who provide the best care take care of themselves first. No one can give their best when they're tired, stressed, or sick.

The same is true for business owners. When you're good to yourself—you're great for those you serve.

Yes, change is inevitable. Fight it or embrace it. The choice is yours.

Andrea Nemeth, the former owner of a non-medical home-care agency, Synergy HomeCare, is now the assistant campus operating officer at Berkeley College in New York. Andrea worked in corporate America for several years as an accounting/finance professional prior to owning the agency and has extensive experience in supporting corporate goals through planning, reporting, and analysis. She is an active and prominent leader of Alpha Kappa Psi Professional Co-ed Business Fraternity (www.akpsi.org), where she was elected the first female president in the history of the fraternity. Andrea can be reached at andrea.nemeth129@gmail.com.

How to Meet Adversity Head-On and Keep Yourself Calm during Chaos

by Audrey Storch

Whether you are a product- or service-based business, Murphy (of Murphy's Law) will visit you. Call it adversity, bad luck, or a challenge—when it hits, you must be prepared. I always like to plan for the worst but hope for the best. I know this is a pessimistic way of thinking, but it is reality and has saved me from losing money and clients. For those who wish to succeed, I can tell you that meeting adversity and challenges head-on will give you your best options.

So take a deep breath, calm down (if you need to), and draw from your biggest resource—your peers. If your adversity/challenge is out of your comfort zone, hire the best you can afford in consulting, legal, accounting, or whatever area of expertise you need. In addition to having the expertise you lack, a professional outsider does not have the same emotional investment as you do. He or she can help you keep your wits, see clearly, and give you objective advice.

Yes, when you are in the thick of battle, this advice might sound placating, but trust me—I have been in the trenches, and I've been in deeper than most others ever will be. As an inventor, my patent was stolen. Then I was sued for patent infringement! My eight years of battle had devastating effects—not only on me and my company, but on my family, too. But as a result of this dirty fight, I grew stronger and more successful.

In fact, I believe this saying speaks to the truth: "Those who stay calm while others panic are the ones that survive." This is not to say that you won't get crazy, feel outraged, and at times, betrayed. My advice is to feel the pain and outrage—but choose to feel them privately or with a confidant—then reboot, get up, and strategize.

Focus on the Solution

When adversity hits, the most important thing to do is to focus on the solution. Of course, this means you must have the problem clearly in hand—so this is when a peer or a professional can bring objectivity to the situation. By focusing on the solution, not only will you gain clarity, but you'll also find hope. Remember, without hope there is no winning. Hope will galvanize you, put you in the right frame of mind, and get you over the hurdles you're facing.

Every business owner faces challenges and adversity. How you deal with them will not only make a difference in the outcome, but in your success as a business owner. When you're faced with adversity, try the following:

- Address the problem. Look it squarely in the eye. Truly see it.

- Deal with the emotions of the problem before you do anything else. Privately address how it makes you feel and what it makes you want to do. After you focus on the emotional aspect, you can attack it professionally. (A life coach can be a tremendous resource.)

- Do *not* react immediately (unless it is life threatening). Take this problem and separate it from your everyday challenges so you can focus on the situation.

- Use every networking resource you have. Of course, this depends on the type of adversity you are facing. You can turn to your peers to share what they've learned during a similar situation, or you can ask them to recommend a professional who can advise you. Do not expect them to do the work or take the burden off you. Remember, you are asking someone to give up valuable time and advice. This thinking will keep your peers answering your calls.

- Now *focus on the solution*. Do not waste time focusing on the problem. Solutions are what you need, so create a "pro" and "con" list for each of your solutions. This will help you think your problem through and assist you during the decision-making process.

- Contact those who can help you implement your solutions. By now you should feel more hopeful of a positive outcome, more confident about your future. When you are proactive, you put the flame to the torch and see the light at the end of your tunnel.

- Under no circumstances do you take the easy way out. Do what is *right*, not what is easy. If your problem takes years, then you fight the right fight for years. Remember, mine took *eight* years! I had to fight a factory that not only stole my patent—but sued me and my company, as well as my clients and my family for patent infringement on *my* product! I did not have the money needed to fight, so I had to become extremely resourceful and use all the techniques I'm sharing with you—plus more!

- When you are feeling beaten, turn to those who will support you emotionally. When it gets so dark and you feel you have used your last molecule of energy, turn to your most loyal supporters. They will refuel your energy and hope tanks so you can come back stronger. You are only human, so it's okay to break down (for a short time)—but *do not give up!*

- Take a break when you need it. It's OK to say, "I don't know right now. Can I get back to you?" Allow time to think things through and recharge.

- Contingency Solutions: If solution A does not work, have solution B ready. If solution B does not work, have solution C ready, and so on. Your plans are like lines of soldiers in battle, when one fails, other lines are behind them ready to take over. By going that extra mile and planning for the worst—developing contingency solutions—but hoping for the best, you have protected your company and yourself against unforeseeable events.

- When the good fight fails. I was forced to shut down my "baby" to end the lunacy because of the expensive and lengthy way the legal system works. After eight years, my solution to this problem was to stop fighting. But I did not give up! Knowing that in a few months I was going to close my company, I formed another with the dim hope of rebuilding in a new direction. Within a few months of forming my new company, success arrived. By using my contingency solution and all the knowledge gained from my previous eight years in business, I realized that, although I lost that battle, I won the war. So, don't be afraid to admit it when your good fight is over; it may actually be a blessing in disguise. It was for me.

- Focus on what means the most to you. Hope returns when you focus on your dreams, goals, and solutions—not on your problems. Follow what your gut tells you and you will make it through this difficult time—better prepared and ready for the next challenge you face.

Remember, you cannot always change a situation, but you *can* change the way you look at it. There is *always* a choice. The important thing is to remember that the choice is yours—and that you always have one.

 **Audrey Storch** is the creator of the world's first and only "huggable picture frame," HUGGEE MISS YOU, and other products sold on QVC, HSN, and in stores around the world. She is a creator, inventor, motivational speaker, consultant, and entrepreneur who has been a guest on national TV and radio shows, profiled in three business books, and written about in over 100 newspapers worldwide, including *The New York Times*. Audrey helps business owners and inventors turn their dreams into reality by working with them on manufacturing, marketing, and sales needed to create, produce, and promote their products or services. When you're ready to make your dream a goal with a real start date, contact Audrey at 973-696-6300 or 973-650-5793 or astorch@huggstogo.com. Visit her website at www.huggeemissyou.com.

Ergonomics for the
Healthy Business Owner

by Ellen Rader Smith

Imagine work without a computer. In today's world, it's nearly impossible to picture how to get through the workday without a computer. After all, you use the computer to maintain contact with business associates, find information, do research, prepare proposals, maintain finances, sell your products and services, take payments, and more. The truth is, your business resides on your computer. And because you rely on your computer to keep your business fit and in top shape, like any smart business owner, you want the fastest Internet connection and best technology possible. I don't blame you.

However, in their quest for the fastest, most up-to-date technology, business owners often lose sight of one very important factor, which is their personal comfort at the computer. Why? Because ergonomic factors, including where the computer is placed, what chair is used, and how users interact with their computer components such as the keyboard, mouse, and screen, are not always considered. This, in turn, can result in muscle fatigue and overuse, eyestrain, and emotional stress.

In addition, busy business owners often fail to consider where or how they use their computer, so the computer could be added to an existing work area or a makeshift home office—or in the interest of having one computer that does it all—a laptop that is used both on the road and in the office. Although working on a laptop placed on the dining room table may be acceptable for occasional users, it is not wise for a business owner to spend several hours looking down at the screen or elevating her arms to access the keyboard or mouse while sitting in a nonadjustable or nonergonomic chair.

Pay Attention to Your Body and Your Workstation

Attention to your work setup, especially the computer workstation, is critical to productivity, well-being, and minimizing stress, as well as any aches and pains in your upper back and neck, low back, hands, or arms. Once the body begins to experience a vicious cycle of muscle, tendon, or other musculo-skeletal stress and strain, it is hard to stop this process without attention to ergonomics—or how you arrange your work area to meet your specific needs. Simply stated, ergonomics optimizes the fit between people and the work they perform to minimize the risk of injury. Therefore, without the ability to make adjustments—whether it be the chair or the work surface—it is not possible for the same workstation to fit the needs of a petite woman and a big, burly man.

In order to get their work done, business owners tend to sit for extended periods without taking breaks. Since the body is meant to move—not remain in one sustained posture—prolonged sitting is another cause of musculo-skeletal stress.

For business owners who experience discomfort while sitting at the computer—from medical and ergonomic perspectives—it's important to assess the causes and address the issues as part of their total effort to feel better or be pain free. While going to the chiropractor or taking over-the-counter pain or anti-inflammatory medications might help, returning to the same contributing stressors will not resolve the problem or eliminate the pain or discomfort. Unfortunately, business owners who are in pain are also not as productive as their pain-free colleagues and staff. Applying ergonomics can help make business owners more comfortable—and as a result, more productive.

Are you contributing to your own discomfort? You might be surprised. Read the warning signs listed below. How many are you guilty of?

- Sitting for extended periods without breaks
- Sitting in a nonadjustable or improperly fitting chair
- Extended hand/arm reaches to the keyboard or mouse
- Mice and keyboards at different work heights
- Screens too high, far away or close, or skewed to one side
- Inattention to the special visual needs of users who wear bi- or trifocals
- Cradling the telephone while writing or keying
- Prolonged viewing of source documents positioned flat on the table
- Reliance on a laptop as the primary computer
- Glare or adverse lighting

Any one or a *combination* of these can contribute to poor work postures and methods, which can become major stressors on the body when they are repeated or even become habits. Over time, they can affect a business owner's daily well-being and, ultimately, productivity.

The good news is that most ergonomic fixes are inexpensive. While some involve purchasing new equipment, others are easy to achieve once you open your ergonomic eyes and make a few of the following changes:

- Break the cycle of sitting, and get up from your seat at least once an hour.
- Take regular stretching breaks to relieve muscle discomfort.

- Invest in a new chair (be sure to try it first, and not just pick it from a catalogue or based solely on another person's recommendations).
- Rearrange your work area so that your keyboard and screen are in line, and no twisting is required.
- Try using an adjustable-height keyboard tray (so your keyboard and mouse are at elbow level when seated) or an alternate, contoured mouse design.
- Use a headset so you can stand and/or move around your office while you're on the telephone.
- Add at least one external component to your laptop setup, for example, a keyboard, mouse, or screen.
- Create an alternate, standing work area.

Sometimes the eyes of an ergonomic expert are helpful, especially when you don't know what you are doing wrong, or you think you are doing things right. Ergonomic evaluations examine not only the chairs, furnishings, and equipment, but also the interface between users and these components. For business owners who have experienced musculoskeletal discomfort or various stress and strain injuries in the past, it is particularly important that your workstations are set up ergonomically, since you are more prone to recurrences.

Now that you have a basic awareness of ergonomic issues and how they can affect your physical and emotional well-being, and ultimate work performance, consider the following each time you sit down to work:

- Prolonged sitting without breaks can be a health hazard.
- Listen to your body. Pain is a warning signal that should not be ignored.
- Take control of your immediate work surroundings.

Most importantly, give yourself the attention that you would your clients.

 **Ellen Rader Smith** is the owner of Ergo & Rehab Services, an ergonomics consulting company that helps you to be more ergonomically correct so you can be as productive as possible at your computer workstation and avoid annoying aches and pains. Ellen is a Certified Professional Ergonomist, Certified Vocational Evaluator, and Licensed Occupational Therapist who has successfully helped many small business owners for over twenty-five years. You can reach Ellen by phone at 973-334-7499, e-mail at ergoers@optonline.net, or by visiting her website at www.ergoers.com.

Simple Techniques to Stay Positive and Be More Productive

by Irina Smirnova

If you are like me, you find yourself thinking that you spend all of your time on marketing, running around meeting people, and other promotional activities instead of doing what you love. And you might be wondering: Is being my own boss really paying off? I'm spending all this time pushing, and I am exhausted, and I even forget why I started this whole business thing in the first place. Things aren't going the way I expected, and I'm working so hard. What do I do? I'm going to take a nap. Yeah. As if that ever helped anything, because the world keeps on going—with or without me.

The truth is, a good number of business owners spend too much energy dwelling on what isn't working and how it isn't working, rather than actually doing the work. Naturally, that time could be put to much better use—even if you use it to take a day off to refuel and jump-start your creative engine. Being negative drains your energy—a lot. To stop the leak, I'm going to reveal four simple techniques that you can use to train your mind to change those negative thinking habits, so you can be more productive running your business and your life. What are these "magical" techniques?

1. **Pick supporters over naysayers.** Surround yourself with friends that believe in you and support you, and avoid the ones who think they are helping you by criticizing your every move. Feedback can be useful, but not in the early stages when you are establishing yourself as an independent business owner.

2. **Draw the line between what makes you feel good and what makes you feel bad.** Examine your skills and the niche you want to develop, then make a list and feel your way through it. Cross out the negatives on your list, and leave only what feels right and makes you feel good. For example, when I was deciding what kind of photography I should be doing, I knew immediately that my focus would not be in the private market because shooting weddings and parties did not excite me. I wanted to deal with something more controlled and organized, so I focused on helping businesses with their advertising and presentation needs.

3. **Catch bad thoughts and switch your attention to what feels better.** This seems hard to do at first because you can't stop your thoughts. And in a "my-glass-is-half-empty" society, ignoring your upbringing is not

easy. But the way you think is really a habit that you can change when you pay attention to your thoughts. After all, the human brain is a marvelous tool, and with a few days of practice, you'll notice remarkable changes in your thinking. Besides, most of your negative judgments aren't even true. When that's the case, think the opposite of your bad-thought statements, and you'll feel better immediately. And if the negative statement *is* true, there is no point in focusing on it. Can't fix it? Switch your attention to something that makes you feel good.

For instance, I used to go to bed at night thinking the market was flooded with too many great photographers and that I could not compete with them. However, as I analyzed the situation, I came to the conclusion that neither of these statements was true. As I studied their work, I realized that many of the photographers were not as good as their presentations suggested. Then I saw that each had a specialty. And just like me, every photographer deals with the same time limitations: twenty-four hours in a day, seven days in a week, and twelve months in a year. Each one of us could only do so much in a day, and most of us have a life outside of work, so there is plenty of work for everyone. Once I realized that, it was easier to breathe, and the world brightened.

4. **Keep an optimistic state of mind.** Yes, it is possible to train yourself to be more optimistic. You can do that by collecting and storing memories that make you feel good. Let me explain: One day I went to the park for a quick run, and met a very cute doggy strolling with his owner. The pup greeted me happily, wagging his tail—his button eyes dancing with delight as he studied my face. When I leaned down and petted his soft, silky fur, I relaxed. My brain snapped a picture of that perfect summer morning: my muscles aching for a stretch, the smell of fresh grass, a happy, little dog showing his affection. I will never forget that moment, and during challenging times, I picture that puppy to bring me back to the state of mind that keeps me positive and productive.

Learn to store your good memories in your mind, and hang on to them. Whether it's a sunrise, a stranger responding to your smile, your child's affection, your loved one's look, a comfortable bed, the smell of fresh laundry—whatever brings a smile to your face or makes you giggle—summon that picture. Carry this precious image library in your heart at all times, and it will keep you going, even during life's toughest moments.

Find the positive in every situation, and pay as much attention to it as possible. This may sound like a cliché, but it is very effective, and if you haven't discovered it yet, when you do, you'll be surprised by the difference it makes. Many potentially mood-killing situations are avoided by using this simple, but powerful technique.

There are many things you can do to become more positive and productive, but these are not complicated, and everyone can practice them. And if you still can't shake your negative thoughts, consider the fact that optimists, in general, live much longer and healthier lives. Isn't it time to choose happiness?

Irina Smirnova is an entrepreneur as well as a spirited, digital artist specializing in commercial "people" photography. From double-spread editorials to promo material—when you want your product to start "talking" to your customers and clients, you won't find a better-suited production company to do the job illustrating it. And when it comes to providing your fabulous self with an appropriate image that reflects your business—creative artist and business head shots are Irina's specialty. To find out more about how Irina will capture your image so you turn heads, visit www.irina-smirnova.com, e-mail her at irina@irina-smirnova.com, and connect with her on Facebook.

Don't Stop Believing in Yourself

by Sue Waldman

You wanted to be your own boss and now you are. Feeling proud of yourself for taking not only the financial, but also the psychological risks that come with success or failure, gives you the courage to move forward. But soon you realize that the honeymoon is over. Although your dream of becoming a business owner has come true, this newly discovered autonomy brings responsibility—some of which you never anticipated. The long days are not what you envisioned when you started out, and you are wondering if it's all worth it. The thought of returning to work as an employee crosses your mind.

After all, you have to meet payroll, and pay taxes and rent. There are health-care costs, expenses, and deadlines to meet. You work fourteen hours a day. There is no time for a vacation in the foreseeable future. You have noticed changes in your eating and sleeping patterns. Fatigued, you are losing pleasure in the activities that provided much joy. Your loved ones complain that you are moody, irritable, and restless.

You feel overwhelmed by the never-ending obligations for which you are responsible. Unable to concentrate, you have difficulty following through with your day-to-day duties and tasks. Your doubts about whether you are capable of meeting the demands of your business place a toll on your mind, body, and spirit. You are easily distracted by unexplained aches and pains. You feel stressed—seriously stressed.

Stop and Think

You knew that owning a business was not going to be easy. You knew it would be hard work. But you also know that you enjoy overcoming obstacles. In fact, you overcame a great deal of uncertainty and fear when you opened your business. You also expected to be challenged. After all, friends describe you as optimistic and inspiring. For you, the glass is always half full. Your accomplishments are the result of your determination, persistence, and courage.

You pride yourself on your integrity and excellent customer service. Your choice to be self-employed was based on your desire for freedom, personal empowerment, and autonomy. Rather than have an external authority control your workday, you wanted to conduct business your way. You are driven by a strong code of ethics and a balanced quality of life. You exude professionalism. You value your work and know that you are at the top of what you do.

Never Give Up

Don't stop believing in yourself—or in your dreams. Facing and overcoming challenges and adversity bring rewards of character, independence, and self-confidence. When you change the way you look at things—the things you look at change.

As an entrepreneur, you recognize that there will be setbacks, moments of doubt, and times of wanting to give up. So be realistic in the expectations you place on yourself. Open yourself to see things differently. Think positively, take action, and creatively release your frustrations.

Brainstorm out of the box, explore your options, use all of your resources, and let go of your self-inflicted limiting beliefs. It is all right to be human, to try and to stumble, to be momentarily weak and vulnerable. The ability to overcome that helplessness with moments of strength, courage, and perseverance is how you will succeed. Remember that the solutions reside within.

Find Balance

Ask yourself: "Is my work satisfying?" "Do I respect myself?" "Am I having fun?" "Are my most important values in life being met?" "Do I enjoy the people I work with?" "Am I moving in the right direction?" If the answers are yes, then stick with it. If you knew you could not fail, what would you do differently?

Face challenges as they arise. When you hit a wall, take a break. Go for a walk. Ask for help and support. Reach out to a trusted colleague and get a fresh perspective. Begin a project that will excite you. Empower and motivate yourself by introducing new opportunities. Delegate responsibilities to interns. Find a mentor. Take a continuing education seminar. Enjoy a meditation class. Don't take things so seriously. Remind yourself to slow down and take a breath. As your troubles recede into the distance, your self-esteem will grow, and your inner doubts will disappear.

Remember

Success is how you define it. Feel a sense of achievement for how you show up in your life. Focus on how much you enjoy what you do. Learn something new every day, so you can be the best that you *possibly* can be. Don't make assumptions or take what others do or say personally. You are never alone. We are all connected. Get out of your way. Stop ruminating about what went wrong. There is no purpose to judge yourself or others. Let go of the past. Make things happen now.

Living an inspired life involves a major shift in attitude in the direction of feeling peaceful, being honest, and assisting others. Remember that dreams take time, patience, a personal commitment, compassion, a sustained effort to overcome obstacles, an openness to endure change, a clear sense of purpose, and a willingness to fail—if they are ever to be anything more than dreams.

Have a Source of Inspiration

My mother is my true source of inspiration. She taught me how to be positive in the midst of chaos. She conquered and survived a two-year battle with lung cancer and never complained. Unfortunately, another form of cancer won the battle, but my mother always played the best game of her life. She held her head high, walked with grace, and radiated beauty wherever she was. Until her last day, her primary care physician applauded her determination and fortitude to live. She would not give up. Above all, I witnessed how she faced each new day as if it were her first—not her last.

Each and every day offers a new beginning—so recognize, acknowledge, and honor the power of who you really are. When you are true to yourself, you will live your life on your terms. Most important, when you believe in possibility and the expectation of miracles being part of life, you come to know that *anything is possible!*

Sue Waldman, LPC, a licensed psychotherapist in private practice for over eighteen years, is a Board Certified Clinical Mental Health Counselor, and Board Certified Personal and Executive Life Coach with specialty certifications in career, health, wellness, energy leadership, and group counseling. Her private practice, Advanced Counseling & Coaching Services, is all about inspiring, empowering, and supporting people to reach their full potential. Sue's passion is guiding people to deeply love who they are and the life they are living. In one-on-one counseling sessions, through her inspirational workshops, networking meetings, and retreats, Sue enjoys creating sacred spaces for individuals to explore their personal growth, spirituality, and life purpose. Sue offers weekly meditation classes, stress management, Reiki, and a coaching group called POSSIBILITIES, which provides support to help you through divorce, a career change, and/or with self-esteem development. Sue is also available for training, teaching engagements, and telephone coaching. She can be reached at 973-857-9090 or Sue@SueWaldman.com. Visit www.SueWaldman.com.

Technology

Ten Proven Strategies
for Developing a Killer Website

by Barbara Zaccone

Even with the popularity of social media, most business owners agree that their website is their most valuable marketing asset. In fact, a website branded to a business is what potential customers rely on to obtain an in-depth understanding of the company's products and services.

So the first step in planning, building, and maintaining an effective website designed to grow your business is to understand and believe in its ability to put your business on the map. This belief will drive you to be proactive. And because websites are the most measurable of all marketing and lead-generating campaigns, you can track and measure your efforts over time.

As an online marketing expert, I have put together the following list of ten website marketing strategies for you to use to your business advantage.

1. Target geographically. Do you serve a local market? A town, suburb, county, or state? It's important for visitors who arrive at your site to immediately see the geography you serve. You can do this with a tag line that says, "Top Web Design Company in New Jersey" or by providing a bulleted list of the areas you serve. This information should be placed at the top of your home page. To appear in local search results, include geographic keywords throughout your website.

2. Grab your visitors' attention. In a matter of seconds—if visitors don't *get* what you are about—a mouse click will take them to your competitor. So, how do you engage your visitors? Easy, focus on them—*not* on you. Communicate engaging benefits to them with clear, concise, easy-to-read content. Keep your home page copy to less than 200 words, and use headline copy, subheads, and both bold and bulleted text to make your pages easy on the eye.

3. Control your own content. If you lack the skills to update your website yourself, hire a Web designer to rebuild your site to today's standards. Software such as WordPress and Adobe Contribute allow you to update text and images with ease. Not only do updates keep your site fresh, but search engines love new and changing content—which should result in increased traffic.

4. Plan for mobile visitors. Make sure you can navigate your website from a smart phone. Older sites built with Adobe Flash do not work on the iPhone or iPad devices. If large numbers of visitors come to your site from mobile devices, consider building a mobile website. To find out, simply check your Google Analytic website statistics.

5. Know the basics of search engine optimization. You don't have to be a search engine optimization (SEO) wizard to implement some basic strategies that will improve your ranking for targeted keyword phrases. By doing research online, you'll be surprised how a little knowledge can go a long way. Perform a Google search on "search engine optimization basics" and pay attention to URL naming, page title, meta description, and link names. Your targeted keyword phrases should appear in these four elements.

6. Develop rich content with hierarchy. Since search engines love content with order, write your content like you would a term paper: page title, heading, subheading, and secondary heading—which should be keyword rich, describing your paragraph content. Targeted keyword phrases should appear in the first paragraphs of the page.

7. Research your competition. Look at your top five competitors—especially when building a new website—and write down what you like about each site. Note how these companies position themselves and what they call themselves. Set up a Google Alert for your competitors to see what they're focused on and to stay informed about your industry. Take it up a notch by noting what larger companies in your industry are doing as well. And if you have time, check out companies that are not your direct competitors—but are in your industry—to see what features and functions they have on their websites.

8. Design for functionality. To make your website more than a brochure with a mouse, think about your customers and prospects, and what they need when they come to your site. How can you use your site to improve customer service and increase your productivity? Perhaps you can offer online forms, an online catalog, or sell products online. A distributor or dealer password-protected area allows access to selling tools and reports.

9. Make your website unique, professional, and memorable. Often, your website is where potential customers first experience your brand and your company. An amateur-looking website leaves a less than desired first impression, so consider using a professional Web design firm. A designer's portfolio will give you a sense of the company's experience and capabilities. Collaborate with your designer, but make sure you give him or her creative freedom. After all, that's why you hire an expert. If your website design is stale or outdated, you could be losing business to competitors with more innovative and professional designs.

10. Bring a personal touch to your website. Quality photography speaks thousands of words about your company. To bring a personal touch to your website, use your own photographs. Stock photos come in handy, but don't rely on *all* stock photography for your site. Whenever possible, hire a professional photographer. Photos of your office, team, plant, customer service department, lab, warehouse, fleet, office building, etc., help visitors connect with your business. Your site will be more engaging when people are in the photos. A site with humans creates a better connection with the viewer compared to sites that just use graphics.

Building a successful and effective website for your business is an ongoing process—not a onetime event. Your site should evolve as your business evolves. Whether your website is up and running—or you are about to create a new one—having a strategy in place will help you craft a story that accurately represents your business. You work hard—and deserve nothing less.

Barbara Zaccone, a Web strategy and online marketing expert, is the president and founder of BZA LLC, an interactive marketing agency. She developed her management, marketing, and sales talents at Hewlett-Packard. BZA helps companies and nonprofit organizations maximize and sustain their return on investment in their Internet presence. Clients include Vira Manufacturing, Yale University, Accurate Box Company, The Big Green Egg, NJ Council for the Humanities, Paterson Public Schools, Paterson Education Fund, American Conference on Diversity, as well as many small- and medium-sized businesses and nonprofits. Barbara's innovative thinking has led to key improvements in the online enterprises of clients, who report significantly increased levels and quality of leads, sales, and customer relationships. Barbara, a frequent speaker on topics relating to her field, can be reached by e-mail at Barbara@bza.com, by phone at 973-890-0880, or by visiting: www.bza.com.

The Right Tech Tools
for Your Growing Business

by Susana Fonticoba

The longer you're in business, the more you can relax, right? Not so much, that is, unless staying at your current level of revenue is exactly what you want. How much you plan to grow is up to you—making sure you use the best tools today's technology has to offer is what my company, Right Click Advantage, does. In order for you to use technology to work smarter, get more done, and grow your business, consider the following:

Make the most of email. Whether you love it or hate it, you can't avoid email, so embrace what you can accomplish with it by using a product that is suited for business, is reliable, and can handle multiple communication avenues. I recommend Gmail or Microsoft Outlook because of the suite of productivity tools they offer. (If you're a Yahoo, Hotmail, or AOL user, continue to use it for your personal email.) For instance, Outlook and Gmail let you store client details in *Contacts*, keep abreast of your action items in *Tasks*, organize your time with *Calendar*, and keep the information flowing with email.

If you use Microsoft Outlook, the following five tips will help you stay organized and productive:

- Use a logical filing system. Let's say your company name is ABC Widgets. You get email about your product and networking events, as well as personal messages. To save time searching for a message, use a prefix for each file folder such as ABC clients, ABC marketing, ABC prospects, NET chamber, NET committee, NET events, PERS family, PERS friends, and PERS volunteer.

- Create *Categories* to sort the inbox contents according to the action you need to take. Categories might include Action Required, Wait for Answer, Schedule Appointment, Pay Invoice, and Read Later.

- Use *Rules* to automatically file incoming email that is not critical. This will keep your inbox organized and prevent a hot item from getting buried in the rubble.

- Use your *Task List* to manage each component of bigger projects, but don't let them sit there. Copy the task to your calendar so you devote time to getting it done.

- Store as much information as possible in the *Calendar* entry. If you plan to attend an event, you can include the address, directions, meeting participants, the contact's cell phone number, whether you've registered, etc.

Gmail can handle many of the same functions—but has different names for them. Instead of *Rules*, you create *Filters*. Instead of *Folders*, you create *Labels*. *Google Calendar* allows you to color code your appointments, as well as create multiple calendars to share with others. When key people in your circle use *Google Calendar*, you have access to their schedules, which makes it easier to plan meetings and other business events.

Keep data safe and accessible. For a monthly fee, there are services that will automatically back up the data from your hard drive every day. But you can ignore that route and use a virtual filing cabinet that is free—or almost free—instead. Now, as long as you have an Internet connection, your data is at your fingertips. And yes, it's safe. This is why companies like Dropbox are monstrously popular and Microsoft, Amazon, and Apple have their own cloud storage products.

The best line of defense against losing your data when (not if) your hard drive crashes (or your laptop is stolen) is this two-layer approach:

1. Use a portable external hard drive (getting less expensive every day) to store your bulk items, such as older files, videos, photos, and extra copies of your work. Don't waste your time or money on flash drives. You'll never remember what data are stored in which, and you'll be juggling multiple little drives. Just one external drive of 500 gigabytes or more is light and easy to carry in your business bag.

2. Use Dropbox or a service such as Amazon Cloud Drive for everyday filing. As long as you can access the Web, your important documents will be available when you need them. You can even access them from your smart phone or tablet—truly instant and portable.

Connect with your customers. My wish for you is that you have more clients than you can possibly hold in your head—and to help you with that, you will use a customer relationship manager (CRM). There are many excellent choices for a growing, small business with changing needs. My personal favorite is Batch Book. With most CRMs, you can customize by creating fields that track the details you need to remember about each person who is vital to your business. For instance, you can track the conversations, transactions, and goals of your prospects and clients. You'll even have the ability to pull up a list of "people I haven't reached out to in a while—but expressed an interest in this new product line."

In addition, a CRM allows you to include how you met the client, the client's preferences, what the client bought from you in the past, and when you should follow up. Your CRM helps you provide outstanding customer service beyond your email address book so you can turn your customers into loyal fans.

Share your expertise. Become the authority figure and go-to person your client reaches for first by sharing information with your audience on a consistent basis, using attractive and polished email marketing. I'm not talking about spam or letting everyone know how great your products or services are. I'm talking about educating your audience, so you become a valuable resource.

You accomplish this with a carefully cultivated contact list and a professional email creator such as Constant Contact. When you feed your clients mouthwatering information, they'll be eager for seconds. Use your account to deliver educational newsletters, postcards to follow up and reach out, brief tip sheets, and holiday greetings. Done right, your information will get filed, not deleted, and your phone will ring and your revenue will grow.

Many business owners—especially entrepreneurs—are either too busy or too weary of the barrage of changes to technology to make it work for them. But when you embrace it, technology can help build relationships and create loyal customers who are willing to buy what you have to offer and come back for more.

Susana Fonticoba is the founder and principle of Right Click Advantage, a subsidiary of Home & Office Computer Training. Her background spans twenty years of systems work at AT&T, where she specialized in project management, software documentation, and client training. Susana specializes in training small business owners to have the computer skills and the confidence in those skills to grow their business. She has served on the Board of the Hanover Area Chamber of Commerce, the Morris Chapter of the New Jersey Association of Women Business Owners (NJAWBO), and the First Presbyterian Church of Hanover. Susana was the president of Morris NJAWBO from 2010–2012 and was voted Business Woman of the Year in 2010. She can be reached by phone at 973-952-0053 or email at Susana@njpctraining.com. To learn more about technology for entrepreneurs, visit www.rightclickadvantage.com.

Marketing: Media

Secrets to Getting
Press in Magazines

by Cathy Black

Did you ever wonder how business owners and professionals you know (perhaps your competition) get quoted or featured in your local lifestyle or business magazine? You might think they have connections with the publication, but they are more likely to have one or more of the following:

- A publicist/public relations firm to pitch them to the editor
- The target publication's editorial calendar
- A great story that aligns with the publication's editorial calendar

How Editorial is Set

Putting together a monthly magazine starts by recognizing what its audience wants to read. Without content that interests its readers, the publication will not attract a large enough readership, which means no advertisers either. Both are the financial lifeblood of any publication—whether print or digital.

From a publisher's perspective, the editorial calendar frames the year's editorial lineup that reflects trends among its audience, community, or industry, and delivers articles that resonate with the magazine's readers.

Ideas for these stories stem from many sources: the editors' understanding of who their readers are (demographics, interests, and hot buttons), readers' suggestions, the advertising reps who bring feedback from their accounts, seasonal or current events, social or local trends (lifestyle publications), or specific industry trends (trade publications).

In terms of getting featured in a magazine, the main question for business owners is: What value, information, or insight do you offer its readers?

How to Pitch Your Business

Here are a few considerations to keep in mind, and some key steps to take, when you approach an editor with your story pitch:

Research the publication. Approach a publication that makes sense for what you do. If you are a retailer of high-end baby items, do not pitch to a commerce magazine unless your angle is business-oriented. Instead, find a lifestyle magazine whose readers want to know about the latest in cribs or baby clothes.

Check the magazine's editorial calendar, which lays out the entire year's stories. The editorial staff takes great care to assemble an editorial calendar for each issue. These calendars are generally available for advertisers and media professionals as a downloadable from the publication's website, or can be mailed upon request.

The editorial calendar breaks down the year by issues and details each edition's feature stories, special advertising supplements (if relevant), and the recurring columns. If your product or service fits, go for it. By reviewing the editorial calendar, you will find opportunities where you can contribute.

Pitch your expertise in a compelling way. Sell your expertise or business in a way that motivates the editor to call you for more information or an interview. If you have never written a story pitch, consider hiring a public relations professional to position you and handle your media relations. A feature press release—which focuses on the interests and concerns of the publication's readers—and a short, tailored story pitch are helpful when contacting an editor to ask him or her to think about including you in a story.

You are marketing your product or service, so a little promotion is acceptable. However, it is best to position yourself as a valuable resource who can provide input for an upcoming story or as a potential contributing writer on your area of expertise (samples of your work are helpful, as is a warm introduction by a mutual connection). If you are a supplier of a service that will be featured, demonstrate with photos and examples/case studies of how your company fits in with the particular article and provides value to the readers.

It's OK to show off your work (lush landscaping, that killer kitchen, the marketing success of the new website you designed), but do so in a way that will educate the reader about how you achieved the end result (and how they can do so as well). Ultimately, it's all about delivering value to the publication's readers.

Send in items for community pages. Many lifestyle magazines and local newspapers have community pages that showcase charity events and the people who sponsor or support them. Publications like to include photos and a short write-up about these events, and this fosters goodwill between you and the community. If you sponsor a charity event or are honored for your community service, contact the magazine to ask if a photographer can cover it. You can also send your own photos and a brief write-up after the event.

Submit your business seminars and workshops. Many media outlets have calendars of upcoming events and will include your business program. Target publications that support the local business community with free listings. Be mindful of deadlines for print publications, which might be months in advance (online versions have much shorter lead times). Keep the listing short and to the point by including the who, what, where, when, and how much. If you're not sure about what to include, model yours after the events already listed in the publication.

If you are sending out a press release, bear in mind that some publications will only print events that are free or that directly benefit the community. For a paid program, many print outlets prefer that you place a paid ad to promote it.

Use your connections. If you have a relationship with a publication, don't be afraid to refer a colleague to the editorial or advertising department. By vouching for your business associate, the editor or sales manager is more likely to listen to what that associate can offer readers. Conversely, don't hesitate to ask someone you know who has an in with a magazine to refer you as a feature subject for an upcoming story or special section.

When you do your homework, get to know your target publications' editorial needs, and polish your pitch—you are more likely to break through the clutter and land a feature role in an upcoming story.

 **Cathy Black** is the president and COO of Vicinity Media Group, Inc., with headquarters in Fairfield, New Jersey. Black joined Vicinity Media Group in its infancy in 1997 as a part-time events editor for its single title, *The Towne Crier*. Over the years, Black's responsibilities grew, and her passion for publishing played a key role in the company's growth. Today as president, she oversees all departments and makes key decisions in the daily operations of the company that produces two of North Jersey's leading lifestyle publications, *Suburban Essex Magazine* and *Vicinity Magazine*, with a combined circulation of more than 92,000. Black runs the company with her husband and business partner, David Black, Vicinity Media Group founder and CEO.

The Changing Face of Media: How to Survive and Thrive in the Blitz of New Media Platforms

by Lorraine LaShell

Thanks to technology, the global media landscape is forever evolving.

The printed word, which has been around for the last 500 years, makes it easy for the world to share knowledge and further the cause of human civilization. Even after radio and television arrived, the print news media thrived.

In the last decade, with the Internet expanding its worldwide reach, the demise of the printed word is becoming more of a reality. Newspapers and magazines are in steady decline, and the economic recession has only exacerbated the problem. And with the Internet pervading almost all aspects of life, people are reading less and increasingly consuming their news and information in ways other than from their morning paper or weekly magazine.

News sources like *The Huffington Post* are using innovative models such as bringing together loosely knit teams of a few hundred unpaid bloggers across the United States—as well as some in other countries—to write articles and posts. In fact, with *The Huffington Post's* model, half the content is derived for free from a team of blogger reporters (in real time), while the remainder is aggregated from news resources across the world. People are willing to write pro bono for *The Huffington Post* and other sites because it is prestigious to have their work read by millions of people online.

The fundamental point is that in the last few years, there has been a huge shift in the way people consume news and information. No longer is the traditional media the sole provider of up-to-date information. Professionally managed blogs and aggregators, offering relevant video and audio inputs (live or recorded) on the same platform, are filling an important void. And the traditional news media is playing catch-up—with most news media websites offering full content with relevant audio-visual inputs and user-generated content. Several blog publications are also available on phones, e-book readers, and tablets.

Adapting to New Media

With print readership falling and ad revenues disappearing, many surviving media companies have turned to the Web as a solution. But the Web hasn't solved the problem of falling revenues because no matter how good a newspaper or magazine's site, advertisers still won't pay as much to reach a Web reader as they will for a print reader. Plus, the print model does not translate well to the online platform, so media companies have had to learn new ways to present content online. Savvy advertisers demand metrics and click-through rates for their online ads. These are usually not good. Advertisers seeing undesirable click-through rates look elsewhere.

Publishers are not the only ones to blame for poor click-through rates. Banner ads tend to be boring and just sit on a site's page. Effective banner ads have interactive features inside the pane: buttons to e-mail the ad content, watch videos, set reminders for events, browse products in the picture, and even relay them via Twitter. Nothing technically fancy, just the addition of some useful functionality.

Media companies are continuing to evolve but are still a long way from successfully transitioning from print to online platforms.

Niche Markets and Silk Purse

There is, however, a bright spot on this horizon. Some niche magazines have successfully come through the worst of times by building their readership bases and using the Web in an intelligent way that does not detract from sales—but encourages them. Old-fashioned, good, incisive writing—as well as humor and fresh ideas—keep readers interested. Many advertisers are still willing to pay for print ads in an intelligent, well-designed magazine or media outlet that reaches a niche market.

Silk Purse Women falls into this category and has been successful because we…

1. Know our audience and stick to it. Founded in 2004, Silk Purse represents New Jersey women, aged forty and older. We don't try to cover the entire metropolitan area, but stay focused on our audience in our target geographic area with relevant editorial and advertising. *Silk Purse Women* has a reputation for authenticity and credibility with readers and advertisers.

2. Created a community. It is not only about the magazine, it has to be about the brand. At Silk Purse, we use our brand platforms to foster community with and for our readers. We produce events and provide environments for fun networking opportunities. We are one with our community and use our network to establish brand loyalty.

3. Provide information no one else does. *Silk Purse Women* is the only publication addressing the unique needs of women over forty in New Jersey. Our readers appreciate that we give them a voice.

4. Keep up with our audience. In a world filled with iPad apps and tweeting, we recognize what our audience expects of our publication in terms of technology. Not all of our readers use Twitter or invest in iPad apps. Although many are tech savvy, they still like to hold a magazine in their hands, flip through pages, and cut out and keep articles. It feels familiar to our demographic. We match our technology efforts with the pace of our audience's adoption.

What's Next?

For those of us in media, a crystal ball would be very useful. However, because that is not a realistic option, the next best is to continue to strive to stay on top of new media developments and to pick and choose what makes sense for our particular situation. We have to keep listening to our audience, respect their needs, and work diligently to give them what works for them.

Lorraine LaShell is executive vice president of sales and publisher of Silk Purse, LLC. She is responsible for the sales and marketing efforts of all *Silk Purse Women* media outlets: print, website, blog, and e-newsletters. Silk Purse has represented the pulse of women over forty in New Jersey since 1999 and has gained a reputation as a respected resource for timely and trusted information. Visit Silk Purse at www.silkpursewomen.com to learn more. Lorraine can be reached at lorraine@silkpursewomen.com or 973-689-4750.

Guerrilla Marketing for Serious Entrepreneurs: How to Build Buzz and Sales through Social, Digital, Mobile, and Other Thrifty Guerrilla Picks

by Pattie Simone

If you are starting or growing a business today, you need to be socially active and "connected" in as many spaces as possible. Why? Because it helps to organically boost your search engine rankings, sending better quality traffic back to your website. Second, millions of people use online sites, social platforms, and mobile tools to learn, research, connect, and ultimately buy products and services just like yours.

Your clients and prospects *expect* you to be accessible and present in real time, so free social spaces can help you reach, respond, and sell to larger numbers of people without leaving your office or breaking the bank. Here are the top eight digital and mobile tools and what you need to know to help leverage (and get better results from) your guerrilla marketing activities.

1. Pinterest—This visually focused channel is one of the fastest growing marketing and intel tools out there. An article posted by *Tonia Ries of The Real Time Report* (which shares nine tips to work this platform) says this: "Pinterest drives three times more traffic to the PediaStaff site than Facebook and has helped PediaStaff build a reputation as a real resource for pediatric therapists." The gist of Pinterest is that you create "boards" that visually showcase your favorite picks/links on any topic or area of interest. My tech startup WomenCentric has boards labeled "Books Worth Reading" and "Empowerment Quotes." Be true to your brand and your core mission, but the more creative you make your boards, the better sharing/follower stats you'll get. All of which helps to expand your digital footprint.

2. Google+—Connects people via "Circles" that Google+ has organized, as well as those you can create on your own, such as "Peers" or "Prospects." You can chat privately or publicly, and post videos, comments, and links, but "Hangouts" are the big thing—allowing you to invite up to ten people at a time to video chat.

Sarah Hill a KOMU-TV anchor has launched one of the first interactive socially charged news broadcasts using Google+ Hangouts, and she was one of the first to exceed 768,000+ in her circles. She does her live TV report, then talks with her preselected Google+ Hangout "crew" via her laptop on the set. The whole thing is broadcast live and recorded so thousands (or potentially millions) of people around the world can catch her interactive Missouri-based show, which she does three times a day.

I was recently interviewed on her live TV show from my kitchen table, while chatting with other Hangout "guests" from Pakistan, Canada, and a bunch of cities throughout America—so the potential learning, connecting, and promotional reach for your company is *awesome!* To see my interview on Sarah's interactive news broadcast, go to http://bit.ly/WomCentKOMU1.

3. YouTube—Authentic, interesting, and entertaining videos can be a gold mine for an entrepreneur. With a small investment (under $200 if you want HD/TV quality results), you can make terrific videos. Post them on a business YouTube channel, add them to your website, or include them in your e-mail marketing—all are *great* Google juice generators. Check out udemy.com, LearningAnnex.com, and YouTube for tutorials with creative scripting ideas, lighting and audio tips, equipment lists, etc., as well as postproduction and editing advice. Be natural, mike and light yourself properly, and share *useful* information. A super example of an easy-to-produce and effective video, filmed by a woman at her desk, can be found at http://bit.ly/WCenVid.

4. Twitter—This microblog lets you communicate, connect, and opine (and create new revenue streams) with current clients and new markets in 140 characters or less; the key is to be valuable. Use Twitter to observe trends and also get smart intel on competitors. While there are a few exceptions to the rule, businesses that steer clear of hype and overt sales messages at least eighty percent of the time can grow a real fan base, which can translate into more website traffic and tangible sales.

5. Facebook—Millions of people are on Facebook, so it's important to have a business page in this space. Your Facebook business page is a great digital guerrilla marketing pick because you can publish *exactly* what you want in order to position yourself as an expert, while positioning your company as a resource for information, tips, ideas, advice, etc.

6. Foursquare.com—A geosensitive mobile app that allows people to "keep up with friends, discover what's nearby, save money, and unlock rewards." Originally developed for restaurants and food service establishments, any business can reach new audiences via their tips option. Simply sign up for a free account and start posting helpful tips soon!

7. Blogging—Blog on your own site and on other people's sites. Search engines *love* valuable, new content, and so will prospects and clients who are actively searching for the kind of products and services you sell. Write editorial, not advertorial, and you'll attract quality traffic and fans.

8. E-mail marketing—This is still an excellent guerrilla prospecting, connection, and sales tool. Sent monthly, weekly, or quarterly, if it's filled with authentic, interesting content, your e-newsletter will get shared, you'll grow your list, and you're sure to gain some revenue.

Whatever you do, know this: make online marketing a key part of your marketing toolkit, whether you have $500, $5,000, or $50,000 to spend. Attend networking events, send out supertargeted direct mail to well-researched prospects, cold call, and post flyers—but also plant as many digital "markers" as you can in order to boost your organic search engine rankings to gain traction and sales. Devote one hour a day to a core group of marketing initiatives and you will start to see results.

Important Postscript

Before you begin any online activity, detail your objectives and know your target markets. Understand what they want, the best way to communicate with them effectively, and the spaces they spend time in. Choose one or two key spaces to be active in, so you can manage your other responsibilities.

Laura Fitton, aka @pistachio, and one of the first women to attract over 20,000 followers on Twitter (go to http://bit.ly/LFittonTwitter for a video interview), says to succeed in business today—whether you are opening a brick and mortar business, selling widgets virtually, or hawking life coaching services—you need to "listen, learn, care, and serve."

But how can "listening, learning, serving, and caring" lead to *ka-ching*? It's simple. People need to see or hear about you multiple times—at least ten times in fact—before you and your brand permeate their radar. If you're a cash-strapped entrepreneur, you can grow your "brandwidth" and sales using a smart mix of the above-mentioned free online spaces *and* some tried-and-true marketing standards such as networking, PR, and promo cards. I recommend an eighty/twenty split: eighty percent digital and mobile guerrilla activities to twenty percent offline guerilla promotions. Be strategic and present on a consistent basis—and watch your business grow!

Pattie Simone is a profit alchemist, small business journalist/vlogger, and consultant. Simone is the CEO of a tech start-up, WomenCentric, a hip directory and connection hub for professional women worldwide, and president of Marketing-Advantage and Write-Communications, innovative branding, communications, and new media agencies. Her tips and insight have been featured in *MORE* Magazine, WCBS Newsradio Wall Street Journal Small Business Report, *The Bergen Record*, MSNBC, ABC and FOX5 TV, and Entrepreneur.com. For information on growing your brand's digital footprint and sales, call Pattie at 845-362-7880 and check out WomenCentric's Facebook, Twitter, Google+, Pinterest, and YouTube presence.

Boost Your Credibility—Get Published!
Share Your Brilliance and Impart Your Expertise
with Your Very Own Book

by Donna R. Thompson

For a business owner, being recognized as an author is a powerful way to boost your credibility with your clients, prospects, and competitors—as well as with the public and the media. Authoring a book gives you the opportunity to show off your expertise and establish your authority. This leads to greater exposure for you and your company, which is followed by speaking engagements, more book sales, and in the long run—business growth.

The big question is: Do you have something to say? The bigger question is: If you write it, will they read it? Since your readers will invest time and money in your book, they expect to learn something new, take away lessons, or be inspired by fresh ideas, especially in an entertaining way. The best-case scenario for your readers would be to come away with a combination of all those things. If they do, expect to receive glowing testimonials and positive feedback.

Get Started

So, where do you start? First, think about your business—the products and services you offer—and how they solve problems and make a difference in people's lives. Do you help people save time, money, energy? Do you teach people how to live with less stress or be more organized? Next, identify your target audience. If you are a Web copywriter, for instance, one market is the people in your industry. In this case, your book could focus on improving copywriting skills: how to write eye-popping, lead-generating squeeze pages, autoresponders, and sales pages. Or, if your audience is business owners, you could focus on how to apply copywriting techniques to blogs and other marketing communications to increase sales. It's all about offering value to your readers.

Collect and Organize Your Content

Now it's time to gather any written content you've created for your business: blog posts, product and service descriptions, mission statement, press releases, Web copy, e-newsletters, articles, profiles, brochure content, etc. Do you provide helpful tips or information readers value? Are your blog posts more than just news about you or your products? If so, you can rework those pieces to form the foundation for your book. For example, you can group your blog posts by topic and create book chapters with them.

After reviewing your content and deciding on a topic for your book, segment your content into chapters by creating an outline. (Remember those outlines for high school and college papers?) Each chapter can be further organized using subheads. And, if your material lends itself to being grouped by major topic areas, you can use sections to house your chapters.

For example, if you're a doctor, your book could contain four sections: prevention, diagnostic measures, surgical options, and rehabilitation. The chapters within those sections could cover different types of preventive, diagnostic, surgical, and rehab methods (four or five chapters per section). And within a chapter, subsections could cover the descriptions and details about specific methods.

The point is to get an overview of what you will be covering in your book and break the material into easy-to-understand sections for your readers. These sections can serve as your table of contents.

Understand Your Publishing Options

When it comes to publishing a book, you have plenty of options. You can try the traditional route or you can self-publish—which has its own list of options. But it all comes down to time and money, as well as expertise, so consider the following carefully:

1. Traditional publishing is tough to achieve for a first-time author, but if it does happen (although it may take years), the author has little or no control over the book's title, content, or cover design. Authors may receive an advance (which is deducted from future royalties), and those royalties represent only a small (ten to fifteen percent) share of the profit on print book sales. You'll have to market the book yourself, too.

2. With self-publishing, one major advantage is going from manuscript to marketplace quicker than traditional publishing—months instead of years—whether a printed book or an e-book, and another is (in some cases) retaining the all-important control of your work. To self-publish, authors can choose from the following:

- Self-publish for free or a nominal up-front cost with an online service, such as LuLu, BookBaby, Smashwords, PubIt!, or CreateSpace, or with an online self-publisher, such as Author House, where you'll pay more. Either way, know that you'll be giving up profit share and/or paying for additional editorial or graphic design services, and with online self-publishers, you may not own your production files unless you buy them.
- Handle all the work and also become the publisher. This includes doing the editing, layout, proofreading, and cover design, and hiring a ghost-

writer if you need help developing your manuscript. Then there's the matter of copyright registration and attaining International Standard Book Numbers (ISBNs) and bar codes for your book. You'll need a different ISBN for each format you publish: softcover, hardcover, iPad, Kindle, Nook, pdf, etc. And you'll have to market and distribute your book yourself, too. Here, you take on all the responsibility to reap all the rewards.

- Work with a professional publishing consultant who handles every aspect of the publishing process. You will pay more for this option, but you will retain the copyright to and should have complete control over your work, and you can also expect to earn all or most of the profits from the sale of your books.

Because your book is a reflection of you (for years to come), you want it to look, feel, and "sound" like the expert you are. For busy business owners, it makes sense to invest in working with a professional publishing consultant—but the choice is yours.

Educate Yourself

Whatever path you decide to follow, visit the bookstore or library and look at the books in the section where your book would most likely fit. Check the competition to see how those books are formatted—how their sections and chapters are designed. Do they include any special sidebars or pull-out quotes or helpful hints? Will any of those features work for your book? There's more to publishing a book than just writing the copy.

The payoff comes when you sell your book in the back of the room at speaking engagements, give it to clients in appreciation for their business, donate it to your local and alumni libraries, and sell it on your website.

Are you ready to take your business to the next level? Then think about how you can share your brilliance, capitalize on your expertise, expand your scope, repurpose your blog content, add to your marketing collateral, and reap the benefits of authorship with a book.

Donna R. Thompson, a publishing professional for more than 35 years, is the owner and publishing director at Woodpecker Press, LLC, Bayville, New Jersey. The company specializes in helping authors self-publish—from idea to printed book and everything in between. Woodpecker Press is also the publisher of the Big Bold Business Book Series. For more information about self-publishing, visit www.WoodpeckerPress.com and also take a look at the books we recommend on our *For the Author's Bookshelf* carousel.

How to Craft the Most Compelling Pitch to the Media

by Inna Shamis Lapin

Oprah, Madonna, Martha Stewart, Rachael Ray, Kim Kardashian—they've all done it! But creating an image isn't just for the rich and famous. Brand credibility, power, and success are largely a matter of public perception. This is why business owners should take the following six steps before any media pitching efforts begin:

Step 1: First and foremost, it's about positioning yourself (your brand) above your competition. Start by asking yourself these three very important questions: (i) Am I an expert in my industry? (ii) Is my brand unique? (iii) What is my value proposition? Your answers will help you to do the following:

- Define the goals of your brand and/or public persona.
- Differentiate your brand from the competition and identify your unique selling point. Is there something unique and different about your brand? Do you provide a solution that did not exist before?
- Visualize your brand with quality marketing collateral. Think logos, website, packaging, images, etc.
- Project a powerful, credible, and believable image to your demographic/audience.
- Support your brand through social media marketing efforts via blog, Twitter, Facebook, LinkedIn, Pinterest, Google+, StumbleUpon, etc.
- Continually reinvent your image to stay newsworthy and timely.

Step 2: Most would agree that we do business with people we like, and we buy brands that we trust. For this reason, telling your story is extremely important and should be used to pitch media, so keep the following points in mind:

- Effective, emotional storytelling convinces and persuades audiences to pay attention and/or to buy!
- Identify what your personal story is (if there is one) and how it applies to your brand today.
- Craft a message(s) that will evoke a response—in other words, an emotional connection.
- Share these message points with media (while staying concise and on point).

Step 3: Every smart brand has the right tools in the toolbox. In this case, brands need the following ingredients in the media kit:

- Company background and history.
- Fact sheet.
- Product/service line sheets and/or look book/catalog.

- Biography of founder/CEO and executive team bios (if/when applicable).
- Most current press release announcement.
- High-resolution (color) headshots/product images (digital).
- Reel or B-roll (video footage if/when applicable).
- Business card/contact information.
- Samples (this applies to tangibles).
- Client/customer testimonials.
- Copies of recent press/articles in which the brand has been featured. Or consider condensing these in a listing of all recent/most prominent media placements in an "As Seen In" one-sheet (single-page) document.

Step 4: A press release is an important element in public relations—but it, too, is just one tool in the toolbox. While it is important to have when pitching the media, please note that press releases should never be sent without a pitch. (You would never send a resume without a cover letter!) Keep the following in mind when drafting a press release:

- Define the objectives of the announcement.
- Is the announcement relevant and timely?
- Make sure the copy is well written and succinct.
- Define your audience.
- Include a call to action.
- Avoid industry jargon or technical terms that most people will not recognize.
- Add quotes for impact of message.
- Follow standard press release guidelines: (i) a compelling headline and subhead; (ii) address the five Ws—who, what, when, where, and why—and how; (iii) include contact information and boilerplate language, which is standard "About Company" information used in press material; (iv) signal the end of the release with this symbol: ###.
- Make the press release interactive with hyperlinks and use SEO-friendly key words.
- Syndicate the press release on your website and with RSS (really simple syndication) feeds (blog).
- Never send press releases or any other materials via attachments to media contacts you do not have a relationship with. Spam filters will bounce e-mails.

Step 5: Now that the media kit is available and the press release is ready to go, to craft the most compelling pitch to the media, follow these guidelines:

- Do your homework. Know your audience; make sure you craft a pitch that will address their interests/concerns.
- Get your timing right. Tie your pitch into a media hot topic, holiday, and/or breaking news story. Does your brand fit in to something that's trending now?
- Media love numbers. Add any interesting statistics/figures; pull information from industry organizations, studies, etc. Frame your pitch in a clear way; show how your story relates to the audience.

- Skip the formalities; get to the point; be clear, concise, and consistent.
- Make sure what you write is well thought out and compelling.
- Spell check!

Step 6: Now it's time to pitch and follow up properly. Here are some pointers.

- Develop a media list.
- Understand lead times and deadlines.
- Know the right (and wrong) time to contact.
- Designate a spokesperson if you don't feel savvy enough to do the outreach yourself.
- Make friends with the media by developing a rapport with your top media outlets/contacts. Call and introduce yourself, even if you're not ready to pitch a story.
- Know your message points before pitching/following up—and stick to them.
- Always provide a phone number, e-mail, or website for those who want more information.
- Answer media requests in a timely manner.
- Provide concise reference materials/information such as a press kit, statistics, website, etc.
- If you have to leave a message, breathe and speak slowly. Say your name, company, and phone number at the beginning and end of your message.
- Be persistent. Since follow-up is key, always do so with an e-mail correspondence or with a phone call. Once you establish a rapport, you will learn their preferred form of contact.
- Be prepared for rejection, but do not let the word "no" stop you!

As you develop your efforts in pitching media, don't forget to keep your website, blog, social networks, and other marketing collateral updated. Finally, once your hard work pays off and you begin to reap the fruits of your labor, do not forget to leverage your media exposure—all of which can be used to drive even more brand awareness and media opportunities!

Inna Shamis Lapin is a seasoned communications expert with over fifteen years experience in PR, marketing, business development, and client management; and has worked with some of the world's most recognized brands. She also maintains extensive global contacts in the media/entertainment, consumer, beauty/wellness, travel/hospitality, and lifestyle sectors. Following a formative career in corporate America, Inna founded AvantGarde Communications Group—a full-service firm that offers expertise in PR, marketing, business development, and creative solutions. Much like a first-class couture designer, the firm tailors programs based on client needs, objectives, and more. Contact Inna at inna@agcomgroup.com, 732-385-1714, or visit www.agcomgroup.com.

Systems and Production

The Virtual Assistant:
The Busy Business Owner's Secret Weapon

by Felicia Lucco

You started your business to do what you love and what you're good at. Those who go into business as a virtual assistant (VA) are just like you. They choose to work as a VA because that's what they love and that's what they're good at. They rely on client referrals to keep working.

A virtual assistant is an independent contractor who works from her own office to support yours. She is a business owner providing a skilled, professional service—administrative support—and is not an under the table employee.

A competent VA has years of experience and can keep your business running smoothly. She will stay on top of the necessary administrative tasks so you don't have to, leaving you free to focus on your business. She can also function as a business partner. Wouldn't it be great to have someone with intimate knowledge of your business to bounce ideas off of, question a decision, or call your attention to something that's not quite right?.

Who Says You Can't Buy Time?

The average small business owner can spend up to sixty percent of his or her time on administrative work. These necessary tasks are at the core of any business, but you didn't go into business to do administrative work. As a business owner, your time should be focused on building your business and making money. This includes planning, marketing, and spending time with your clients. The biggest benefit you'll get from partnering with a VA is *time*.

A VA can be an invaluable asset when it comes to the tactical implementation of your marketing strategies. She can do the following:

- Set up and maintain your social networks.

- Update and maintain your website.

- Organize your contacts into a database from which she can execute e-mail campaigns, direct mail, newsletters, or personal calls.

- Create a customer relationship management system (CRM) to follow up with prospects and clients, and track your sales and marketing efforts.

This saves you hours and hours of time, maximizes your efforts, and potentially brings in new business.

Working with a VA Saves You Money

Think you can't afford it? Consider the cost of hiring a virtual assistant against doing the work yourself. If you spend ten hours per week on administrative tasks, and your bill rate is $100 per hour, that's $4,000 a month you're *losing* by not doing billable work!

You may have a hard time grasping how to work with a VA and insist on having someone in the office. But think about all the things you do online that just a few years ago were done in person, which include banking, taxes, registering your car, shopping, even dating! Today's VA keeps her skills up to date and knows how to work with online technology. She will be able to recommend the most efficient tools and methods to get your work done efficiently. With "in the cloud" computing, you and your VA can collaborate to work faster and smarter.

And working with a VA is more cost effective than hiring a full-time employee. A virtual assistant can condense a forty-hour workweek into ten to twenty hours, and you pay only for productive time on task. Plus, you save money on overhead expenses because a VA works out of her own office using her own equipment and does not require payroll, medical insurance, employment taxes, or a 401(k). In September 2011, the average cost for employee compensation was about 30.6 percent, according to the U.S. Department of Labor.[1]

Do the Math

The hourly wage for a virtual assistant is likely to be higher than the hourly wage of a full-time employee, but don't let that fool you. Do the math.

- Let's say you hire a full-time employee at $25 per hour: ($25 × 40 hours × 52 weeks) + 30.6% (taxes/benefits) = $67,912 annually.[2] (This also includes nonproductive time, plus the cost of office space and equipment.)

- Let's say you hire a virtual assistant at $45 per hour: $45 × 20 hours × 52 weeks = $46,800 annually—saving over $21,000! (This is for 100% productivity; when you're not using VA services, you don't pay.)

For small businesses operating from a home or shared office, hiring a VA just makes more sense. A VA is also a great choice for larger companies that have a staff, but need an extra hand on occasion or to cover extended absences. Oftentimes, a virtual assistant can supplement your current staff with additional skills.

How Do I Hire a VA?

When you hire a VA, you are contracting for a service just like you would hire a marketing expert or an accountant. Ask for referrals, or if you are considering someone you don't know, ask for testimonials and references. You want to ensure that your VA is reliable and trustworthy. Determine what you need, and then make sure she has the necessary skills to support you.[3]

Prices will vary depending on an individual's skill and experience. Remember that you get what you pay for. There are VAs who are trained and certified in specific areas such as social media, online event planning, bookkeeping, or realtor support—the kid next door is not. An experienced VA will have an agreement in place covering all of the details of her service, including confidentiality. Personality is also important, so suggest a trial period during which you can test your working relationship.

You may not find just *one* VA skilled in all aspects of your back-office needs. You may need several. This is where an experienced administrative consultant comes in. Acting as a project manager and coordinator, she will be your single point of contact and can facilitate building and managing your virtual team.

As with any purchase or expense, you must look past the dollar amount and consider the value. Partnering with a VA will add hours to your week— time you can spend nurturing your company's growth. What will you do with more time?

References

1. http://www.bls.gov/news.release/pdf/ecec.pdf; date accessed: Dec. 29, 2011.
2. According to Salary.com, the median salary for an administrative assistant (min. 5 yrs experience) in Essex county is $53,221 (approx. $25.58 per hour); date accessed: Dec. 29, 2011.
3. Very important: treating any VA as an employee can have serious implications with the Federal Government. See http://www.irs.gov/businesses/small/article/0,,id=99921,00.html for details on the distinction between an independent contractor and an employee; date accessed: Dec. 29, 2011.

Felicia Lucco, an administrative consultant and owner of *Your Cyber Partner*, focuses on supporting small businesses. With twenty-plus years in corporate, she has supported many sales and marketing teams, handling everything from basic administration to product documentation and participation in trade shows, including on-site supervision and logistics, keeping each project on track and on time. She later worked as a documentation specialist and technical writer, and has created several online help systems. Always a part of the marketing team, Felicia also earned a certificate in graphic design. With such diverse experience, Felicia now helps businesses save time and increase revenue using online technology to manage the back office. To find out how Felicia can help you, visit www.yourcyberpartner.com, call 201-258-4593, or send an e-mail to felicia@yourcyberpartner.com.

A Five-Point Efficiency Tune-up to Turn Your Business into a Peak Performer

by Donna Wasiak

Even the best run companies need to trim costs, purchase more efficiently, and create more defined policies and procedures. In fact, keeping costs in check and running a streamlined, efficient business are the building blocks to long-term success. To turn your business into a peak performer and leave your competition in the dust, follow these five steps.

1. Conduct a comprehensive business analysis. This detailed examination includes evaluating every aspect of your business including facility conditions, processes, employee responsibilities, ordering, billing, receiveables, payroll, and purchasing. For the best results, always include your employees. Interview them to assess morale, hear their concerns and ideas, and gain a clear understanding of how tasks are performed and completed.

The results will dictate the next steps and be used to develop a new work flow, sound budgeting, and facility updating, and to overhaul the existing policies and procedures manual (or draft a new one). Even solo practitioners or small businesses with a few employees can benefit from this type of analysis.

2. Employ a sourcing strategy. Cost-effective purchasing starts with a sourcing strategy. Through strategic sourcing, a company evaluates the products and services it purchases, which includes suppliers as well as expenses, to find ways to increase profits without compromising quality. Put simply, the goal is to identify waste, and to implement cost-effective, innovative approaches for sourcing goods and services.

3. Negotiate better prices. To get this ball rolling, examine invoices. Look for the high-volume items and how they are ordered. You'll often find hidden costs and overspending that can be remedied by negotiating better prices. Also, getting several bids for products and services can help you secure volume discounts or locked-in pricing for a specific time frame.

Work with vendors who offer corporate buying programs for stock items. Businesses with multiple departments or locations can benefit from these programs by getting better pricing on materials, services, and maintenance contracts through centralized purchasing.

Businesses with high-volume or multi-unit accounts typically receive more favorable pricing, especially from suppliers and distributors with national sales managers. Manufacturer rebate programs and long-term pricing locks also provide financial boosts for companies that qualify. Whether you have a single location or are a multi-unit retail chain, always ask about volume pricing, rebates, and long-term pricing programs.

Of course, relationships with vendors are crucial to maintain cost savings and on-time deliveries, so transparency is the rule. This means informing vendors of your status in a bidding process with other suppliers, sending a formal request for proposal (RFP), and soliciting recommendations on other noncompetitive sources.

4. Streamline workflow. Many established companies rely on policies, procedures, and systems that are obsolete and inefficient—especially in an age of computers and burgeoning technologies. The first step is to evaluate how your employees work, which could result in labor cost savings. You might discover that you can automate tasks, streamline workflow, or have employees share responsibilities or equipment.

For example, a firm that owns or leases a high-quality copy machine will save money and time because employees can do their own low-cost copying in house. Sending printing to one central printer/copier eliminates the need for and expense of individual printers at every workstation, and saves money on ink cartridges, too.

Of course, you want your employees' input. Get them involved by asking them what they do and how they do it. Once they're on board, show them how any improvements make their jobs easier without cutting corners. Besides boosting morale, you'll see improved productivity.

Other productivity boosters include using wireless technology in new ways, customizing software to your systems, or creating systems where there were none before. Be aware that implementing new efficiencies could lead to reducing staff. This difficult decision is typically based on your balance sheet and fiscal goals.

Don't have employees? Solopreneurs who often "do it all" themselves also benefit from learning where and how to institute time- and cost-saving measures.

5. Institute change management. Rather than force new ideas and systems on management and expect change to just magically happen, educate and train your managers so they become part of the process. As they change their thinking about how the company operates, it will resonate with all employees. By supporting management's goals and helping employees adjust to new systems, management will gain a firm understanding of the efficiencies. As a result, every employee develops new skills that save time and money.

Change is hard at first, but when employees see their environment is nicer and the workflow is more efficient, they'll buy into the new culture and become allies of positive change in the workplace. That's change management.

What does it take to analyze a company's operation and recommend changes that will save money and manpower and result in higher profits? The following is a list of key factors:

- A basic accounting background: To spotlight areas of opportunity for savings; this includes the ability to evaluate profit and loss statements, cash flow statements, and balance sheets.

- An analytical mind: To develop a strategic plan of how to save money.

- Creative thinking: To see the big picture and how all the pieces work together when shaping the sourcing strategy and operational efficiencies.

- Negotiating skills and experience with purchasing: To go after better pricing from vendors.

- Good people skills: To help managers and employees accept and integrate change into the operation.

Are you, the business owner, up to the task? Whether you hold all of these skills or your management team works together to analyze your company's operation, an outside efficiencies consultant can help you frame the process and initiate the changes that will improve systems, ramp up productivity, and increase profitability.

Donna Wasiak is the owner of Custom Purchasing and Business Solutions (www.custompbs.com), a business efficiency consultancy practice. Donna applies her extensive background in all phases of hospitality operations to her work with businesses in a wide range of industries to identify cost-savings opportunities. Key areas where she helps businesses become more efficient and improve the bottom line are purchasing, policy, and operational procedures. To start getting your business expenses under control, and increase your firm's profitability and employee productivity, e-mail Donna at Donna.Wasiak@gmail.com or call her at 973-868-3470.

Buried by Your Business?
An Organized Office Keeps You on Top

by Maria-Elena Grant

Don't be fooled into believing an unorganized office is not a distraction. Often, when people have stacks of paper cluttering their desk, office floor, and chairs, they claim to know where every piece of paper is and can easily find what they need. In reality, they are only fooling themselves and I believe they are just making excuses.

The truth is that an organized office has tremendous benefits in the following three vital areas:

- First, it is important to your financial performance. Being organized allows you to bill your clients sooner, pay invoices on time, and meet important financial deadlines because all of your financial papers are in the proper place.

- Second, it helps you to be more productive. An organized office allows you to easily find contact and project information. Time is not wasted looking for a phone number or a particular piece of correspondence.

- Third, an organized office shows that you are a professional. Stacks of paper are a sign that you are too lazy to file and can't manage your time. When clients, coworkers, or associates come into your office, they see an unprofessional, disorganized person—a person who cannot prioritize which papers, projects, and people are important.

So, how do you start to create a work environment that allows clearer thinking, higher energy levels, and improved concentration? There are two solutions, namely, hire a professional organizer or try (once more) to take it on yourself.

If you have failed at your previous attempts to get organized, it's time for help. Organizing is a professional service. It's a lot like working with a personal trainer. You know you need to go to the gym, eat less, and exercise more—but you need a trainer for motivation. Just like a trainer gets you in shape, a professional organizer gets your home and office space in shape.

Or, perhaps you worked with a business coach. Just as you benefit from working with a business coach to help you reach your career goals, a professional organizer will help you reach your goals of gaining control of your time and space.

If you do decide to work with an organizer, here's a tip: Organizers are not housekeepers. They are experienced at identifying and understanding the root cause of your disorganization. They pair this with their knowledge of solutions and systems that will help you function at optimum productivity. The proper organizing solution is one that is custom designed to your situation and needs.

However, if you still want to try it on your own, the following procedure makes organizing simple—not overwhelming:

- Begin with your files, the biggest contributor to office clutter. Commit to spend thirty minutes each day for one week purging your existing files. On day one, purge files A through E; on day two, files F through J; day three, files K through O; day four, files P through S; day five, files T through Z.

- Purge is the key word. Most filed documents never come out of the cabinet, so think about what you really need. When purging, look for duplicate papers, outdated guidelines and policies, drafts of documents that have been finalized, and clients or accounts that you no longer serve. Purge with a vengeance.

- If you must save documents for legal purposes, find a specific place for them. Archive them to a designated file cabinet, or store them in a different location.

- Standard documents can be recycled. Sensitive documents should be properly disposed of by shredding. If you need to shred on a regular basis, schedule quarterly service visits with a shredding company. If your needs are less, establish an annual shredding event.

- Once your files have been properly arranged, plan a yearly purge. I always schedule this for the week between Christmas and New Year's. It's a slow period for work activities, so I have the time to create and set up my files for the new year.

- Outdated technology is another overlooked source of office clutter. Do you still have some old equipment that you are holding on to just in case—equipment such as an old monitor, keyboard, or mouse? Digging deeper, do you still have supplies for equipment you no longer own, such as a carton of old fax paper or cartridges for an old printer that is long gone?

If you hesitate at the thought of disposing of equipment, you're not alone. It's hard to part with, especially an expensive purchase or an item that worked when you last used it. I understand. It's difficult to dispose of something that is still in working condition. However, it is outdated and difficult to donate. Schools and charitable organizations cannot use outdated equipment. They have the same need to keep up with technology as everyone else. There is no need to keep this equipment. Technology has moved on, and so should you.

- Conquer cord clutter, too. First, check that all the cords are actually connected to something. Almost every time I do an office organization job, I find cords and cables all tangled up, no longer connected to anything.

- If you happen to be upgrading your office desk, consider purchasing one with built-in power strips. These allow for hookups of computers, monitors, printers, cell phones—almost any device.

It all comes down to the fundamental concept of organization: You only need what keeps you current and moves you forward. Think about the level of achievement you have set for yourself, and don't allow clutter to slow down your business. My advice to business owners boils down to this: Having an organized office shows that you are on top of your business, not your business on top of you.

 **Maria-Elena Grant** loves to hear her clients say, "Wow!" She is the principle interior decorator and organizing consultant for Awesome Rooms, LLC. The company offers decorating, organizing, and staging services. It can best be described as providing any service that transforms your space into rooms that are awesome. Maria-Elena also teaches, lectures, and conducts seminars on a variety of decorating, organizing, and staging subjects. Awesome Rooms has designed rooms for charities, helping to raise funds for their causes. Maria-Elena holds a certificate for interior design and is a custom decorating consultant for Metropolitan Window Fashions in Paramus, New Jersey. To find out how to put the *wow* into your home or office space, contact Maria-Elena by phone at 973-853-8126 or e-mail at awesomerooms@optonline.net.

Launching Innovative Products in Today's Competitive Marketplace

by Zoe Vaklinova

All great ideas are born in the mind of a single person. Conceived through a sudden moment of inspiration, great ideas have the power to transform into innovative products that change the world. Think of Thomas Edison's work with electricity, and Steve Job's vision behind Apple's revolutionary products: the iPod, iPhone, and iPad. Today, we could not imagine our lives without those inventions.

As an inventor and an entrepreneur myself, I would like to share some insight on how to best launch your products. By outlining the four key lessons I learned on my journey, I hope to bring clarity and direction to where entrepreneurs and business owners should focus their attention in order to succeed.

Lesson 1: Clear Vision Is a Must

The first thing innovative products have in common is a clear vision of what they should look, feel, and be like as finished products. In 2010, when I came up with the idea to create a dairy-free version of cheese that I could incorporate into my newly adopted vegan diet, I knew exactly what I wanted it to look, taste, and feel like. Growing up in Bulgaria, my grandmother, who was a master in fermentation, made some of the most delicious dairy cheeses and yogurts I have ever tasted. Her version of Feta cheese was outstanding!

With determination, I set out to create a nondairy version that closely resembled the Feta cheese I fondly remembered from my childhood. Using organic, raw cashews as the base, I applied my grandmother's fermentation technique—and after much experimentation, my Feta-style Nut Cheeze was born.

Having a clear vision of your finished invention makes it easier to execute and perfect the product you are working on. The last thing you want to do is use up your funds, time, and resources on a broader concept that may or may not work. The more precise you are, the more likely you are to succeed.

Lesson 2: Research and Development

Launching an innovative product is not an overnight process. Unlike existing products, new ideas do not come with manuals or guarantees to work. From the moment of conception to the moment of finalized production, be prepared to invest much time and effort in research and development.

It took two years for my Cashew Nut Cheezes to evolve into better versions. From conducting tasting events, to gathering feedback, to sending samples to food science labs, to studying shelf life, to tweaking ingredient ratios, to refining taste—I was able to gauge what appealed to the customer and what needed improvement. Consequently, my latest version is *so* much better than the initial version.

Rushing your invention out the door before it has undergone adequate testing may set the stage for disappointments and failure. Take the time to research thoroughly and make improvements before releasing your product or service on the market. You only get one shot to impress your customers, and if you miss, you may lose them for good.

Lesson 3: The Power of Trademark

Once you have an innovative product, it is only appropriate to give it a unique name so that it can stand out in the crowded marketplace. Following months of search, combining all kinds of words and phrases, RAWbundant was born out of "raw" and "abundant," standing for foods abundant in raw ingredients. When I typed it in Google and saw almost no results, I knew I found the right name!

Within days of finalizing my company name, I filed for trademark with the U.S. Patent and Trademark Office (USPTO). Nine months later, I received an approval, and RAWbundant is now a registered trademark. When you Google RAWbundant, all the results point to my company. And from a search engine optimization (SEO) standpoint, we have already established a dominant place on the Web.

Picking a unique name for your innovation and registering it as a trademark will give you protection from future imposters, and a significant advantage of brand recognition once your product is out in the marketplace and people are searching for it. To learn more about trademarks, visit www.uspto.gov.

Lesson 4: To Patent or Not to Patent

A patent for an invention is the grant of a proprietary right to the inventor, issued by the USPTO. Generally, the term of a new patent is twenty years from the date on which the application for the patent was filed. It gives the holder the legal right to exclude others from making, using, or selling the invention.

Unlike trademarks, filing for a patent can be a costly and long process. Based on the complexity of your invention, an attorney may charge you fees ranging from a couple of thousand dollars to several thousand dollars to file the application. For a new entrepreneur starting with little to no funding, this may present a considerable challenge.

Another factor to consider is that patents require full disclosure of how your invention is made, which becomes public record. You may be protected from others trying to copy your exact product, but it does not stop them from making alterations and selling similar products. To determine what is best for your invention, visit www.uspto.gov and consult an attorney who specializes in intellectual property.

No matter what industry you specialize in, considering these four lessons will put you on the right path to a successful product launch by streamlining the process, which will save you money, time, and effort. Think of them as the foundation of a house. If you don't build it strong and resilient in the beginning, everything you add will crumble when destructive forces strike.

I would like to add one last piece of advice: Bringing an idea to life is a very exciting but very challenging journey. Be prepared to go through many ups and downs. Recognize that failing is part of success. Learn from what doesn't work, so you can better yourself and your product with each new trial. And remember that an idea powerful enough will find its way to realization as long as you are one hundred percent committed to bringing it to life.

Zoe Vaklinova is the president and founder of RAWbundant, a line of premium living foods based out of Linden, New Jersey. Prior to launching her business in 2010, Zoe worked in the public relations and special events field, where she gathered invaluable experience and knowledge on the best practices to launch and execute marketing campaigns. She started RAWbundant after undergoing successful weight loss and improving her health on a high–raw food diet. An avid health and wellness blogger, Zoe credits her desire to help improve the lives of others as what inspired RAWbundant to life. Her products are organic vegan foods, free of processed sugar, dairy, soy, and gluten, making them appealing to a wide range of people with specific diet needs, allergies, and lifestyles. Learn more about RAWbundant at www.rawbundant.com or at www.zoevblog.com. You may contact Zoe directly at zoe@rawbundant.com.

Go with the Flow:
How Workflow Optimization Maximizes Profitability

by Diane A. Lombardi

Every corporate goal has one or more of these underlying objectives:

- Make money
- Retain customers and keep them happy
- Optimize the employees' work environment to generate the highest productivity levels.

With the exception of the people component, the only thing that really matters is the "how." Once you add the "how" to the "who"... "It's ALL About the Process"®.

Every task you perform has the components of a manufacturing production process: Raw Materials, Work In Process, and Finished Goods.

For example, to make your morning coffee, you gathered your Raw Materials of water, coffee, electricity, etc. While it is brewing, it is your Work In Process. When the coffee is in the cup and ready to drink, you have your Finished Good. Or, when you buy a house, your application, credit report, appraisal, etc., are your Raw Materials. When your application package goes through processing, underwriting, etc., it is Work In Process. When it closes, the Mortgage and Note are your Finished Goods.

Therefore, as a business owner, it would make sense to use the best quality, most cost-effective Raw Materials, while expending the least amount of high-caliber effort to convert those Raw Materials into optimum Finished Goods. So, to optimize the process and maximize your profits, you must first analyze your process flows.

In our daily lives, most of our tasks are performed without a focused thought process. When you made your coffee, you did not need to create a written plan, you simply performed the steps. So how does this apply to your workflow in your business environment?

Assuming you have established your business goals and plans, along with the associated risks, you can now look for opportunities to optimize. In this arena, the approach is formalized to include the following steps:

1. Analyze the workflow processes
   a. Assess the technology

Jersey Women Mean Business! Big Bold Business™ Advice from New Jersey Women Business Owners 293

© 2012 Diane A. Lombardi
Published by Woodpecker Press, LLC

2. Identify the needs

3. Select a solution(s)

4. Implement the solution(s)

This approach uses Flow Diagrams to capture all inputs and outputs of the work process, whether automated or manual. The initial Flow Diagram will depict only your major tasks. Then, as you proceed with the analysis, each major task will be broken down into its components, each with its own diagram, and then those components into more diagrams, and so on, until you have the details for each individual step in the workflow.

Figure 1 shows the simplified flowchart symbols that we will use for our diagrams. (Creative liberties have been taken with the definition of these symbols.) A benefit of diagramming your workflow utilizing flowchart symbols is that technical people understand them. So, when you are trying to communicate your needs to IT, you can always show them your picture.

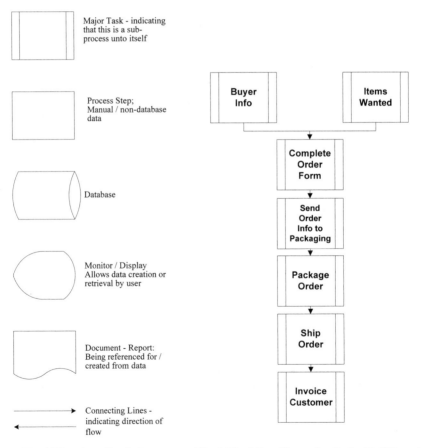

Fig. 1 Flowchart Symbols   **Fig. 2 Workflow Example: Order Fulfillment**

Figure 2 uses these symbols to define the workflow of the sample business process of order fulfillment.

Choosing to expand the task "Complete Order Form," we can add the inputs and outputs, along with the tools currently used to provide them. However, before adding the annotations for these tools, you need to do a technology assessment to determine if your technology is:

1. 100% outsourced or 100% in-house
2. A combination of outsourced and in-house
3. None of the above
4. What's "technology"?

Now, with the addition of the above components, Fig. 3 shows what our expanded task looks like.

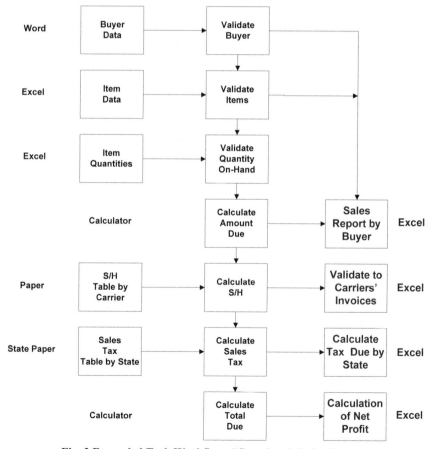

Fig. 3 Expanded Task Workflow: "Completed Order Form"

As you were expanding the task, you were able to identify specific process issues, including:

- Holes
- Bottlenecks
- Duplicate efforts
- Frustrating current practices
- Pure needs

But before you move forward with this information, it is important to spend time with staff and management to create a list of their thoughts and ideas regarding the existing workflow.

Utilizing the task's Flow Diagram, the identified process' issues, and the "Thoughts and Ideas" list, you are finally ready to answer the following questions:

- What do we *really* need to be 100% effective and efficient?
- What existing processes need to be changed?
- What currently automated processes need to be modified/upgraded?
- What automation (technology) can be leveraged to improve the process methodology? (Remember: NEVER automate for the sake of auto-mation.)

Now, keeping those answers in mind, go back and update the "Thoughts and Ideas" list, categorizing each entry as follows:

1. **Must** = Must Change
2. **Need** = Need to Change
3. **Nice** = Nice to Change
4. **Hmmm** = Brainstorm

Next, you have to prioritize these needs, bearing in mind that you must also be able to define both your tangible and intangible gains. Once you have created your list of requirements, annotate the process Flow Diagram (see Fig 4.) to identify these needs.

Now you know:

- Where you are
- Where you want to go
- The critical components necessary to get you there

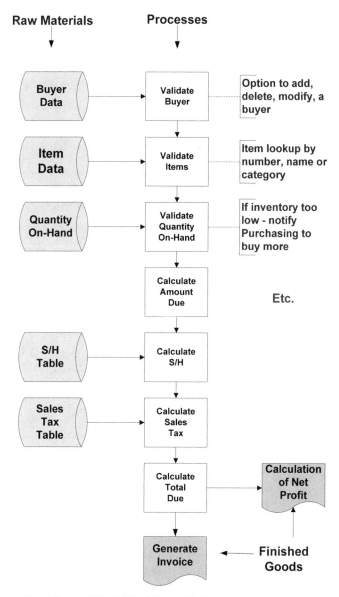

Raw Materials **Processes**

Buyer Data	Validate Buyer	Option to add, delete, modify, a buyer
Item Data	Validate Items	Item lookup by number, name or category
Quantity On-Hand	Validate Quantity On-Hand	If inventory too low - notify Purchasing to buy more
	Calculate Amount Due	Etc.
S/H Table	Calculate S/H	
Sales Tax Table	Calculate Sales Tax	
	Calculate Total Due	Calculation of Net Profit
	Generate Invoice	← Finished Goods

Fig. 4 Revised Task Workflow with Requirements Defined

But there are still a lot of tasks ahead of you. You have to:

- Select your Solution
    - Decide if it can be provided in-house or if outside resources are necessary
    - Determine your ROI (Return On Investment)

- Bring key players up to speed, remembering that their buy-in is essential.
- Create your Project Plan with milestones
- Complete the Project
- Update your Flow Diagrams, Process Analysis documents, etc.
- Create your User Guides
  - Process Manuals
  - Quick Reference Guides
- Train your staff
- Implement your Solution—Go Live!
- Perform a Post Implementation Review (aka a Post Mortem)

As you can see, once you begin to use Flow Diagrams to analyze and then optimize your workflow, your business cannot help but be profitable while outdistancing the competition.

Diane A. Lombardi is the CEO of MindBulge, a company that specializes in process reengineering, productivity management, and custom software solutions. MindBulge helps her clients achieve their corporate goals while minimizing expenditures, condensing time frames, and maximizing profits—enabling them to gain a competitive advantage in the marketplace while acquiring and retaining clients. With more than thirty years of professional experience in the Information Systems and Technology field, both domestically and internationally, Diane has a unique combination of skill sets in that she speaks both "business" and "geek." Her senior-level management experience is very diversified, having worked in banking, manufacturing, finance, distribution, human resources, sales force automation, Internet start-ups, website design/development, and e-commerce. Most recently, she has held CIO, CTO, and Sr. Vice President of Operations positions in the Mortgage Banking industry. She has taught Information Systems and Technology courses, as well as Project Management, for the University of Phoenix Online. She holds a B.S. in Accounting from Elizabethtown College, and an MBA in Management Information Systems from Rutgers University. To find out more, contact Diane at 973-734-1733 or Lombardi@mindbulge.com, or visit www.mindbulge.com.

Work-Life Balance

Making a Life
versus Making a Living

by Bonnie Jerbasi

This is your life. Do what you love, and do it often. If you don't like something, change it. If you don't like your job, quit.

Work is such an integral part of our lives that we should not settle for anything less than a job we love. Yet the trick to having a balanced life and blending work and play lies not in what you do, but in how you view what you do. If you are stuck in a dead-end job and believe you cannot quit, change your attitude and become more positive, being grateful for all that is working well in your life. View your job in a new light, and watch how your life takes a positive turn.

I am here to assure you that you will survive a change of jobs or even careers. You can quit your job and start your own business if that is your dream. The important thing to remember is the goal of every day of your life should be to experience joy. This is the number one rule of being a successful businessperson, whether you "work for the man" or are an entrepreneur. The old adage, "Do what you love, and you'll never have to work a day in your life," holds true.

I have been a New Jersey lawyer since 1986. Over the years, I have worked for the man as well as run my own businesses. I prefer the latter. The freedom you experience from having your own candy store outweighs the fear and lack of security that goes hand in hand with starting out on your own.

Who Will You Follow: Fang or Buddy?

If you approach entrepreneurship on an organic and instinctive level and follow your intuition along the way, you will succeed in making a life for yourself that integrates work and joy. As sociologist and author Martha Beck wrote in her article, *How to Tune in to the Voice Within*:

"This very day, two individuals are vying to be your personal adviser. The first, whose name is Fang, dresses in immaculate business attire, carries a briefcase full of neatly organized folders, and answers all e-mails instantly, via BlackBerry. In a loud, clear, authoritative voice, Fang delivers strong opinions about how you should manage your time . . .

"The other candidate, Buddy, wears shorts, a tank top, and a rose tattoo. If you question the professionalism of this attire, Buddy just smiles. When you ask advice on a pressing matter, Buddy hugs you . . .

"Who will you hire to advise you?"

Of course, the world trains us to follow Fang in order to survive a cutthroat culture, especially in business matters. Fang tells us we don't measure up, and that we need to work harder and worry more and be organized to within an inch of our lives.

Buddy, on the other hand, brings peace and joy into our lives. He doesn't take himself too seriously, and he takes the time to smell the roses. Buddy can be my consultant any day of the week!

But this is not to say that Fang does not have a place in your business. Business plans and budgets are useful tools. However, many people who start with a business plan and budget quickly plummet from the exhilaration of being their own boss to the terror of feeling they can never do enough to make it succeed. No matter how prepared you think you may be, running your own show can be overwhelming.

House Call Attorney

When I ventured out on my own, I did what I most often do in my life: I followed my heart. I wanted to have a unique approach to law, and I came up with the idea to offer house calls to my clients. After doing research and discovering that no one in the area offered house calls, I grabbed up the domain names, set up a website, and ran with it.

Today I am the "House Call Attorney." I meet clients in their homes, offices, assisted-living facilities—even Starbucks. I like the fact that I am not stuck behind a desk all day. I practice family law and I am a trained divorce mediator. I also have a general practice as well. My business model has enabled me to meet some extraordinary people. I have done wills and estate documents for those too ill to make a trip to an office, and I have built my business through referrals—the best way to organically grow a company.

But when I first started House Call Attorneys, I discovered that instead of working a fifty-hour week, as I did in the law firms, I worked a seventy-hour week that included midnight brief writing and weekend work. That is not what I signed up for. Add to this the fact that I was not only the rainmaker—networking and bringing in new clients—I was also the bookkeeper, receptionist, accountant, and lawyer.

Most entrepreneurs wear many hats at the beginning, and that is fine. However, once there is extra income, it is wise to start delegating tasks. Using a virtual office can be a lifesaver. These organizations offer a wide array of services, from receptionist to bookkeeping, for businesses. By taking advantage of the professionalism and convenience of the virtual services, you will be free to concentrate on the aspect of the business you enjoy.

Eventually I learned I could have it all: a successful practice and free time to live my life outside of work. Simple solutions such as setting up boundaries for my workday and shutting off the business cell phone at 6:00 p.m. each week night, and turning it off completely on the weekends and holidays, did the trick. Did I lose a client or two by doing this? Probably. But the upside is I have a life.

Balance is the key to success in any endeavor. Being a successful entrepreneur is no different. While it is tempting to get carried away with working long hours when you are your own boss, it is important to remember that your clients will suffer if you are not well rested and balanced.

When you live your dream and share your passion, the way you make your living will automatically afford you a good life. So follow your intuition and truly enjoy what you do for a living. So what if you don't make that million-dollar mark? If you're happy every day—that's priceless.

 **Bonnie Jerbasi, Esq.,** founder of House Call Attorneys, has practiced law in New Jersey since 1986. She is experienced in diversified legal areas, including complex civil litigation, family law mediation, collaborative divorce, contested divorce, commercial law, contract law, chancery matters, real estate, wills, estates, guardianship, and business law. Bonnie is a Court-Approved Family Law Mediator. Personal energy management and life balance are cornerstones to success in both her work and personal life. Spiritual growth and helping others, as well as time spent with family, are her joy. To learn more, contact Bonnie by e-mail at bonnie@housecallattorneys.com, phone at 973-459-5923, or visit www.housecallattorneys.com.

Seven Healthy Habits of Highly Productive Business Owners

by Donna Perillo

Are you guilty of neglect? Yes, you, busy business owner—I do mean you. I know you never stop thinking about ways to grow and improve your business. Whether it's keeping up with the latest technology, adding products or services, establishing a social media presence, or building stronger customer relationships—you pay attention to the things that will help you produce more and grow your business.

And like most business owners (including me), you have systems in place and procedures to follow that help you and your staff stay productive and keep your business running smoothly. This is all well and good, but what about you? Do you pay attention to *you*?

Owning a business is demanding and stressful, so when you don't pay attention to your most valuable asset—which is *you*, busy business owner— you are guilty of neglect. And the one thing that can make a huge difference in your stamina and productivity—but often gets the least amount of attention—is your health and well-being.

Optimal Health: What You Can Do to Be Your Best

Nothing feels better than feeling good. You exude energy and enthusiasm. You know it, and so do the people around you. But how do you sustain that energy? You start by paying more attention to *you*—and what you do—or don't do—in these three major areas: physical, emotional, chemical.

Put simply, physical includes movement and exercise, emotional includes your attitude and belief system, and chemical includes the food you eat, the products you use—even the air you breathe.

In your quest to be your best, assess how you're doing in each of the seven categories listed below. Once you know where you stand, you can develop a routine to stay healthy and highly productive. Of course, make sure you check with your health-care provider before you begin any new program.

Physical

1. Exercise: Start moving. Regular exercise controls weight, fights diseases such as high blood pressure, and lifts your energy and mood. Aerobic exercises such as walking or biking build heart and lung capacity. Strength-bearing exercises such as circuit training or lifting free weights help increase muscle mass and bone density. Yoga increases flexibility and induces relaxation.

2. Chiropractic Care: Regular chiropractic care helps to keep your muscles and joints healthy. Most people think of chiropractic for back and neck pain because it is so effective for these conditions. However, did you know that a chiropractic adjustment allows your nervous system, which controls every function in your body, to function more efficiently? It also allows your blood vessels and lymphatic vessels (part of your immune system) to flow more freely.

Emotional

3. Attitude: Do you see the glass half full or half empty? To improve your attitude, pay attention to your thoughts and emotions. This is not an easy thing to do, but with practice, it gets easier. Try to stay in an uplifted, happy state, especially when dealing with people. What message do you send to the people around you? How do you treat your family, your friends, and your team? How do they perceive you? Ask them, but be prepared for some honest feedback.

4. Visualization: This is a powerful tool that most people do not take advantage of. We all daydream and let our imagination run wild. The question is, what do you think about when you are daydreaming—or at night before you fall sleep? Are you thinking about the good things that happened during the day, or about the negative or bad things that happened? You are in control of your mind, so visualize yourself in positive situations. Visualization is a powerful tool; use it to your advantage.

Chemical

5. Diet: What's on your plate? Most people think they eat well, but don't. Why? One major reason is they try every new "miracle" diet available. But diet and nutrition are not cookie cutter in nature. There is no such thing as "one diet fits all." For instance, do you suffer from food allergies or sensitivities? Do you have digestive issues such as reflux, constipation, diarrhea, or irritable bowel syndrome? Do you have any conditions such as diabetes or heart disease? Are you taking any medications? All these factors must be considered when you seek the best diet for *you*.

6. Supplements: Do you take anything to supplement your diet? If so, how do you know you are taking what you need? Assessing your nutritional status is very important, and there are many ways to do it. There is blood testing, which most people are familiar with, but there are also other ways to test your health status. Hair analysis for mineral and heavy metal status, saliva testing for hormones and neurotransmitters (brain chemicals), and muscle testing (kinesiology) are just a few methods available to health-care providers to pinpoint nutritional deficiencies and recommend steps for improvement.

7. Environment: Where you live, the air you breathe—even your food and beverage choices—can be toxic. Do you realize that toxins can cause many diseases such as cancer and autoimmune disease, as well as fatigue and weight gain? Do you do anything to remove the toxins from your body? There are many ways to do this. A colon cleanse, liver cleanse, detox foot baths, far-infrared saunas, enemas, and chelation therapy are a few ways to rid your body of toxins. Your environment impacts your overall health, so don't ignore it.

As a business owner, your patients, clients, or customers depend on you to help solve their problems. And if you're like most business owners I know, you rarely take time off, even when you're ill. That's why it's important to adapt healthy habits based on these seven categories. Not only will you reduce or eliminate your sick days, but you'll have more energy and be more productive. But here's a final thought: Wouldn't you rather take a well day than a sick day? You can—busy business owner—when you stop neglecting *you*!

Dr. Donna Perillo, DC, NMD, CNS, has combined her experience as a chiropractor, nutritionist, naturopath, musician, and composer to help her patients achieve a state of optimal health and well-being. Testing and treatment is customized to the needs of each individual. If you are interested in improving your health and boosting your productivity, contact Dr. Perillo by phone at 973-872-2133 or e-mail at drperillo@aol.com, and visit njtotalhealthcenter.com and arthriticise.com.

A Blissful Business Journey: What Passion and Confidence Do for Your Business

by Philomena Servodio

I'm sure you've heard this before…

If money is your passion and you work hard enough, you will acquire it. If power is your passion and you work hard enough, you will obtain it. If material abundance is your passion and you work hard enough, you will possess it. But when your work is your passion, it's no longer work, but a joy, because you are blissfully engaged.

Applying this wisdom to the work that you choose begs the question, "What is your passion?" Do you know your essence? What drives you to do what you do? Why are you in the business you are in? Do you like it or love it? Is it the work that motivates you or the by-product of the work?

So, how does one discover passion, increase it, or better yet—develop it? Passion is not an organizational skill that you can simply learn. The most prominent universities cannot instill passion; they can only provide you with the tools to pursue it. Passion is innate. When you are passionate about something, you feel it.

Passion (or lack of it) is evident in everything you do in life. It's *that* something that lies deep within you, burning strong and yearning to come out. It drives you and your business. It is a part of who you are and your belief system. It is *that* something that defines your life and pushes you to work past your fears and insecurities. Your desire to fulfill your passion will sustain you when facing obstacles—the bumps in the road and the growing pains that all businesses experience. That is reality.

Your belief in who you are, what you do, and how you do it will empower you to rise above the setbacks. That's the kind of fire you need to persevere and manifest your dreams. This path, however, is not for everyone. Some people have limiting beliefs and choose to play it safe, so they remain within their comfort zone. But when you have big aspirations, passion will ignite you. Passion will keep the fire within burning.

Worst Moment Inspires Business

Personally, I have been caring for my mother since her liver transplant in 1993. My mother's medical needs inspired me to become a social worker, specializing in geriatrics. I later resigned from my position because my father was diagnosed with terminal lung cancer. I found myself having to provide care for both my mother and father.

The eight months of caring for both parents left me drained and vulnerable. Regardless of my vulnerability, one reality remained the same: I had to earn a living. When my father passed away, it became clear to me that I did not want anyone else to endure the type of pain I had experienced while caring for him. My passion was ignited by the love for my father and my sense of responsibility to my mother. Therefore, the worst moment of my life became the inspirational moment that motivated me to follow my path, so my first business was born.

When Passion Isn't Enough

Unfortunately, passion alone was not enough to make that business a success. My heart was in the right place, but I lacked the other key ingredient—confidence. I knew I had excellent credentials, but I did not have enough real-world business experience. I did not possess the know-how—the knowledge to make the business a success. I was very good at being a social worker, but I was far from a savvy business owner. So I dissolved the business and went back to work to gain more experience.

Eight years later, I established my second business, Medicaid Pros, LLC. Now clients, as well as other professionals, refer to me as an expert in my field. The years I spent working for someone else gave me time to mature, gain experience as a professional, and acquire the business skills I needed to run my own business. For instance, I had to become proficient in areas that I wasn't as concerned about as an employee, including networking, time management, marketing, technology, and even public speaking. (It also gave me the confidence to write this chapter for the book you are reading.)

My first business could have been perceived as a failure, but it was actually a launching pad to my future success. This is because the passion to serve never left me. Time allowed me to turn a true passion into a needed business that enables me to serve my clients at the highest level.

In my current business, I am successful because my passion is in *balance* with my confidence. Confidence is the reflection of your skills, knowledge, and life experience. You need to believe that you really are good at what you do, be able to project that to others, and exude your confidence in a healthy, positive manner. You do not need to become an egomaniac, but a strong sense of who you are as a business owner is a requisite. Your desire to grow and to improve within your field should be a lifelong process.

My advice to you, which I strongly recommend, is that you pause and get to "know thyself" before you pursue future business endeavors. Knowing where your passions lie and being totally confident in what you do will determine your level of success. Although it is important to know how to develop a business, you can learn that. But if you are not passionate and confident, you may end up with great skills and a business that does not thrive. Following your heart's desires in a prepared and intelligent manner will earn you a blissful life.

I have been inspired by the late Joseph Campbell, who said, "Follow your bliss and the universe will open doors where there were only walls." I wish all of you who are feeling inspired a blissful journey.

 Philomena Servodio, LSW, is the founder and president of Medicaid Pros, LLC, a geriatric care management company located in Nutley, New Jersey. She has years of experience as a medical social worker, where she was responsible for patients' psychosocial assessments, applying for state/federal benefits, discharge planning, patient education, and advocacy. She also has expertise in hemodialysis, where she provided supportive therapy, benefits coordination, and care planning to patients with end-state renal disease. The company focuses on meeting clients' specific needs, which can range from home care to long-term placement. Philomena's emphasis is on long-term care planning, and she specializes in Medicaid. She has been in the geriatrics field since 1996 and a caregiver for her mother since 1993. Philomena holds a bachelor's degree in psychology, a master's degree in social work from New York University, and postgraduate certification in geriatrics from Rutgers University. She can be reached at 201-993-3104 or info@medicaidpros.com or by visiting www.medicaidpros.com.

Is Your Subconscious Sabotaging Your Success or Producing the Results You Desire?

by Joy S. Pedersen

Do you struggle to bring in enough business, money, or clients? Do you feel uncomfortable with sales? Do you work hard, do all the "right" things, and yet fail to get the results you desire? Your subconscious holds the key to success, as well as the cause of the challenges you experience throughout life. Learning to work with the subconscious can help release the blocks that prevent you from building a thriving business.

If you have never worked with your subconscious as a way to have greater fulfillment, you are not alone. Although my work is unconventional and not for everyone, after years of failing to reach their goals using a variety of business models, a number of my clients have had breakthrough success after learning how to use their subconscious. If you are open to a new experience—to a new way to have what you desire, especially a thriving business—read on.

You are made up of three selves: the superconscious, the conscious, and the subconscious. Yet most people focus on and live life from just the conscious mind. However, it is the subconscious that not only holds hidden and valuable information—it is the part of you that manifests what you desire. Unless you know how to work effectively with the three selves, you won't produce the results you want or achieve them easily.

To attract new business, you might have no problem defining your target market and reaching them. But for some reason, your phone doesn't ring. When your phone doesn't ring, you might blame your current circumstances and reevaluate your marketing strategy. If you're like most people, you do not look within to determine what is going on inside to attract those less-than-stellar circumstances. Yes, *you* attract those circumstances. Your subconscious beliefs attract what you experience. Therefore, no matter what you think you want, if your subconscious mind has other ideas—you will sabotage your efforts.

Clarity Leads to Business Success

The first step to business success is to clarify what you want. Once you clarify what you want, look within to determine if your subconscious is in alignment with your thoughts and actions so that you achieve what you desire.

This can be the tricky since most people aren't tuned in enough to their subconscious to know what it actually believes. But your outside results can help you identify what your subconscious believes, because your outside world is a reflection of your inside world. So, if your outside world reflects an abundance of business that comes easily, then you know your subconscious believes that this is a comfortable reality for you. If, however, abundance is not reflected back to you, you know there is something in your subconscious that is sabotaging the results you crave. What could be sabotaging the results you desire? The memories that the subconscious holds go back to the beginning of time. They include memories of this life, past lives, and the lives of your ancestors from all the lifetimes you have lived. Those experiences are an accumulation of judgment, perspective, decisions, and emotions that become attached to those memories—and you operate your life from them.

Your past sabotages your future because memories wreak havoc when they trigger something within that sets off an alarm signaling you to avoid the outcome you seek—such as acquiring new customers. With the ability to see past lives and the sabotaging thoughts of the subconscious, I help clients identify their sabotaging memories and clear the cause of them, using an ancient spiritual process.

For example, you attend a networking event, gather cards, and then fail to follow up, so you lose the momentum created for any potential new business and blame your busy schedule. What may be at the root, however, are, for example, your subconscious memories of being forced into a loathsome lifestyle of stealing from innocent victims and then selling the items for survival. Although the choice was made in order to survive during a past life when there were few options, the memory is so distasteful that any thoughts about selling cause you to avoid selling. Lifetimes of servitude also block success. I often end up identifying and clearing these memories when working on financial issues with business owners who work long hours for little or no money because they worked for little or nothing in past lives.

When a client complained of attracting prospects who couldn't afford her fees, I identified two lifetimes that were affecting this situation. First was an impoverished lifetime in which she tried to sell flowers in a neighborhood where the people couldn't afford them. She avoided the neighborhood where people could afford her flowers because she was embarrassed by her shabby appearance. In another lifetime of poverty, she was a man who begged in order to survive, and suffered the guilt of watching his wife and son starve to death because he could not support them. After clearing those lifetimes, my client reported receiving two new paying clients that very afternoon.

Attract What You Desire

Guilt often blocks you from attracting what you desire. Because you aren't conscious of past memories and the guilt attached to them, you don't realize that you sabotage the very same results you seek. Until you let go of the negative memories and emotional charge attached to them, you will continue to live from those memories.

Not all memories are triggered and active at once. A chance meeting or a new experience can be the trigger that activates the memory. Once the memory is activated, the subconscious begins to operate from it and the fear of repeating an unpleasant experience prevents you from achieving the results you long for.

When you set a goal and notice what thoughts emerge, you will begin to identify the subconscious beliefs surrounding it. If you don't notice the thoughts, but notice you aren't achieving what you desire easily, those thoughts may be more hidden than others. At those times, consider seeking assistance to identify them.

Remember, your results identify what you really believe and show you if you are in harmony with what you desire. Using life as a mirror helps you identify what is out of alignment. Looking within to the subconscious is not only the key to resolving the discrepancy—it is the key to your success.

 **Joy S. Pedersen** founded Express Success to help individuals, as well as their businesses, succeed quicker and easier. A gifted healer and channel, she is a Licensed Spiritual Healer, Certified Spiritual Health Coach, Certified Law of Attraction Practitioner, Doctor of Divinity, and author of *Wisdom of the Guardian: Treasures From Archangel Michael To Change Your Life*. She works with her clients virtually, helping them change their lives by clearing the cause of their challenges as well as their path ahead. For a free report on "How to Work with Your Subconscious to Successfully Manifest Easily and Effortlessly," e-mail info@expresssuccess.net with "How to Manifest" in the subject line. For more information, visit www.ExpressSuccess.net.

Put Self-Care on Your Daily "To-Do" List: Your Business Success Depends on It

by Ellen Goldman

I've a question for you. Why did you decide to go into business for yourself?

If you are like most entrepreneurs, at some point you recognized that you have a talent or skill that is making money for someone else, rather than you. Perhaps it was a passion you weren't fully expressing at your current job and a burning desire to do so. Or maybe you wanted to be your own boss, in charge of your own schedule, making your own decisions. In any case, you took the leap and set out to create the business and lifestyle of your dreams.

How is it going? Are you feeling the same excitement and drive you felt when you first started your business?

When attending meetings or speaking to business groups, I am struck by the many entrepreneurs struggling to maintain the focus, energy, and productivity needed on a daily basis to run a business. I see women who are overwhelmed, exhausted, stressed, out of shape, overweight—or plagued by all of them.

It's not because they aren't bright, industrious, and ambitious. It's because somewhere along the journey of building a business, the boundaries between personal life and work got blurry. In the never-ending quest to do all that is needed to run a successful business and meet the demands of home, family, and friends, self-care got pushed to the bottom of the daily "to-do" list.

If you are thinking self-care is a luxury or selfish when you have so much else to do, I want to explain why this isn't so. Self-care is made up of the activities that allow you to function at peak performance: exercising, eating healthy, getting sufficient sleep, making time for leisure activities, and spending quality time with family and friends.

We were designed to do purposeful work, and when doing so, we feel well and happy. However, we only have limited resources. Rest and rejuvenation are just as important as work. When you deprive yourself of rest, and don't take time to refuel, you burn out.

Burn out takes its toll. It saps your energy to stay alert, focused, and productive. This leads to stress, an overwhelmed state, exhaustion, and disillusionment. In the worst-case scenario, you become sick. This is a recipe for disaster for the business owner. If you fall apart, so does the business—because you are the business.

Here are five habits that lead to a healthier, happier, calmer life—*and* a more productive workweek:

1. Elevate self-care to the highest priority. How sad would it be to close your business, not because it wasn't a viable idea, but because you feel you can no longer keep up the pace you've set? Self-care is not a luxury—it is a necessity. Self-care is not selfish—it is essential.

2. Develop clear boundaries between home life and work life. Don't answer business calls during dinner or when conversing with family or friends. Shut off the computer by 8 p.m. Declare one weekend day work free. Stop multitasking things that are important, especially your relationships. It's one thing to watch TV while folding laundry. It's a whole other problem to be answering e-mail while having a conversation with your kids.

3. Create a support team, delegate, and drop the perfectionist attitude. With the myriad of tasks necessary to run a business, you can't possibly do it alone. Household help, babysitters, virtual assistants, and your spouse should be part of your team. Be clear about what you need help with and when—and trust them to do it. Not all things need to be perfect. Sometimes good enough is just that: good enough.

4. Establish a consistent, systematic approach to planning your week. Whether it's marketing, handling clients, scheduling programs, or getting exercise into your day, have a plan. If you don't have a consistent way to plan out your week, you'll find yourself reacting to daily urgencies, rather than focusing on what's important.

5. Embrace healthy lifestyle habits, and schedule them into your daily calendar first.

- **Include thirty minutes of exercise or movement into your schedule most days of the week.** It will pay you back tenfold in energy and stress management. Three ten-minute bouts of exercise have been shown to produce the same benefits as thirty continuous minutes. Take ten-minute walking breaks in the late afternoon. Walk to pick up lunch rather than drive. Go bowling on weekends with your friends or kids. Investing in your health is investing in your business.

- **Strive for seven to eight hours of sleep every night.** You may think staying up late to finish work is productive, but efficiency dramatically decreases when you are sleep deprived. Chronic sleep depravation leads to decreases in reaction time, increases in errors, declining productivity, and escalating anxiety and irritability. Exhaustion is not a client magnet.

- **Eat often and eat light.** Never go more than four hours without a meal or snack. This will keep your blood sugar levels even, which is your fuel for mental energy. You can't possibly think sharply and stay alert if you run out of fuel.

- **Take a break every sixty to ninety minutes.** It is too challenging for the mind or body to sustain attention for longer periods. Set an alarm on your computer to take breaks. Grab a healthy snack, walk around the block, or have a quick chat with a friend. You'll come back to the task refreshed and more creative than before. You'll also avoid the muscular fatigue that accompanies sitting in the same position for too long.

- **Have something fun on your calendar at least once a week.** You created your business because you believed it would make your life better, not take over your life. Whether it's meeting friends for dinner, going to the theater, or crawling into bed with a great book, schedule "me" time into your calendar and enjoy it guilt free.

We've all been told that people want to do business with those they know, like, and trust. We like and trust those who are happy, calm, confident, healthy, and self-assured. The best way to achieve those attributes is to make sure self-care is on your daily "to-do" list. There is absolutely no reason why you shouldn't thrive both professionally *and* personally.

 **Ellen Goldman** created *EnerG*coaching, LLC, to help over-extended business professionals and entrepreneurs who are worried about their health and happiness, and are exhausted, burned out, out of shape, or overweight—or all of the above! She shows clients how to integrate health into their busy lifestyles with simple, small steps that lead to massive change, resulting in greater energy, focus, productivity, and happiness every day. Ellen is a Certified Wellness Coach and Certified Personal Trainer. She holds a BS and MS in physical education, and is certified by the American College of Sports Medicine, Aerobic and Fitness Association of America, and Wellcoaches Corporation. To learn more about Ellen and her wellness programs, visit www.EnerGcoaching.com or contact her at Ellen@energcoaching.com or 973-535-8891.

Author Index

Chapter Title Index

About the Editor

Joyce Restaino, an award-winning writer and editor, is a cofounder of the Big Bold Business Book Series. She leads Grow Your Business Write, a company that helps businesses, organizations, and entrepreneurs polish their image through the written word.

Using the power of the written word to boost visibility and credibility, the company specializes in creating and cranking out content for clients by transforming their knowledge and know-how into articles, blog posts, newsletters, e-zines, tip sheets, and special reports. Joyce is also happy to ghostwrite or coauthor an e-book or hard copy book with individuals who dream about becoming published authors.

For six years, Joyce worked as an editor for The Economics Press, a business-to-business newsletter publisher with over 100,000 paying subscribers. She was responsible for the content of six newsletters, and worked closely with top industry thought leaders in sales, motivation, peak performance, leadership, and relationship building, including Jeffrey Gitomer, Bob Bly, Barry Farber, and Rob Gilbert.

For eight years, Joyce's consumer column, "Saving Makes Cents," appeared in two weekly Northern New Jersey newspapers. The column received a first-place award from the New Jersey Press Women in the category of "personal informational column." Joyce's work has also appeared in *The New York Times*, *The Star-Ledger*, *The Record*, *Woman's Day* special edition magazines, the *ParentPaper*, *House Beautiful*, and *New Choices* (no longer published)—a *Reader's Digest* publication. She also coauthored the helpful, handy homeowner workbook *New Jersey Property Tax Assessments: A Homeowner's Guided Tour to Understanding Assessments, Appeals, Revaluations, and Reassessments* for property tax–burdened New Jersey homeowners.

Joyce is also the "essay expert" for *Ask Your College Advisor*, a college consulting company started by her husband, Patrick. *Ask Your College Advisor* helps guide high school students and their parents through the college admissions process. A former middle school English teacher, Joyce also taught English composition at the college level. In addition, she developed and taught a writing program for high school students with learning disabilities. Joyce was trained for and has scored the college admissions essay requirement for the College Board's SAT® Writing section.

When she isn't writing or doing research, Joyce recharges by heading outdoors for a good four- to six-mile run or by riding the beautiful back roads of the USA with her husband on their motorcycle. A huge sports fan, especially of college football, Joyce looks forward to Saturdays in the fall when she can root for her favorite teams.

What Are You Waiting For?
Publish Your Big Bold Business^{TM} Book Now

Do you belong to a business organization, association, club, or mastermind group?

If you do, you're sitting on a gold mine of knowledge, know-how, and expertise that can put you and your organization in the limelight.

If you want to…

- ➤ Raise the profile of your organization
- ➤ Gain recognition for individual members
- ➤ Tell your organization's story
- ➤ Share your successful business strategies
- ➤ Grow your membership
- ➤ Attract new customers
- ➤ Take your business or career to the next level
- ➤ Promote your cause

Will your book be next in the Big Bold Business Book Series?

The Big Bold Business Division of Woodpecker Press works with organizations, associations, clubs, and mastermind groups that want to self-publish a business book to promote their organization, their cause, and/or their individual members.

Best of all, publishing a Big Bold Business Book is rewarding and easy.

Rewarding because you get to share your expert knowledge to help others, support your organization, and add "author" to your credentials.

Easy because the Big Bold Business Team takes your information and turns it into a value-packed, influential book that every member of your organization can be proud of.

If you believe in your organization, in its work, and in its members, share your knowledge and know-how by publishing your big bold business book.

To learn more, contact info@WoodpeckerPress.com or visit:

www.BigBoldBusiness.com
www.WoodpeckerPress.com

Jersey Women Mean Business! Big Bold Business Advice from
New Jersey Women Business Owners: Practical Pointers, Solutions,
and Strategies for Business Success

BOOK ORDER FORM

Order Online:
www.WoodpeckerPress.com/Our-Books

E-Mail Orders: info@WoodpeckerPress.com

Mail Orders: Woodpecker Press, LLC
P.O. Box 316
Bayville, NJ 08721-0316

SHIPPING ADDRESS: (PLEASE PRINT):

NAME _____

STREET ADDRESS_____

APARTMENT OR BUILDING NUMBER: _____

PO BOX _____

CITY _____ STATE_____ ZIP _____

COUNTRY _____

PHONE WITH AREA CODE (_____) _____

E-MAIL ADDRESS _____

QUANTITY ORDERED:___ @ $28.00 SUBTOTAL $_____

SALES TAX   Add 7% sales tax (USA only) $ _____

SHIPPING & HANDLING Add $6.00 each (USA only) $ _____

TOTAL: $ _____

International orders, please contact info@WoodpeckerPress.com for shipping costs.

PAYMENT METHOD

Make check payable to: Woodpecker Press, LLC (US funds only)

To pay by credit card, order online at

www.WoodpeckerPress.com/Our-Books